Dan Nelson's biography of George Whitefield is a wonderfully engaging chronicle of a truly great life. I love the rich insights into Whitefield's personality and opinions. Whitefield had an amazing gift for proclaiming the Word of God with tremendous passion and power—even in the most hostile environments. As a result, he was enormously influential in his generation, and he left a long-lasting mark on the culture of both the United Kingdom and America. Evangelicals in the current generation desperately need to rediscover Whitefield and imbibe a fresh dose of his faith and his love for the Word of God.

—JOHN MACARTHUR
PASTOR, AUTHOR, PRESIDENT
THE MASTER'S SEMINARY

George Whitefield is a towering figure in the story of evangelical Christianity. Knowing his life is essential for understanding the roots of modern evangelism. Dan Nelson has done a superb job of bringing a man to life that you will enjoy getting to know. As you read this book, you will understand why those who come to know his story yearn for him to be widely known among those who follow Jesus today. Yes, one life truly can make an enormous difference in the world.

—CHUCK KELLEY
PRESIDENT
NEW ORLEANS BAPTIST THEOLOGICAL SEMINARY

George Whitefield is among the premier examples in Christendom of how a preacher ought to live. Now Dan Nelson has brought this fabled preacher back to life. No one can read this volume and remain unchanged.

—PAIGE PATTERSON
PRESIDENT
SOUTHWESTERN BAPTIST THEOLOGICAL SEMINARY

George Whitefield was the most powerful preacher of awakening in Britain and America, yet he remains strangely forgotten today, even by many evangelical Christians. There are signs of an evangelical recovery of Whitefield, however, and I hope that Pastor Dan Nelson's book will introduce many readers to this great luminary of the eighteenth-century revivals.

—THOMAS S. KIDD
PROFESSOR OF HISTORY
BAYLOR UNIVERSITY

Through Dan Nelson's clear and edifying portrait of George Whitefield, readers will be stirred as they encounter Whitefield's life, ministry, vision, and evangelistic burden.

—CHRIS MORGAN
DEAN AND PROFESSOR OF THEOLOGY
SCHOOL OF CHRISTIAN MINISTRIES,
CALIFORNIA BAPTIST UNIVERSITY

The story of George Whitefield is one that every generation of the church needs to hear afresh, and that because of its power to remind us of the glory and power of the great God of the eighteenth-century evangelist. Dan Nelson has written a popular account of Whitefield's incredible life and ministry, laying it out in strict chronological order, and showing us clearly how God used this man in the hurly-burly of his day. Running through his narrative is a passion for the very same thing Whitefield knew and experienced: heaven-sent revival. May this book be a means to such an end!

—MICHAEL A. G. HAYKIN
PROFESSOR OF CHURCH HISTORY & BIBLICAL SPIRITUALITY
THE SOUTHERN BAPTIST THEOLOGICAL SEMINARY
LOUISVILLE, KY

The legacy of George Whitefield on the continuing work of his "beloved Bethesda" cannot be understated. Whitefield as founder, spiritual guide, visionary leader, and even as a pragmatic manager, continues to impact this ministry that he first established in 1740. Today, Bethesda Academy still holds true to the value equation Whitefield dictated, "a love of God, a love of learning and a strong work ethic." Dan Nelson's work provides profound insights into how one man's passion for Christ can still inspire leaders and believers generations later.

—T. DAVID TRIBBLE
FORMER PRESIDENT, BETHESDA ACADEMY

This compelling biography of the premier evangelist of the English language, George Whitefield, is a priceless treasure for the church. Here is a well-researched, concisely-written account of one of history's most prolific figures, the "Grand Itinerant" who ignited flames of revival on both sides of the Atlantic. The life and ministry of Whitefield is one of the most remarkable stories you will ever read and is sure to inspire you. These pages, I believe, will stir your spiritual blood and move you to action for the cause of Christ.

—STEVEN J. LAWSON
PRESIDENT OF ONE PASSION MINISTRIES,
PREACHING PROFESSOR IN THE MASTERS AND DOCTORAL PROGRAMS,
THE MASTER'S SEMINARY

A Burning and Shining Light

The Testimony and Witness of George Whitefield

BY

Dan Nelson

LifeSong Publishers, Somis, CA

ISBN 978-0-9799116-7-5

A Burning and Shining Light
The Testimony and Witness of George Whitefield

By Dan Nelson

LifeSong Publishers
P.O. Box 183
Somis, CA 93066
www.LifeSongPublishers.com
805-504-3916

Photos used by permission:
The Works of George Whitfield, © 2000 Quinta Press
Meadow View, Weston Rhyn, Oswestry
Shropshire, England SY10 7RN
http://www.quintapress.com

Cover: Original Painting by Margo Ewing ©2017, based on multiple paintings which are public domain. Design by Laurie Donahue.

All Scriptural quotations or citations are taken from the King James Version of the Bible unless otherwise indicated.

All other quotation sources throughout the book have been footnoted or indicated within the text.

Internet addresses (Web sites, blogs, etc.) and telephone numbers printed in this book are offered as a resource to you. These are not intended to imply endorsement.

Library of Congress Control Number: 2017942026

DEDICATION

This work is dedicated to all who practice evangelism and place
the winning of others to Christ as their most important
venture in life, as Whitefield exemplified.

This work is also dedicated to the memory of my parents:
L.R. and Irma Lois Nelson, who were my teachers in school.
They fostered a love for learning through history and writing
that is very much a part of my life. They were wonderful parents
and motivational teachers who inspired
all who studied under them.

CONTENTS

PREFACE

HEROES ALWAYS SEEM TO BE IN SHORT SUPPLY when needed, and the world is constantly in need of them. Our highly sophisticated technological age does not exclude that need. Indeed, the age probably magnifies the need for heroes, because we are constantly looking for a cause bigger than ourselves. We especially applaud someone rising out of nowhere to answer needs in the day and age we live.

George Whitefield was such a hero to his generation. His influence lives on in movements we probably take for granted. Whitefield lived in a time when he was desperately needed because of the decline of morals and church influence. His conversion and call to preach were dramatic. Praises were showered upon him with rapid succession. One hardly notices his short life in comparison with life spans of today because of all God accomplished through him. Those who seriously study his life will quickly see the significant place Whitefield has in the history of Christianity and evangelism.

Whitefield clarifies the affinity we have for those in the Kingdom of God through our shared beliefs in the gospel. His preaching was very influential; he was not only the talk of his day but the model for generations. The ministry of George Whitefield on two continents was far-reaching. Frank Mead wrote a thrilling biography of Whitefield in his *Ten Decisive Battles of Christianity*. He placed Whitefield's ministry in the strategic position it maintains today.[1]

Whitefield was a leading figure in Colonial America. His establishment of the Bethesda orphanage in Savannah, Georgia left a lasting legacy. He

---

1   Mead, Frank S. *The Ten Decisive Battles of Christianity* (Bobbs-Merrill: New York, 1935), 105.

made a significant contribution to the colonization of America through the establishment of Bethesda. The evangelist's popularity in America was far-reaching and he was a fixture in the English colonies because of the seven trips he made here.

Studying Whitefield's ministry is an adventure because of his extensive trips for someone of his time. His constant travel and continual preaching in spite of hardships were major accomplishments.

I grew up in the era of the Billy Graham Crusades. In the decades of the 60s, 70s, and 80s, he maintained a wide cultural exposure. But the beginning of the mass evangelism movement could quite possibly have its beginnings as far back as George Whitefield.

The history of the awakening movements and their influence on the culture of their time are monumental to our nation's history. Jonathan Edwards, John Wesley and Whitefield were all famous leaders during the Great Awakening. My Ph.D. dissertation was on "The Evangelistic Preaching of the 18th Century Awakening Leaders." I contrasted their preaching styles, beliefs and leadership. Whitefield's constant travel, dynamic preaching and influential life were impressive, and I knew there was still more to uncover on Whitefield beyond what I had found earlier in my studies.

The primary source for my research on Whitefield was Arnold Dallimore's *George Whitefield: The Life and Times of the Great Evangelist*. His two volumes are comprehensive and followed Luke Tyerman's example of a century before.

Other recent books have been written on Whitefield. Some of their themes have been his political influence on the colonies before the American Revolution, his devotional life and other various aspects of his ministry.

When I began my work at Southwestern Baptist Theological Seminary, I unearthed numerous biographies on Whitefield. My research revealed basic information of Whitefield's life and ministry. John Gillies wrote the first biography in 1773. He also preserved Whitefield's early journals dealing with the evangelist's upbringing, college days, conversion, call, and inauguration of ministry during the early days of his ministry in America. The other sources gave ample information to write a complete chronological account of Whitefield's life.

My biography omits much of Whitefield's correspondence with various individuals and does not extensively discuss doctrine. This work offers a fresh comprehensive biography of Whitefield's life relating to his travel and trips to America. The chronological account has been an arduous task, piecing together sermon quotes, biographer's assessments and meticulous documentation. This book will help readers understand more about Whitefield and his ministry.

The world is in need of Christian heroes like never before. Whitefield was one of the catalysts for the Great Awakening in Great Britain and America whose example and energy are impressive and motivational in overcoming life's obstacles. The 300th anniversary of Whitefield's birth revives a study of his life that will help students see how God wants to use us, as well. He demonstrated a tremendous evangelistic zeal and influenced untold multitudes for the cause of Christ.

I want to especially thank Laurie Donahue, of LifeSong Publishers, who published my book and worked with me diligently to finish the book through numerous edits and design. She has done a marvelous and thorough job. Ellen Kersey, professor of journalism and writing at Corbin University, thoroughly reviewed my final draft suggesting needful changes to help the book be more readable. I fully appreciate her review and suggestions. I am grateful for my wife, Janice, and her patience with my long periods of hibernation in my study when I was working on the manuscript. Special thanks to my administrative assistant, Amy Cranage, for helping gather information from all my sources and the formatting of some of the manuscript. Cindy Thomas assisted me greatly in several edits of the work, alerting me to some better ways to phrase my writing. She selected various items appearing in the glossary of terms needing more definition. Her help was invaluable.

The exact years of Whitefield's life are copied from Luke Tyerman's massive two-volume work of the 19th century. His record was the clearest chronology I found in all the sources I researched.[2]

Digby James, newfound friend and editor of Quinta Press in Shropshire, UK, graciously allowed me to use pictures he has taken on his trek to all the major historical places in Whitefield's ministry.

---

2   Luke Tyerman, *The Life of the Rev. George Whitefield*, 2 Volumes (London: Hodder and Stoughton), 1877) reprinted by Need of the Times Publisher, Azie, TX: 1995, vol.1 vii-X, vol.2 iii-viii.

I am thankful for the use of these valuable visual aids to show where Whitefield ministered.

The various quotes have been somewhat modernized particularly in the area of punctuation and style to be more understandable to the reader.

I hope you enjoy and learn from Whitefield's life and ministry. May you be motivated through Whitefield's example to be the witness he was to those who need our influence.

Dan Nelson,
Camarillo, CA

INTRODUCTION

A COLONIAL FARMER IN MIDDLETOWN, NEW JERSEY, named Nathan Cole, describes a life-altering event he experienced through a vivid narrative. He dropped his farming tools, ran to get his wife, hitched his horse team, and pushed the team as fast as he could to get to a large assembly of people. These masses of people were easily identifiable by the huge cloud of dust surrounding them. All were doing as Cole was, seeking to get to a certain locality as quickly as possible.[3] When they arrived at a certain juncture, they joined the crowd waiting with anxious anticipation and eagerness because of one grand declaration: "Whitefield will preach tonight!" George Whitefield was there, speaking with authority and anointing by the Lord. Many were moved to tears, repentance, and conversion. This scene was a typical preaching event in the Great Awakening when George Whitefield preached.

The format was a familiar one for the roaming evangelist. He preached to masses of people with constant regularity in the American colonies and in Great Britain. These meetings featured the largest crowds ever assembled to hear the gospel in his time. The dynamic preaching of the gospel was in full display as many heard the Word of God in a way they had never heard it before.

Why did one man evoke this response on both continents? Extended research of Whitefield's life and ministry have led me to believe three main truths that explain the phenomenon of his ministry.

---

3   Arnold A. Dallimore, *George Whitefield: God's Anointed Servant in the Great Revival of the Eighteenth Century* (Crossway: Wheaton, Ill., 1990), 90.

(1) His Confidence in the Word of God: His messages were filled with the great doctrines of the faith. His hearers were captivated by biblical truth. Whitefield immersed himself in the study of God's Word, from his conversion at Oxford until his dying day. He loved preaching the dynamic themes of the Scripture with power and purpose and brought its redemptive message to his audience.

Whitefield was constantly devoted to the Scripture; his confidence in it never wavered and its teaching captivated him. God used him to bring the Bible to life and expose the contents of the Bible to his hearers. He urged hearers to see all the glories of God's revealed word and His divine revelation through it.

(2) A Zeal for Souls: Whitefield was always on the gospel trail for souls. His seven voyages to America are evidence of his energy in sharing the gospel. His evangelistic efforts were all encompassing, and he was comfortable with any audience. He faced opposition to his preaching with a certain fearlessness, while threats on his life were secondary to the furtherance of the gospel.

The force of Whitefield's preaching was a direct result of his deep burden for the unconverted. Response to his preaching was evidenced through his long hours of counseling after his messages. Whitefield's ministry was constant on the sea or in the uncharted territory of America. His overwhelming pace drove him to an early grave. As an evangelist, he desired to reach as many as possible for the sake of the gospel. Those who converted came from all walks of life.

(3) Animated, Dynamic Preaching: Whitefield gave full expression to such themes as heaven, hell, the cross, and the way of salvation through his effective preaching. The masses awaited his arrival and bemoaned his departure. Sinners stopped in their tracks. Children understood Whitefield's preaching because of his sincerity and compassion toward them. People from all walks of life were drawn through the Holy Spirit's power and the way he preached. Actors envied the dramatic tone of his preaching. Whitefield preached with power, authority, confidence and a sense of purpose.

John Newton, the famous English clergyman, who converted from slave trading and writer of the famous hymn Amazing Grace,[4] recalled Whitefield's style of preaching:

> I have had opportunities of looking over the history of the Church in past ages, and I am not backward to say that I have not read or heard of a person, since the days of the apostles, of whom it may more emphatically be said, "He was a burning and shining light" than that of the late Mr. Whitefield. The Lord gave him a manner of preaching, which was peculiarly his own. He copied from none, and I never met anyone who could imitate him with success. Those who attempted generally made themselves disagreeable. Other ministers perhaps could preach the gospel as clearly, and in general could say the same things, but no man living could say them in his way.[5]

The highpoints of a cenotaph to his memory read:

> GEORGE WHITEFIELD, born at Gloucester, England, December 16, 1714: educated at Oxford University: ordained 1736. In a ministry of thirty-four years he crossed the Atlantic thirteen times, and preached more than eighteen thousand sermons. Over two centuries have passed since Mr. Whitefield passed into glory on Sept. 30, 1770.[6]

- What are the influences that led to God using Whitefield's preaching on two continents?
- What made him the popular preacher he became?
- Why did crowds rush to the spot or church where he was preaching?
- What led Whitefield to begin field preaching?
- In what ways did his preaching stand in stark contrast to the typical sermons of his day?
- What were Whitefield's motivations in spite of the many obstacles he faced?

This work will seek to answer these questions. By discovering answers to these questions, readers will be able to understand the man, the preacher, the evangelist, the orphanage organizer, and the encourager to church leaders regardless of denominational stripe.

---

4   John Newton, *Amazing Grace The Hymnal* (Word Waco, TX), 1986.
5   Tyerman, vol.2, 624-625.
6   Joseph, Belcher, *George Whitefield, A Biography with Special Reference to His Labours in America* (American Tract Society: New York, 1938), 444.

George Whitefield made a solid commitment to God after his conversion and call to ministry. He never looked back or regretted anything God had done in his life. Although he was tempted to cut back or even quit at times, he continued his ministry until the day he died. He often was miraculously rejuvenated after his health wavered and he seemed to lose all his physical strength. "A good pulpit sweat was the cure for what ailed him."[7] His inspirational life speaks volumes to those today that have many more conveniences that aid them in ministry.

Whitefield's ministry can be compared to a rapid comet. It was fast-paced and fiery. The holy flame of God that burned in his soul was caught by many hearing him and associating with him.

Whitefield was a spiritual leader the world needed. Churches were desperate for a preacher with his degree of "gospel authority."[8] Churched and unchurched alike knew they were hearing a man of God, preaching the truth of God, from the Word of God.

Whitefield's example has influenced former generations immensely. Hopefully, we will see that same influence rediscovered in this generation. His example is worth the effort of uncovering. The work before you is a comprehensive study in understanding his life and influence. The holy fire in him progressed to a burning blaze and was not extinguished until the day he died. His example is one worthy of emulating. My purpose for writing this will be accomplished as readers experience his example and are inspired to be used in the same manner as Whitefield. May the account of his life speak to you as you experience Whitefield's ministry, testimony and witness in this text.

Dan Nelson,
Camarillo, CA

---

7   Tyerman, vol. 2, 599. This was a common phrase used by Whitefield revealing his belief that preaching actually helped restore his health. Whitefield used the phrase on the night he died in response to Richard Smith, his traveling companion's concern for his physical well-being.

8   Arnold A Dallimore, George Whitefield, The Life and Times Of (Banner of Truth: London, 1980), vol.1, 97. This phrase was used by Whitefield to describe the power he experienced in preaching his first message at St. Mary de Crypt church on June 27, 1736.

1

CHILDHOOD

AND UPBRINGING

(1714-1732)

GEORGE WHITEFIELD WAS BORN IN GLOUCESTER, England, on December 16, 1714.[9] His father Thomas and mother Elizabeth Edwards were from the Bristol area.[10] Whitefield's great-grandfather, Samuel, was a distinguished clergyman in the established Church of England. His grandparents lived on an estate near Bristol with their fourteen children. Thomas, the oldest, was a wine merchant in Bristol. He afterwards became proprietor and owner of the Bell Inn.[11]

The Bell, located in Gloucester, was the largest and finest establishment of its kind. The inn was comprised of three stories, was nearly one hundred feet long and its depth with its carriage yard and stables extended all the way to the street beyond. Its main hall was the

---

9   Great Britain changed to the Gregorian calendar in 1752. The 16th was under the Julian calendar. According to Digby James, editor of Quinta Press, he describes Whitefield, writing after 1752, referring to the 27th of December as his birthday. Biographers' are split on the birthday with Frank Lambert indicating he was baptized as a baby on Christmas day and Joseph Belcher here listing it as December 16th.

10   Dallimore, vol.1, 40.

11   E. N. Hardy, *George Whitefield, The Matchless Soul Winner* (American Tract Society: New York, 1938), 19.

center of social activity with plays staged there.[12] The hall was one of the two auditoriums used for entertainment in the city.

Thomas Whitefield's promising career was cut short when he died unexpectedly. History does not record the reason he passed away on December 13, 1716, but he was only thirty-five years old. Young George's mother raised him by herself since the time he was two years of age.[13]

Thomas Belcher shares a concise history of Whitefield's earliest years. He was the sixth son born to Thomas and Elizabeth. Concerning his father and mother, he wrote, "The former died when I was two years old. The latter died December 1751 in the 71st year of her age." Whitefield's mother was very ill giving birth to her youngest son.[14]

Young George was a victim of various hardships. At four years of age, he had a bout with the measles, leaving one of his eyes dark blue and causing a squint. His eyes were lively while he preached and did not diminish his countenance, nor did the squint detract from the charm of his glance. The defective eye became a source of ridicule in later years with scoffers and railers giving him the nickname "Dr. Squintim."[15]

After his father's death, Whitefield's mother married Capel Logden, who mismanaged the Bell Inn. His father had been the mayor of Gloucester and was well known. Logden's skills, however, were deficient to this undertaking. His marriage to Elizabeth Whitefield was far from ideal and dissolved a few years after they were married.[16]

The events of Whitefield's early life, losing his father at an early age and assisting his family in their work, greatly influenced his future path. He grew up in the environment of the Bell Inn. Although it was a famous place, noted for its respectable and elegant accommodations, the tavern associated with it was not as attractive. On a cold, wintry day, young George could be found drawing a bucket of ale to serve drunken ruffians who became more delirious as they continued drinking. Young George faced difficulty in overcoming these circumstances. The inn was hardly helpful in the upbringing of the future evangelist, but this environment influenced him in his formative years.

---

12   Dallimore, vol.1, 43.
13   Ibid., 45.
14   Belcher, 26.
15   James Patterson Gledstone, *George Whitefeld: Supreme Among Preachers* (Ambassador Publications: Belfast, 1998 reprint), 2.
16   Dallimore, vol. 1, 52.

His mother and stepfather enlisted young George in the ongoing upkeep of the inn. This rough place was not healthy for his moral well-being with the convergence of exposures that were prevalent at this time. He heard criminals tell of their exploits against the upper class of England. Whitefield's exposure to individuals such as these was constant and this working environment could not be avoided as it was his job.[17]

The condition of the tavern mirrored England's spiritual decline at the early part of the eighteenth century. There was a dead formalism in the state church's worship. Orthodox doctrines were threatened with the enlightenment movement in full bloom. A former century of religious fighting had given way to lethargy and apathy toward personal religion.

The decline featured a spiritual ignorance of the things of God from the pulpit. The people in the pews suffered because of the lack of preaching on the new birth and the need for personal salvation. The doctrines of the faith and biblical exposition were generally unheard. This ignorance had resulted in rampant sin and disregard for moral law.

In Puritan times, England featured strict adherence to scriptural standards. In the days of Oliver Cromwell, the strict enforcement of those standards led to decent moral behavior. King Charles II brought significant changes with the restoration of the monarchy. Persecution of non-conformists (although religious toleration was achieved under William and Mary) had fostered religious in-fighting. Weariness with religion had brought England to this apathetic condition. Many Puritans representing the devout religious non-conformists had fled to America, seeking freedom to worship God without any governmental interference. The remaining group's influence was minimized. A high-church atmosphere and little spiritual instruction was the order of the day.[18]

Deism afflicted many clergy's pulpits. Arnold Dallimore said, "Deists carried on a vigorous warfare against supernatural religion and biblical Christianity and in doing so made loud boasts about the reasonableness and logic of their views."[19]

The greatest tragedy resulting from this attack was that the preaching

---

17   Dallimore, vol. 1, 48.

18   Historical Data based on a cursory view of British history in the 16th century from the author's knowledge of such events as a teacher.

19   Dallimore, vol. 1, 20.

of the gospel in the established church was generally unheard. Belcher especially enumerated doctrines in this omission:

> But as to preaching of the gospel, in the established church there was none. The distinguishing doctrines of Christianity, the atonement, the work and office of Christ, and the Spirit, were comparatively lost in pursuit of other diversions. The majority of sermons were miserable moral essays totally devoid of anything calculated to awake and convert, save, or sanctify souls.[20]

The lethargy of the church led to the debauchery that young Whitefield experienced at the inn. Edwin Ninde explained his opinion for this regression: "In large measure, the church had lost its power. Not that the nation was utterly depraved, for both pulpit and pew had some godliness but their number was comparatively small."[21]

Whitefield was influenced by the spiritual climate of his day. His religious experience before his conversion was not unlike the normal countrymen of his time. Frank Lambert told of Whitefield's initiation into the church and his family's involvement in it:

> On Christmas Day, Rector Matthew Yates baptized George at the parish church of St. Mary de Crypt in Gloucester. The Whitefields were active and prominent members of the Anglican congregation situated less than a hundred yards away from the same side of the Southgate Street as the Bell Inn: The family business and residence. His father, Thomas, had served in major lay offices—overseer, vestryman, and church warden and as a wine merchant, who supplied the church with wine for communion. After Thomas' death in 1716, George's older brother, Richard, followed his father both as proprietor at the Bell and as family leader at St. Mary's.[22]

The family involvement in the church subsided somewhat with all the circumstances changing around them. Despite all of these factors Whitefield still maintained an interest in the church and particularly preaching. Steven Mansfield describes Whitefield's penchant for learning from sermons he had heard:

> He spent hours recreating what he had seen or read and became so accomplished that he could also perform Sunday sermons with greater affect than the original. Once, when he was acting out a sermon for the entertainment of some guests at the inn, he noticed some of them began to weep. It was a

---

20   Belcher, 16.

21   Edward Summerfield Ninde, *George Whitefield: Prophet-Preacher* (Abingdon Press: New York, 1924), 42.

22   Frank Lambert, *Pedlar in Divinity: George Whitefield and the Transatlantic Revivals, 1737-1770* (Princeton University Press: Princeton, NJ, 1994),16.

sign of what lay ahead, but George was too young and too impressed with the attention to realize what was happening.[23]

Whitefield possessed a deeply religious nature, as well as a mischievous one. His behavior was often confusing. Mansfield asserted, "He stole money from his mother's purse then used it to buy religious books. He would fight vicariously with boys in the streets and crawl weeping on the floor of his bedroom to pray for the souls of those who he had just pummeled."[24]

The education Whitefield received in Gloucester was different from most young men in England. James Gray shared, "Gloucester was one of the few places in England at the time where poor boys could secure anything of an education."

Robert Philip revealed how Whitefield developed a love of drama: "Thus he contracted the taste of theatrical amusements, which gave rise to well-known insinuation, that he learned his peculiar style of oratory upon the stage."[25] Young George particularly liked drama, possibly because he longed to withdraw from the loudness of the place he labored. The young actor loved to memorize dramas in his school, St. Mary's de Crypt, housed in the church of the same name. He also regularly read from *The Manual for Winchester Scholars*,[26] which contained prayers for the use of the Scholars of Winchester College by Thomas Ken.[27] He believed his reading of this book was of "great benefit to his soul."[28]

It was through drama that young George felt he reached his true nature and was able to express himself. This interest delivered him from the bleak future awaiting him as a table server.

Despite the privilege of St. Mary's, Whitefield left the school at age fifteen to go back to work.[29] George left school despite his rapid progress and his love of learning because his family needed him to work full time

---

23   Stephen Mansfield, *Forgotten Founding Father: The Heroic Legacy of George Whitefield* (Highland Books/Cumberland House: Nashville, 2001), 40-41.

24   Ibid., 40.

25   Robert Philip, *The Life and Times of George Whitefield* (George Virtue, Ivy Lane: London, 1842), 5.

26   Dallimore, vol. 1, 50.

27   Ann Arbor, MI; Oxford (UK): Text Creation Partnership, (2003-07), http://name.umdl.umich.edu/A47224.0001.001, (accessed September 23, 2015), see Glossary of Terms for further explanation.

28   Dallimore, vol. 1, 50.

29   Joseph M. Gray, *Prophets of the Soul* (Abingdon Press: New York, 1936), 68.

at the inn. Life was hard, and he was essential help. His brother Richard became the proprietor of the Bell and employed him vigorously in many menial tasks.[30] The evangelist described the transition that gave occasion to renew his religious interests: "I began to assist her (his mother) occasionally in the public house, till at length I put on my blue apron and my snuffers, washed mops, cleaned floors, and in one word became professed and a common drawer for nearly a year and a half."[31]

Belcher observed, "In the midst of the activities, he was called for in such a situation that pleased God to renew his religious impressions, which induced him, at least at intervals, to attend with such earnestness to the concerns of the soul."[32] Leaving school afforded Whitefield more time to reflect on spiritual things.

Whitefield was encouraged when someone mentioned his going to Oxford as a student. It touched a nerve as the hardened life of a young man had tempered him to accept almost any challenge. The challenge to go to Oxford was a worthy one and a way out of the darkened path ahead of him.

Whitefield was also encouraged in spiritual things by the preaching of a dissenting pastor, Thomas Cole, who was nicknamed "Old Cole," and served the Southgate Independent Church.[33] Cole, who used many stories in his sermons, made an impression in a strange way on the evangelist's future ministry. Whitefield gave particular attention to his dramatic gestures and the way he preached. He did not intentionally preach like Cole, but generally had some of his mannerisms and style. Whitefield and Cole died in the same manner, shortly after each had preached a sermon. Cole heard of Whitefield's similarity to his preaching many years later. He reacted: "I find that young Whitefield can now tell stories as well as old Cole."[34]

Whitefield's interest in preaching and preparing sermons seemed puzzling to his friends because of his surroundings. He revealed his

---

30   John Gillies, ed., *George Whitefield's Journals* (Banner of Truth Trust: London, PA, 1960), 40.

31   Belcher, 28.

32   Ibid., 28.

33   Harry S. Stout, *The Divine Dramatist: George Whitefield and the Rise of Modern Evangelicalism* (W.B. Eerdmans: Grand Rapids, MI, 1991), 5.

34   John Gillies, *Memoirs of Rev. George Whitefield* (Hunt & Son: Hartford England 1853), 40-41.

growing interest in preaching by disclosing, "Notwithstanding, I was thus employed in a large inn, and had sometimes the care of the whole house upon my hands, yet I composed two or three sermons—frequently I read my Bible when sitting up at night."[35] It is unclear what his motives were in these efforts since he was unconverted at this time, and the Bible had not yet transformed his life.

Whitefield continued work with his brother Richard as his assistant in the management of the inn and as an aspiring tradesman. It appeared he was directed away from formal education, although he still had a desire to go to college. His responsibilities increased when his mother retired and allowed the business to be managed by her sons.[36]

Whitefield's interest in education gave him a sense of purpose. He wanted to rise above others' expectations for his life. George needed to escape the ebbing tide of moral erosion consistently around him. He had a quest for learning and a supportive mother wishing the best for her son. He aspired to excel in school, eventually, go to Oxford and pursue the finest course of study offered in England.[37]

One of the future evangelist's great strengths later in his life would be his identification with the lower class. His mingling with undesirables in the tavern, his hard work in the inn and his constant association with the lower class made it easy to relate to the common people. But assisting his brother did not benefit his educational interest. The income from any job he had at the Bell would not begin to pay for an Oxford education. He worked for his brother to have lodging and waited for a break to go to school. [38]

God began to deal with young George. In his journal, he said he was "much pressed to self-examination and found myself very unwilling to look into my heart... Frequently I read the Bible when sitting up at night. Seeing the boys go by to school has often cut me to the heart. And a dear youth, now with God, would often come entreating me, when serving at the bar, to go to Oxford. My general answer was, 'I wish I could.'"[39]

---

35 Hardy, 26.
36 Lambert, 37.
37 Dallimore, vol. 1, 55-56.
38 John Gillies, ed., *George Whitefield's Journals*, 40-41.
39 Ibid., 40.

Something traumatic did happen, turning Whitefield's sights beyond the inn, as he related in his journal:

> After I continued about a year in this servile employment, my mother was obliged to leave the inn. My brother, who had been bred up for the business, married…and I being accustomed to the house, it was agreed that I should continue there as an assistant. But God's thoughts were not as our thoughts. By His good Providence, it happened that my sister-in-law and I could by no means agree; and at length, the resentment grew to such a height, that my proud heart would scarce suffer me to speak to her for three weeks together. But notwithstanding I had much to blame and I used to retire and weep before the Lord.[40]

Whitefield wanted to get out of his job. Uncertain of his future, he shared, "One morning, as I was reading a play to my sister, I said, 'God intends something for me which I know not of. As I have been diligent in business, I believe many would gladly have me for an apprentice, but every way seems to be barred up,… I think that God will provide for me some way or other that we cannot apprehend.'"[41]

Whitefield shared his response to an impression concerning a call to preach:

> One night being on an errand for my mother an unaccountable, but a very strong impression made upon my heart that I should preach quickly. When I came home, I innocently told my mother what had befallen me; but she like Joseph's parents, when he told them about his dream turned short upon me, crying out, "What does this boy mean? Prithee hold thy tongue, or something to that purpose." God has since shown her from whom that impression came.[42]

Whitefield shared how he took the sacrament, fasted frequently, attended public worship, and generally became more interested in spiritual things. He revealed to his sister a dream he had that made a deep impression on him. In the dream, he had seen God on Mt. Sinai. He also revealed the dream to a lady who had known him from childhood. She interpreted the dream: "Thus, George, this is a call from God." The dream was meaningful, for he said, "I grew more serious after the dream."[43] The dream had great influence in shaping the future destiny of

---

40   Ibid., 40.

41   Ibid., 42.

42   Ibid., 44.

43   J. B. Wakeley, *Anecdotes of Rev. George Whitefield Sketch* (Hodder and Stoughton: London, 1900), 65-66.

the dreamer. God was using various means to call young George to His work though he was still unconverted.

The constant grind of the inn precluded any serious involvement of the Whitefield family in spiritual matters and church in general. Although George's mother did not relish the fact that her family had a loose association to the church, life was hard; the time and effort in the upkeep of the Bell was constant. Spiritual blindness had played heavily on the family. The thought of a personal relationship with God was remote and overshadowed by a religion that was ritual and routine. Whitefield's experience of personal religion was to come through exposure to godly influences at Oxford. Elizabeth Whitefield's shallowness is seen through the response she had to his interest in preaching. She probably looked on it as a boyhood fancy.

Whitefield was able to go back to school and finish his education after the disagreement with his sister-in law. He speaks of re-entering school and being welcomed back. He did continue this time till his course of study ended. He remarked, "God was pleased to give me a blessing and I learned much faster than I did before."[44]

A friend of the family was willing to recommend George and sponsor his entrance into Oxford. He saw the potential in the young man who thrived on memorizing dramas free and natural, with gestures accompanying the expressions of popular plays he had learned.[45] Although he had the beginnings of a master communicator, the path to exercise this gift was not yet determined. A good Oxford education would go a long way to nurture the gift he possessed.

A former schoolfellow and family friend, a servitor at Pembroke College, Oxford, paid a visit to Whitefield's home. The youth's proud boast was that by his delicate service he had been able to discharge all his college expenses and have money left. Whitefield's mother saw an Oxford education as an achievement, not only for this servitor, but for her own son. She exclaimed, "This will do for my son!" She cried and almost in the next breath asked Whitefield, "Will you go to Oxford, George?" The lad replied sincerely, "With all my heart!"[46]

---

44   Gillies, ed., *George Whitefield's Journals*, 42.
45   Ibid., 42.
46   Ibid., 42.

Other friends aided their visitor and helped Whitefield complete the application to Oxford. Mother and son soon rejoiced to know the recommendation would be used to secure Whitefield a servitor's place in Pembroke College at Oxford University.[47] Whitefield's attainment of this position through the interest was an open door he would charge through.

According to John McConnell's book linking evangelicals with the revolutions of the time, he believed, "The hand of God was on George Whitefield's shoulder and he entered Oxford with great anticipation. His decision to attend Oxford would prove to be a turning point for him. God had placed the opportunities before the future evangelist for his life to be totally transformed and connected to His will."[48]

Young George was looking for a break in life to catapult him out of the milieu of despair surrounding many of his age: Many young men were in less fortunate circumstances, trapped with no opportunity to change their destiny. Whitefield wanted his life to be different from what it had been to this point. He developed a new interest by leaving home, thus free from previous enslavement to his circumstances which had served as obstacles to finding a personal relationship with God. All these factors were about to change with his acceptance at Oxford University and his leaving Gloucester to pursue an education.

---

47   Gledstone, 8.
48   John Francis McConnell, *Evangelicals, Revolutionists and Idealists* (Abingdon-Cokesbury Press: New York 1942), 79.

2

OXFORD LIFE

AND CONVERSION

(1732-1736)

GEORGE WHITEFIELD SAW OXFORD AS A DIFFERENT world than the one he been raised in at Gloucester. He entered the most prestigious school in England at a slower pace because of his financial situation. The aspiring student was hired as a servitor and attended young men his age coming from affluent families. The newly enlisted servitor cleaned students' rooms, served meals at parties, ran errands and performed other menial jobs. He also checked to make sure students were in their rooms, guaranteeing an adversarial relationship with upper class students.[49] Young George did not see this work as demeaning because it gave him an opportunity to study at this famous school. Dallimore explained the functions and the status of a servitor in detail:

> The servitor, in exchange for free tuition, served as a lackey for three or four more highly placed students. He might be required to wake them in the morning, black their shoes, run their errands and tidy their rooms, and might be asked to do their college exercises for them. He received what money, discarded clothing and books they chose to give. His inferior position was marked by special garb he wore and custom forbade students of a higher rank to talk to him. The Statutes ordered that the servitors were not to take part in the weekly

---

49   Stout, 18.

Disputations in Philosophy, but were to dispute for themselves on a different day, and even when a whole college attended the Holy Sacrament, the servitors were still separated and partook at another time.[50]

The stark contrast between the servitors and regular students, a situation that reinforced efforts to keep them separate, made the distinction constant. Whitefield tried to apply himself to hard work and studies, but something was lacking at this pivotal place in his life. The future evangelist had seen the affluent students who spent time in drunken parties and took their opportunities to study lightly. His strange appearance and the old clothes he wore as a servitor made him the target of teasing, but he was used to that in his work at the Bell Inn.[51]

The distinction of being a beginning student did not hinder Whitefield's ability to learn, because he was not lacking in intellectual skill. Hardy explained that Whitefield was a capable student: "Concerning Whitefield's scholastic data, there is a wealth of accredited data. He was well trained in preparatory schools with a retentive memory, ardent love of books and a firm determination to make the most of his college privileges; he experienced no difficulty in meeting his college requirements and received his college degree in regular order."[52]

Whitefield met fellow student, Charles Wesley, through a chance encounter at Oxford. Charles and his brother John gathered with several other students for prayer, spiritual edification and partaking of the sacrament. Charles Wesley invited him to a meeting of these fellow students in a group nicknamed the "Holy Club." They were also known as "Methodists" because of their rigidly prescribed lives. These devout students majored in discipline and strict adherence to a set pattern of living governed by the benevolent standard set forth in the New Testament. Because they were becoming a popular group on campus for a variety of reasons, Whitefield had previously known of the young men living by these strict rules. Other not-so-flattering names they were given included "Bible Moths" and "Bible Bigots." They were ridiculed and nicknamed, but the "Holy Club," was the most popular description of the group.[53]

Their leader, John Wesley, was an ardent student of languages and

---

50   Dallimore, vol.1, 61.

51   John Pollock, *George Whitefield and the Great Awakening* (Doubleday: Garden City, NJ 1972), 4.

52   Hardy, 37.

53   Dallimore, vol 1, 66.

excelled in these studies. His academic excellence and benevolent spirit left an indelible impression on the group that met in an environment influenced by the enlightenment movement in their studies. John fasted and gave away to the poor the income he had left after expenses. He visited prisoners and on several occasions prayed with those facing execution.[54]

John Wesley led the group to be "holy" in the midst of an "unholy school environment."[55] When young George attended a meeting of the group the first time, his heart knit with the others in the group. Here were young men of sincerity and piety. They were heavily influenced by the Pietist movement, emphasizing the spiritual side of religion.[56] They sought to break away from the rigid formalism affecting the church, although they were loyal members of the Church of England. Whitefield stated, "They were dead to the world and willing to be accounted as the dung and offscouring of all things, so that they might win Christ. Their hearts never so much glowed with the love of God, and they never prospered so much in the inward man as when they had all manner of evil spoken against them falsely without."[57] Whitefield's inclusion into the Holy Club was swift. An introduction to the little brotherhood followed. Soon he began to live the way they did.

Whitefield's experience with the Holy Club completely changed his outlook on his education at Oxford. He related how "the course of my studies I soon changed. Whereas, before, I was busy in studying dry sciences and books that went no further than the surface, I reserved now to read only that which entered into the heart of religion and which led me directly to the experimental knowledge of Jesus Christ and Him crucified."[58]

The Holy Club had a single-hearted devotion. Here were men committed to a purpose, and it deeply moved Whitefield. He met with them regularly, and they accepted him as a member of the group as one who had great promise. The study of the Scriptures sent Whitefield into deep personal introspection. The group and Whitefield, in particular, were heavily influenced by William Law's *A Serious Call to a Devout*

---

54   Gledstone, 12.
55   Dallimore, vol 1, 66.
56   See Glossary of Terms for definition of Pietism.
57   Gillies, ed., *George Whitefield's Journals*, 48.
58   Ibid., 48.

and Holy Life.[59] Whitefield began to strive for holiness through various measures. All young men in the group were familiar with Christianity because of their association with the Church of England from childhood. Being baptized into the church, confirmed and catechized had put them on the road of religion.

Whitefield quickly entered into the Holy Club's activities. He shared:

> I now begin to be like them to live by rule, and pick up the fragments of my time that not a moment may be lost. Whether I ate or drank, or whatsoever I did, I endeavoured to do all to the glory of God. Like them, having no weekly sacrament, although the Rubric required it at our own college, I received every Sunday at Christ Church. I joined them in keeping the stations by fasting Wednesdays and Fridays and left no means unused, which I thought would lead me nearer to Jesus Christ.[60]

Dallimore illustrated how due to his association with the Holy Club, Whitefield said, "I walked openly with them and chose rather to bear contempt with those people of God than to enjoy the applause of almost-Christians for a season."[61]

Whitefield's association with the Holy Club was more of an outward appearance of godliness that would keep him from the personal God, revealed in Christ. He saw no need for the new birth, of which he was not aware, because of his teaching and experience. Whitefield followed the group's example which sought acceptance by God through good deeds and habitual practices. The search for acceptance by God led the impressionable student on a journey to have a closer walk with God that was more than he had ever experienced before as a member of the Church of England.

Philip shares how the group did not find salvation in these practices:

> Their regular habits and rigid virtue were proverbial throughout the University and the city. They were the friends of the poor, and the patrons of the serious. But, with all their excellencies of character, the Wesleys united much enthusiasm, and almost incredible degree of ignorance in regard to the gospel. Their avowed object in all their voluntary privations and zealous efforts, was to save their souls, and to live wholly to the glory of God; a noble enterprise, certainly; but undertaken by them from erroneous

---

59   Philip, 16.
60   Gillies, ed., *George Whitefield's Journals*, 47.
61   Dallimore, vol. 1, 69.

motives, and upon wrong principles. For any relief proclaimed which their consciences seem to have obtained from the death of the Son of God, and the free salvation proclaimed in the virtue of it, the gospel might have been altogether untrue or unknown; so grossly ignorant were the whole band at one time.[62]

Whitefield's method of seeking a more personal religion was to develop a deeper devotion to God. He went through a crucial time of seeking to earn God's favor through various stringent means. Stout discloses how "...he convinced himself that Satan was out to wrest his soul.... Constant fasting, works of piety, and confrontation with students brought him to the edge of a breakdown."[63] Whitefield shared his struggle: "All power meditating, or even thinking, was taken from me. My memory quite failed me. My whole soul was barren and dry, and I could fancy myself to be like nothing so much as a man locked up in iron armor."[64]

When Whitefield tried to live a life of self-abasement through fasting or eating moldy bread, he became weak in body and felt faint. His sole purpose was to gain a greater awareness of God's presence in his life and be accepted by Him. His involvement in the Holy Club had sparked an interest in pietistic practices. He wanted desperately to experience God in a personal way, but his self and pride got in the way and was perceived as barriers to knowing God more fully.[65] These practices were a contrast to a formalistic route to God through liturgy and symbolism.

The self-abasement Whitefield endured was a means of continuing to try to find God and His will. His studies became secondary to his quest for godliness. He did his first few years of study in Pembroke College at a regular pace, but his new venture served as an interruption in his path to learning. He began to miss assignments and caused concern among his instructors.[66] His very life seemed consumed by this deep search for God's favor. He even sequestered himself from other members of the group, maintaining fellowship with them, but from a distance.

Whitefield was on a personal journey that led to drastic practices

---

62   Philip, 14-15.
63   Stout, 25.
64   Ibid., 25.
65   Ninde, 23.
66   Thomas S. Kidd, *George Whitefield: America's Spiritual Founding Father* (New Haven, CT: Yale University Press), 31.

that still left him unfulfilled. He tried meditating on certain portions of Scripture and the passion of Christ for hours. He secluded himself in his room and prostrated himself on the floor, forming a shape of the cross with his arms.[67] Whitefield now subjected himself to extreme self-abasement.

The suffering in this struggle, Ninde explained, brought the desperate young man to a boiling point:

> ...whole days and weeks were spent in lying prostrate on the ground, writhing under satanic torments. At last, when his condition grew serious, his tutor was alarmed and called a physician. Whitefield's tutor and friends in Gloucester, hearing of these things, were sure the young man had gone mad. He was not mad, but he was struggling toward the light, and he had not yet learned to say, "In my hand no price I bring; simply to thy cross I cling."[68]

Whitefield's life, as he knew it, came to a halt until he found what he was looking for in his relationship with God. Pietistic practices were common among the early Methodist, but Whitefield carried his methods of discipline to the extreme. He was to suffer from the abuse of his body for the rest of his life.[69]

In the meantime, abuse heaped on him by students coming from aristocratic families continued. Whitefield appeared to be as Paul, when Agrippa accused him of being mad because of his religion (Acts 26:24b).[70] Other Holy Club members were viewed by other students in similar fashion. The involvement of the revelers in the church was all-dutiful, but did not touch their lives, for they were constantly engaging in raucous activities and late night partying. The Holy Club seemed odd to them and out of place in a school designed for intellectual pursuit and off-hour wild living.[71] If the Holy club looked odd, Whitefield looked doubly odd. He appeared simply crazy with his unkept clothes, poverty, his ascetic eating habits and strange acts of devotion. Nothing else mattered to him, however, but to find peace with God.

Unexpectedly, Whitefield obtained a copy of a book bringing into

---

67   Mead, 106-107.

68   Ninde, 23.

69   Stout, 27.

70   All Scriptural quotations or citations are taken from the King James Version of the Bible unless otherwise indicated.

71   Kidd, 24.

focus the full understanding of the new birth and how one enters into a personal relationship with God. He began to read Henry Scougal's, *The Life of God in the Soul of Man.*[72]

Scougal illuminated Whitefield's understanding, helping him see that a man may be a member of the church, take the sacrament, do good deeds and still not know God. He may practice an outward form of religion and be a good person, but not have "the life of God in his soul."[73] All this disturbed Whitefield because he knew he was outwardly sincere and devout, but he also realized that he lacked God's life in him. He realized that when God began to be formed in men's souls, the experience of external religion would be natural, and the power to overcome sin and live the Christian life would be evident in all they did.[74] The revelation from Scougal was the breakthrough Whitefield needed. He possibly meditated on Scriptures containing truths concerning the inward change in salvation. Some Scriptures were especially piercing. These verses taught truths that Whitefield could come to understand: "Christ in you the hope of glory," (Col 1:27b), "that Christ may, be formed in you," (Gal. 4:19) but especially, the Scripture, "Except a man be born again he cannot enter the kingdom of God" (John 3:3).

Whitefield knew God wanted to live in him and be manifested in his life, instead of his outwardly trying to please God with good deeds. Hardy describes the glorious revelation he experienced: "The teaching of the book filled him with 'unspeakable joy' when he read that true religion is the union of the soul with God, or Christ formed within us. 'A ray of Divine light' instantaneously darted upon his soul and from that moment he knew that he must be a new creature."[75]

Whitefield sought God's salvation with his whole heart and began to turn to God in a new way, without works, trusting in God to save him. He believed Jesus' death was given for his sin and its penalty. He opened his life to God and trusted personally in what Christ had done for him. It was enlightening and peaceful to enter into a personal relationship with God after the turmoil he had been through. The light

---

72   Dallimore, *George Whitefield: God's Anointed Servant in the Great Revival of the Eighteenth Century*, 16.

73   Dallimore, vol. 1, 73.

74   Henry Scougal, *The Life of God in the Soul of Man* (Harrisburg, VA: Sprinkle Publications, 1986) 73, 92.

75   Hardy, 41.

broke to his soul, a new day dawned, and he was gloriously saved.[76]

When the joy of Christ came to George Whitefield, he had the distinction of being one of the first members, (if not the first) of the Holy Club to arrive at a full understanding of Christianity's main doctrines. He found Luther's truth and rediscovered the power that converted Augustine, while the Wesleys continued to grope in darkness for three more years until their conversion experience in 1738.[77] The new birth Whitefield experienced was a testament to his deep devotion to God and his attentiveness to God's Spirit and His Word.

Whitefield revealed how the light of God began to dawn on his soul:

> **About the end of the seventh week, after having undergone innumerable buffetings of Satan for many months, inexpressible trials by night and day under the spirit of bondage, God was pleased at length to remove the heavy load, to enable me to lay hold on His dear Son by a living faith, and by giving me the spirit of adoption, to seal me, as I humbly hope, even to the day of everlasting redemption.[78]**

Luke Tyerman shares Whitefield's elaboration of his experience: "Thus were the days of mourning ended. After a long night of desertion and temptation, the star, which I had seen at a distance before, began to appear again, and the day star arose in my heart."[79]

Michael Haykin relates how the evangelist later reflected on his conversion experience: "Being convinced by the free mercy of God that my own righteousness is filthy rags and he is only a true Christian who is one inwardly; with strong crying and tears, that cannot be uttered I beseech thee visit me with thy free spirit and say to these dry bones, 'Live!'"[80]

It seems strange that a man destined to preach to thousands was saved by himself with God and His Word, with Scougal's book serving as a guide, the key elements leading to Whitefield's new birth and salvation. His experience was real, for he later said, "I know the place it happened!

---

76   E. A. Johnston, *George Whitefield: A Definitive Biography* Vol. 1, (Trent, England: Tentmaker, 2008), 26.

77   Dallimore, vol. 1, 72.

78   Albert D Belden, *George Whitefield: The Awakener, A Modern Study of the Evangelical Revival* (London: Sampson, Low and Marston, 1930), 22.

79   Tyerman, vol.1, 25.

80   Michael A.G. Haykin, ed. *The Revived Puritan: The Spirituality of George Whitefield* (Dundas, Ontario: Joshua Press, 2000), 210.

It may be superstitious, perhaps, but whenever I go to Oxford, I cannot help running to that place where Jesus Christ revealed himself to me and gave me the new birth."[81] He was confident God's life was now his life. He was saved, a new creature through the new birth. Whitefield would never be the same again, and neither would the world because of his experience.

---

81   Dallimore, vol.1, 77.

3

ORDINATION

AND BEGINNINGS OF MINISTRY

(1736-1738)

GEORGE WHITEFIELD WAS NOW A NEW CREATURE in Christ through his experience of the new birth. He wanted time to digest his experience and find where to go next. He needed to get away, and like Paul when he went into the desert to sort through what God was doing in his life and where He was leading him (Gal. 1:15-18). Whitefield left Oxford and returned to Gloucester. He had been weakened by his severe fasting and deteriorating health through a path of battling illness that would haunt him the rest of his life.[82]

Whitefield went home to the Bell Inn and his family where his brother was now managing the Inn. Returning from Oxford, he was a different young man; he was close to earning a degree and would return to school. For the time being though, he was home. His bearing in his life had changed, and his family noticed it. They saw a confident and mature young man turning twenty-one. Despite his self-abasement in his religious pilgrimage, there was a joy in his life because of the new birth.

Whitefield began to immerse himself completely in the study of the Scriptures. Gledstone shared how Whitefield had a hunger for the Bible:

---

82   Gillies, ed., *George Whitefield's Journals*, 59.

> He cast aside all other books, and on his bended knees, read and prayed over the Holy Scriptures… stimulating him still to search; every search brought treasure; all fresh treasure caused fresh searching. Experience confirmed his faith in the doctrine of the Holy Spirit, who was to him a living Comforter, the Power of God. He seemed filled with the Spirit from the time he was born again.[83]

The Bible's influence on Whitefield was evident through the rigorous way he studied it and incorporated it into his life. He stated:

> My mind being now more open and enlarged, I began to read the Holy Scriptures… it proved meat indeed, and drink indeed, to my soul. I daily received fresh life, light, and power from above. I got more true knowledge from reading the book of God in one month, than I could ever have acquired from all the writings of men. In one word, I found it profitable for reproof, for correction, for instruction in righteousness, every way sufficient to make the man of God perfect, thoroughly furnished unto every good word and work.[84]

Whitefield's deep respect and reverence for God's Word is evident in his testimony. He stayed to himself with the Bible and returned to scenes of his childhood. The changed young man would visit St. Mary's de Crypt's school, housed in the church bearing its name. A burning that began in his heart was satisfied through a call to vocational ministry. Since he had made this wonderful discovery of the new birth, he wanted to share it with everyone he met. The initial talent God had given him in drama would be employed in sharing God's Word with others. The need for a voice crying in the wilderness was great.

Whitefield visited St. Mary's church and made his situation known to Bishop Martin Benson, the rector of the church, through his introduction to him by a certain noble lady, Lady Selwyn. He shared his call to pursue holy orders and be ordained into the ministry of the Church of England. Whitefield's call to the gospel ministry came after months of soul-searching. He was to be a minister of the gospel, not a parish pastor. The calling God was placing on his life was great. [85]

God had burned a message in his soul, the message of the new birth. From his own experience came a burden for others to know what God had done for him.

---

83   Gledstone, 23.
84   Tyerman, vol.1, 36.
85   J. C. Ryle, *Select Sermons of George Whitefield, with an Account of his Life* (Banner of Truth, Carlisle, PA: 1958), 16.

Whitefield's life work was set before him. He would preach with the fervor of the high and holy calling God had placed on his life. He would do it using his natural skill through the abilities God had given him. At first, the task of preaching the Word and receiving holy orders was overwhelming. He viewed his calling and future ministry with great humility. The young preacher felt he was not worthy to follow the course God was directing him to follow but he knew he could not escape this calling.[86] A career began differing from a traditional ministry. Whitefield would deliver the message of God's Word with the same burden God similarly gave to Old Testament prophets.

Good Bishop Benson saw Whitefield as Nathaniel, "an Israelite in whom there was no guile" (John 1:47). He saw potential in him due to the excitement God had placed in his soul. The Oxford education he would soon complete made him doubly appealing. Here was a young man who disproved his reputation as a wild enthusiast. The young man had been rumored to be one producing much heat without much light, but Benson saw otherwise. A consuming passion for study, a beginning ministry to the poor and prisoners, and a devotion to pursue God's will, whatever the cost, became hallmarks of his life.[87]

Whitefield was unlike the typical minister of the day, for here was a young man willing to throw selfish care to the winds and be obedient to the heavenly vision God had given him. He was subsequently set aside for holy orders through the laying on of hands by Bishop Benson.[88]

The scene was set before him; the beginning of Whitefield's ministry was leading to something tremendous. The confirmation for the divine call was to be sealed through his first sermon at St. Mary's church. Whitefield had been accustomed to speaking by memorizing lines and presenting dramatic pieces. Preaching would be different, but he used the skills of communication he had learned in drama. His initial sermon required finding God's message and giving it to people so they would hear a word from the Lord. Whitefield's first sermon was an important occasion in his life, a testimony to where God had brought him in a few short years.

Belden described the scene of Whitefield's first sermon:

---

86   Ibid., 16.
87   Gillies, 9.
88   Gledstone, 28-29.

Sunday, June 27th, 1736 was the great day—a day that carried momentous issues in itself, not only for George Whitefield, but for his age and for succeeding generations on two continents. Only five years had elapsed since this youth of twenty-one was a common tapster in a local public-house. Now he was on the verge of acquiring his Bachelor of Arts degree from his University, and was about to preach his first sermon as a deacon in Holy Orders.[89]

The church was filled with people having known Whitefield as a boy. Many were there to see the boy from the Bell speak to them.

Stout related Whitefield's anticipation:

Curiosity, as you may easily guess, drew a large congregation. The sight at first a little awed me, but I was comforted with a heartfelt sense of the Divine presence and soon found the unspeakable advantage of having been accustomed to public speaking when a boy at school and of exhorting and teaching the prisoners and the poor people in their private homes while at the University.[90]

As Whitefield approached his first sermon, he was captivated by the drama of it all and the fact that God would use him. When he rose to speak, he was momentarily overwhelmed by the realization that many had known him as a lad at the Bell Inn. The title of his message was "The Necessity and Benefit of a Religious Society."[91] He preached on the new birth, and the audience was captivated by his persuasive style. Whitefield described his sermon as having been energized by the Holy Spirit: "As I proceeded the fire kindled, till at last, though so young and amidst a crowd of those who knew me in my infant childish days, I trust I was enabled to speak with a certain degree of gospel authority. Some mocked, but most of the present seemed struck…"[92]

Here was a young man speaking to their hearts, not just reading a manuscript. He gave the message he had to give, overflowing with ethos. They not only listened but were struck by the divine tone of his preaching and considered the Spirit accompanying his message.

John Pollock also shared the confidence and power with which Whitefield preached:

89   Belden, 27.
90   Stout, 32-33.
91   Tyerman, vol. 1, 51.
92   Dallimore, vol.1, 97.

Next Sunday half Gloucester came to St. Mary-de-Crypt. He had not only written a sermon so long that more than half the sand ran out of the pulpit hour-glass, but had also commandeered every art remembered from his play-reading days. He let his deep voice reach effortlessly right across the box-pews of the quality to the very last of the free benches at the back.[93]

The response to Whitefield was quite a scene. Spontaneously, people began to moan and weep, as they fell under the conviction of their sin. Here was God speaking to their condition through a young man connected to a divine message.

Comments on the message were as varied as the people who heard it. Bishop Benson heard mixed reactions to Whitefield's first sermon as described:

People told him that no sermon had ever been delivered so well, and he blushed and fought down pride. But others complained to the Bishop that Whitefield had driven fifteen people mad; to which the Bishop replied: "I hope this madness continues." [94]

The subject of his first sermon was probably the same sermon he afterwards preached at a quarterly meeting of religious societies at the Bow Church in London. This impressive sermon was immediately published. "I shall displease some," said Whitefield, "for I am determined to speak against their assemblies."[95] How he fulfilled this determination was fully seen in an extract from his sermon:

I warn you of the great danger you are in, who, by their superscriptions, presence, or approbation, to promote Societies of a quite opposite nature to religion. And here I would not be understood to mean not only those who by public meetings are designed manifestly for nothing else than revilings or banquetings, for chambering and wantonness at which a modest heathen would blush to be present; but also those seemingly innocent entertainments and meetings, which the politer part of the world are so very fond of, and spend so much time in; but which notwithstanding, keep as many persons out of a sense of true religion as intemperance, debauchery or any other crime whatever. Indeed, whilst we are in this world, we must have proper relaxations, to fit, us both for the business of our profession and religion. But then, for persons who call themselves Christians, that have solemnly vowed, at their baptism to renounce the vanities of this sinful world, and are commanded in the Scripture to "abstain from all appearance of evil," and have their "conversation in heaven,"—for such persons as these to support meetings that

---

93   Pollock, 28.
94   Ibid., 28.
95   Tyerman, vol.1, 51.

(to say no worse of them) are vain and trifling, and have a natural tendency to draw off our minds from God, is absurd, ridiculous, and sinful.[96]

This message was the first of more than 18,000 sermons he preached. Judging from the response, it appears he challenged the false-complacency that some were under as unconverted church members. This first sermon had early direct and personal characteristics. The young preacher spoke to the heart of those in attendance, causing much introspection about their spiritual lives, or lack of them.

His specific and pointed preaching brought many under conviction and to a full awakening of their lost condition. Direct preaching spoke to the deception many were living under in Whitefield's day, driving them to the necessity of the new birth.

The after-effects of Whitefield's first message sent a rippling wave through his hometown. The beginnings of lifetime opposition followed him wherever he went. The message Whitefield preached was new; his listeners had never heard a sermon like the one he preached. This variation from tradition explained the differing reaction to his message. Some who were not ready for this type of preaching fired back and blamed him for disorder in the service.[97] At this juncture in Whitefield's early ministry, Bishop Benson shone as a beacon of encouragement. He offered the young preacher two parishes in Gloucester, but Whitefield turned down these opportunities that came his way, believing that his call was to an itinerant ministry.[98] Benson would stand up for the young man he believed was destined for great things through God using him. This support was crucial for the young preacher's early ministry. The call to an itinerant ministry played heavily in declining the Bishop's offer.[99]

This inscription on the sounding board in the church to this day marks the momentous occasion:

This Sounding Board
(Formerly suspended over the pulpit)

Here reverberated the wonderful voice of
The Rev. George Whitefield, A.M.

---

96   Ibid., 51-52.
97   Stout, 33.
98   Tyerman, vol. 1, 50.
99   Ibid., 118.

He preached his first sermon here
On the Sunday following his ordination by
Dr. Benson, Bishop of Gloucester,
27th June, 1736.
George Whitefield was a Gloucester Man.[100]

Tyerman shared the response to Whitefield's first sermon. He said, "Thus did the renowned evangelist begin his ministry. Great was the effect produced. A few mocked; but most of the congregation displayed profound emotion,"[101]

Bishop Benson himself was probably not present at Whitefield's first sermon because of reports given to him. He displayed generosity toward the young preacher. Whitefield wrote of the bishop's generosity: "Our good bishop was pleased to give me another present of five guineas, a great supply for one who had not a guinea in the world."[102]

Whitefield went back to Oxford to finish his degree, after ten months of piecing together God's call. While returning to Oxford and completing his degree, the young preacher was undoubtedly still in contact with Bishop Benson; he was ready to launch out on his own as doors opened up for him to preach.[103] Whitefield's family's reaction to his life's calling is relatively unknown, but no one stood in the way of what God was doing through him.

The Young preacher bore the title of an ordained minister in the Church of England with nobility. He remained loyal to the church, although he would preach in any church in both England and America. He had a great hearing in "dissenter churches," not aligned with the Church of England. Whitefield subscribed to the Thirty-Nine Articles of the Church of England and its catechism. He administered the sacraments of the church with great reverence and humility.[104]

Serious studies begin to enlighten Whitefield in the Doctrines of Grace. He read Matthew Henry's commentary with the Bible and was significantly influenced by Henry's Calvinistic theology.

Whitefield revealed, "About this time, God was pleased to enlighten my soul and bring me into the knowledge of His free grace and the

---

100   Dallimore, vol. 1, 98.
101   Tyerman, vol. 1, 50.
102   Ibid., 50.
103   Gillies, ed., *George Whitefield's Journals*, 70.
104   Ibid., 62.

necessity of being justified in His sight by faith only. This was more extraordinary, because my friends at Oxford had rather inclined to the mystic divinity."[105]

Whitefield's deep studies were soon interrupted. A friend in Broughton apparently believed Whitefield's reticence was holding him back. The friend renewed the request that he supply in his pulpit at the Chapel of the Tower of London. He thus began his ministry in the London area there.[106]

Whitefield was amazed that the meetings and places he preached were thronged with masses of people coming to hear him. The young preacher's messages were a clear expression of God's Word awakening the souls of needy people in his day. The crowds continued to grow. Whitefield's future societies were knit together for the preaching of the gospel and the fellowship his supporters had in the revival happening throughout the land.

These supporters and societies would remain within the Church of England and not separate from it. Throughout all this early and later success, Whitefield remained loyal to the Church of England, choosing to be supportive of its teachings. Whitefield never left the church. Some within the church left him, but God used the First Great Awakening to revive the true spirit of the Reformation in England. His preaching was centered on the doctrines the Protestant reformers had discovered.[107]

The early beginnings of Whitefield's ministry were overwhelming. As the crowds flocked to hear him speak, they discovered the uniqueness of his preaching. He was unlike any other minister. Curiosity was possibly a factor but biblical truth was being proclaimed boldly. The soil for the gospel was fertile all around him, as many responded to his messages. The spiritual climate of Whitefield's early preaching was encouraging during the start of his ministry. It was a marvelous time to be alive, and the gospel was being proclaimed in a tremendous way.

Whitefield had an extensive preaching circuit during his early days in London. He initially was viewed with skepticism as he preached in a

---

105 Dallimore, vol.1, 84.
106 Ibid., 104-105.
107 The distinction of these groups in America meant they would be labeled New Lights and in England, they would form societies that differed from the formalism within the established church.

church in London. Whitefield reported his activity:

> On Sunday, August 8th, in the afternoon, I preached at Bishopsgate
> Church...those in the stairs almost all seemed to sneer at me on account of my
> youth; but they soon grew serious and exceedingly attentive, and after I came
> down, showed me great tokens of respect, blessed me as I passed along, and
> made great enquiry who I was. The question no one could answer, for I was
> quite a stranger to them.[108]

God began to exalt Whitefield in a status unparalleled for a young man his age. He shared how he wrestled with pride:

> God sent me something to ballast it. For as I passed along the street, many
> came out of their shops to see so young a person in a gown and cassock. One
> I remember in particular cried out, "There's a boy parson;" which served to
> mortify my pride and put me also upon turning that apostolic exhortation into
> prayer, 'Let no man despise thy youth.'(II Tim. 4:12).[109]

From Whitfield's first sermon to his departure after two months, his popularity in London continued to increase. The crowds were vast, making it necessary to place constables both inside and outside of churches to preserve peace.[110] He recalls, "Here I continued for the space of two months, reading prayers twice a week, catechizing and preaching once, visiting the soldiers in the infirmary and barracks daily. I also read prayers every evening at Wapping chapel and preached at Ludgate prison every Tuesday."[111]

The response was even greater as the boy preacher's impact grew. Dallimore revealed the magnetism of Whitefield's earliest ministry:

> Whitefield's ministry at the Tower lasted for two months and proved
> a steady attraction. A number of young men, probably from the religious
> societies, were drawn to hear him discourse. He says, "on the new birth," and
> some of the titled persons of London, who later were numbered among his
> followers, first became aware of him at this time.[112]

The breadth of Whitefield's ministry was summarized by Tyerman: "In 1737, Whitefield's appearance, voice and pulpit eloquence drew around him thousands... in a succession of public services which

---

108   Gillies, ed., *George Whitefield's Journals*, 77.
109   Ibid., 76.
110   Belcher, 42.
111   Ibid., 77.
112   Dallimore, vol. 1, 105.

literally startled the nation."[113] Having heard nothing of this sort before, England was convicted by his preaching. God used his initial ministry for tremendous results.

Whitefield's hectic pace in ministry was remarkable. He wrote about how consumed he was in his ministry as he recorded in his journal:

> Last week, save one, I preached ten times in different churches, and the last week seven; and yesterday four times and read prayers twice, though I slept not above an hour the night before, which was spent in religious conversation and interceding...I now begin to preach charity sermons twice or thrice a week, besides two or three on Sundays, and sixty or seventy pounds are collected weekly for the poor children. Thousands would come in to hear, but cannot.[114]

This statement confirms his notoriety that quickly became his trademark throughout his ministry.

The question of why Whitefield was popular in his preaching and the reason for his notoriety is disclosed by Dallimore:

> Moreover, we may be sure that the people found something highly attractive in the young preacher himself. He was always exceptionally neat about his person—an element of his concept of Christian discipline—and his manner was gracious and easy. At this stage of his development, he was still marked by an unassuming youthfulness, but his consciousness of being called of God gave him an extraordinary spiritual authority and courage. To many of his listeners he seemed as a messenger from heaven; his countenance was radiant and he stood as one sent from God, and, like Charles Wesley who spoke of him as "an angel guest," many were beginning to refer to him as "The Seraph."[115]

Whitefield's ministry would be unlike any typical minister of the Church of England. God had called him to preach the gospel to the entire world as an evangelist. The criticism Whitefield endured later was eased by the confidence placed in him by Bishop Benson. There would always be mixed reaction to Whitefield's ministry.

The criticism of his age of 21 was defended as unusual but proper, given the completion of his degree and passion for fulfilling the divine mandate on his life. Confidence tempered by the humility of God's call on his life drove Whitefield. This combination exhibited in Whitefield's ministry sent him into unparalleled avenues of preaching the gospel.

---

113 Tyerman, vol.1, 64.
114 Ibid., 114.
115 Ibid., 116.

4

MISSIONARY ASPIRATIONS

FOR GEORGIA

(1738)

THE WORLD WAS NOW IN GEORGE WHITEFIELD'S view as he discovered the explosive power of the gospel. The dynamic youthful enthusiasm of his personality met the need in England for spiritual revival of the greatest order. The news was out about this young preacher, who was making quite a stir in the spiritually starved nation.

Preaching opportunities opened up to Whitefield. People were hungry for the message of Scripture preached with dynamic power. Edwin Cashin, in his book detailing the history of the Bethesda Orphanage, explains the expansion of the young preacher's ministry:

> Blessed with a strong, resonant, melodious voice that he could play with the skill of a born actor, he began preaching with the assurance of one of the elect—with astounding results. His sermons were printed and widely read, and by the time he reached London to board ship on his first trip to America, he had become quite a celebrity. He marveled at this sudden fame: "I could no longer walk on foot as usual, but was constrained to go in a coach from place to place, to avoid the hosannas of the multitudes."[116]

---

116 Cashin, Edward J., *Beloved Bethesda: a History of George Whitefield's Home for Boys, 1740-2000* (Atlanta: Mercer University Press, 2001), 5.

The force of the message from Scripture was strong and it was evident that "the boy preacher" was taking England by storm. His notoriety resulted in some opposition and critics referred to the wild enthusiasm that accompanied the results of his preaching.[117] Whitefield encountered the same type of opposition that David had when he volunteered to fight Goliath, but his brothers sought to quench his enthusiasm for God (I Sam.17:28). The opposition plagued Whitefield wherever he went because his message was contradictory to the majority of the established clergy's teaching. The enlightenment movement heavily affected the clergy. They were content to read moral platitudes and have a semblance of religion dealing with outward deference to religious duty. The inward change wrought through the new birth was a foreign concept. Whitefield later said, "They were unaffected by an unfelt, unknown Christ."[118] He began to have an understanding for those hungry to hear the gospel as many of the churches were closed to him.

Changes were afoot for the "Holy Club" at Oxford with most of its initial members now graduated and in ministry and mission work, scattered throughout the world. John Wesley had gone to Georgia, which had been newly established as a colony for debtors, prisoners and orphans, but he was still confused concerning the "new birth." Wesley thought being a Christian rested largely on external things. His understanding led him to a deeply pietistic life. The inward change God could give was unknown to him since he hoped to be accepted by God because of his works. Dallimore revealed that Wesley stated in his journal his reason for going to Georgia as a missionary: "My chief motive," for he had then declared, "is the hope of saving my own soul." He had thought of salvation by way of the Holy Club type of discipline and believed that a continuation of such practices, assisted by the ending of privations in the colony, would serve toward that end."[119]

Keith Hardman explained the plight of the Wesleys in Georgia:

> **On October 14, 1735, the Wesley brothers had gone to Georgia, Britain's newest colony, to work among the colonists. They were in the same primitive spiritual state that Whitefield had known and outgrown at Oxford. Ritualism**

---

117 Dallimore, vol. 1, 119.

118 Sydney, Alstrom, *A Religious History of the American People* (New Haven, Conn.: Yale University Press, 1970), 284.

119 Dallimore, vol. 1, 145.

was their byword. They asked him (John Wesley) to come to Georgia and share
their labors, which he did, sailing from England on December 28, 1737... By
then the Wesleys' austerity had caused the people to reject them, and they
returned to England as bitter men, half-aware that their inadequate religion
was the cause of their problems.[120]

While the Wesleys went to Georgia, Whitefield continued to
enjoy great freedom and open opportunities to preach the gospel. The
direction of his ministry was being dramatically shaped. Because the lure
of a wandering gospel preacher was always appealing to Whitefield, John
Wesley's venture to Georgia intrigued the young preacher.

The Wesley's missionary journey caused Whitefield to yearn to
"preach the gospel where Christ was not known, lest he build on another
man's foundation"(Rom. 15:20). Charles Wesley had returned before
his brother John and excited Whitefield about Georgia. Wesley saw
the great need of children who had lost parents with no one to care
for them. Shortly after his spiritual rebirth, Whitefield received a letter
from Georgia, written by John Wesley, telling him God's work needed
to be done in Georgia. "The harvest is truly plenteous, but the laborers
few" (Matthew 9:37). Would someone heed the call? "What if thou art
the man, Mr. Whitefield?"[121] he asked. This summons came soon after
Whitefield saw the need in Georgia and he took it to be God's clear
message.

Charles Wesley made Whitefield's mission clearer when he wrote
an update about how a fever had raged in Georgia, leaving children
orphans. The young preacher credited Charles Wesley with the idea of a
Georgia orphanage: "It was first proposed to me by my dear friend, Mr.
Charles Wesley, who with General Oglethorpe, had concerted a scheme
for carrying on such a design, before I had any thought of going abroad
myself."[122]

Unfortunately, things weren't going well for Whitefield's friend
John Wesley in Georgia. His adaptation to Georgia from England in
his approach to ministry was difficult and seemed futile. Relationship
problems with the settlers and his unconverted state hindered his

---

120   Keith J. Hardman, *The Spiritual Awakeners* (Chicago: Moody Press, 1983), 82.
121   Cashin, 3.
122   Ibid., 3.

ministry. These events led to his leaving Georgia in a depressed state.[123]

Dallimore recalls the reason for Wesley's departure from Georgia:

> John's stay in the colony was brought to a close by an innocent but unwise love affair. Sophia Hopkey, was the young lady of his affections. He could not make up his mind regarding marriage; suddenly she married another man. John was deeply wounded and shortly thereafter debarred her from the communion service. This was a foolish action which crystallized the feelings of the people against him. Sophia's husband sued Wesley for £1,000 for defamation of her character, and a notice was posted for his arrest. John was able, however, to escape under cover of night to Charleston, South Carolina, from whence he quickly sailed for home.[124]

Wesley's rapid departure from Georgia was necessitated by the romantic catastrophe, but it was also due to his failure to relate to the colonists in Georgia. He left Georgia disappointed about fruitless labor.

Wesley had been dealing with his own salvation when he came to Georgia. Moravian missionaries, led by Augustus Spangenberg, were on the same ship as Wesley and they witnessed to him. When the ship they were on encountered a violent storm, Wesley feared for his life, but saw peace on the Moravians' faces. This conflict of reactions led Spangenberg to inquire whether Wesley knew Christ. Wesley had no clear answer and admitted, "I was afraid to die."[125] When Wesley left Georgia frustrated, he must have pondered Spangenberg's question.

Wesley returned to England still a zealous, hardworking churchman, but unconverted. His association with the Moravians was to last throughout his life and greatly influenced him. His connection with the Moravians also resulted in his going to Fetter Lane, an unused chapel in London, where services were led by Moravian leader, Peter Bohler.[126]

Wesley subsequently found Christ personally at this meeting place for the Moravians on Aldersgate Street. Thomas Kidd, author of the latest biography on Whitefield, shares the circumstances and certainty of Wesley's conversion after he heard the reading of Luther's preface to Romans. Wesley described his conversion experience clearly, as he said, "I felt my heart strangely warmed. I felt I did trust in Christ alone

---

123 Dallimore, vol, 1, 146-148.
124 Ibid., 147-148.
125 Ibid., 145.
126 Ibid., 173-174.

for salvation."[127] Wesley's conversion influenced by the Moravians was a landmark for the Methodist movement. His conversion meant Whitefield would have a co-laborer of equal stature in his initial ministry.

Whitefield's interest in going to Georgia was also encouraged through General James Oglethorpe, the first governor appointed to Georgia. "Shortly after obtaining the charter, he sailed with one hundred and sixteen intended colonists. They reached the spot where Savannah now stands, without encountering any delay or difficulty. Oglethorpe set to work at once to carry out his three leading ideas, the cultivation of silk, the conversion of the Indians and 'no slavery.'"[128]

J. R. Andrews explained the early colonization of Georgia:

> During the first two years of its existence as a colony, Parliament voted upwards of thirty thousand pounds for its support, and everything was done to tempt over (persuade) colonists from the mother country. In the third year of its formation, the Wesleys arrived, followed shortly after by George Whitefield and several others, men who went with all the health and energy necessary for so arduous an undertaking.[129]

Whitefield's vision for Georgia was tied to the anticipation Oglethorpe had in his schemes for the burgeoning colony.[130]

As Whitefield eyed Georgia, he discovered the colony's need for a Minister of the Church of England through Parliament's supervision. He decided to entrust his safekeeping to God; he would go to Georgia for a preliminary visit. His plans were to visit Frederica and Savannah and preach as the designated Minister of the Church of England, appointed by the trustees to the colony.[131]

Oglethorpe would be sailing again for Georgia in the near future. Whitefield had two months to prepare for the voyage with the colony's founder. In receiving the message that Oglethorpe would be leaving, Whitefield shared how it "gladdened many hearts, though I cannot say it did mine; for I counted the hours, as it were, till I went abroad. I preached, as usual, about five times a week; but the congregations grew,

---

127 Kidd, 51.

128 J. R Andrews, *George Whitefield, A Light Rising in Obscurity* (Morgan and Chase: London, 2nd ed. 1930), 36-37.

129 Ibid., 37.

130 Ibid., 37.

131 Robert G. McPherson, *The Journal of the Earl of Egmont* (University of Georgia Press: Athens, GA), 360-361.

if possible, larger and larger."[132] It appears that Whitefield had mixed emotions about leaving England, yet the need was strong in his heart to minister in Georgia. His misgivings seem to revolve around leaving behind many followers converted during the beginning of his ministry.

The days before Whitefield left for Georgia marked further development in his ministry. According to Dallimore, "Before leaving London he had begun to pray extempore, and while at these down-river ports he added extempore preaching—a form of ministry without which his later open-air preaching would have been impossible."[133]

Dallimore described what Whitefield felt in going to Georgia:

> We may well wonder if Whitefield did not feel some tinge of regret in leaving so great a work as had been his in England. "Large offers were made me," he writes, "if I would stay in London"; yet he was relinquishing all of this in order to become a missionary to a sparsely populated colony in a wilderness area of America. The little vessel meant weeks of confinement, poor food and a passage that could hardly fail to entail sickness and danger. But when some of the Gloucester people wrote, urging him to remain, he replied, "Let not my friends trouble me with temporal offers. I shall accept no place this side Jordan."[134]

Whitefield's followers were anxious to hear of his missionary aspirations. They had resigned themselves to the reality that he would be leaving for Georgia to initiate a missionary effort there. In Bristol, Gloucester, and London, hundreds of people prayed for him, bought his printed sermons and impatiently awaited the reports of his activities abroad that he had promised to send to James Hutton.[135]

Dallimore continued describing the events whirling around Whitefield as he went to Georgia:

> Charles Wesley, who had returned from Georgia a few months earlier, viewing the marvelous results of Whitefield's preaching wrote: The whole nation is in an uproar...Similarly, James Hervey exclaimed, "All London and the whole nation ring of the great things of God done by his ministry." And on board the Whitaker, Whitefield, apparently thinking of the strange troubles the Wesleys had encountered in Georgia, prayed, "God give me a deep

---

132 Gillies, ed., *George Whitefield's Journals*, 84.
133 Dallimore, vol. 1, 140.
134 Ibid., 140.
135 Ibid., 140.

humility, a well-guided zeal, a burning love and a single eye, and then let men or devils do their worst!"[136]

With this preparation, Whitefield felt led by God to go on the journey that would change his life and ministry forever. Whitefield had not begun his correspondence as a regular communication tool, yet it would become a trademark of his ministry. It seems strange that there was no correspondence between Wesley and Whitefield on the new birth. The lack of communication possibly was a result of the seclusion Whitefield surrounded himself with at Oxford, and his departure from the school to recuperate.

Going in a different direction, John Wesley had missed hearing of Whitefield's conversion experience when it happened. Whitefield was still introspective through finding himself a new believer as he retreated to Gloucester. The new convert was excited about his faith and the new gospel power he found in preaching. Wesley had returned disillusioned to England before the Aldersgate experience of his conversion.

Georgia offered Whitefield the same adventure to preach in the New World that Paul, the apostle, had on his journeys to preach the gospel. At the invitation of the trustees, Whitefield went to Georgia just as John Wesley was returning. Wesley did send a letter to Whitefield after the young evangelist had embarked on his initial trip to Georgia. In the letter, Wesley tried to persuade Whitefield not to go to the rough colony, even though he never talked with him directly.[137]

Tyerman reflected on Wesley's delayed correspondence:

> It is a remarkable fact that two days after this, while the ship Whitaker was still at anchor, Wesley, at half-past four o'clock in the morning, landed at Deal, on his return from Georgia. Great was his surprise to hear that Whitefield was close at hand; and still smarting from the wrongs he had suffered at Savannah, he immediately dispatched a letter advising the young evangelist to relinquish his mission.
>
> Who can estimate what would have been the consequences of Whitefield's yielding to Wesley's wish? Had he returned to London, the probability is he would never again have started for America; and, in such a case, many of the brightest chapters of his history could never have been penned.[138]

---

136   Ibid., 140.
137   Ibid., 150.
138   Tyerman, vol.1, 114-115.

Whitefield's preparation for going to Georgia meant taking a team of young men with him. Dallimore described how "He took with him five young men, having selected them with a view to certain requirements of the colony."[139] These men, each with specific responsibilities, assisted Whitefield in various tasks when he got to the rustic colony. "Two were teachers, for he planned to establish schools for the settlers' children. Two others were servants. He intended to have them do the housekeeping—a prudent arrangement which would mean a totally male household, and would avoid the necessity of bringing in outside (particularly female) help."[140] This arrangement appears to be by design, removing any sense of impropriety from the young men.

The fifth man, James Habersham, was to be Whitefield's personal assistant. He saw good qualities he hoped to cultivate in Habersham. He wrote, "O that I may be made an instrument of seeding him up for God."[141] Whitefield cherished the hope of establishing an orphanage in the colony and aspired to build an orphan house using Habersham as its superintendent. On board ship, the young instructor gave Whitefield lessons in Latin.[142]

The Whitaker, the ship on which Whitefield sailed, encountered stiff winds and veered toward Spain. Whitefield's time in a full-fledged Catholic country made quite an impression on him. He perceived their ritualism as substitutes for true religion. He shared, "After morning exposition in the church, went and saw the Roman Catholics at their High Mass; and shall only make this remark: That there needs no other argument against Popery, than to see the pageantry, superstition, and idolatry of their worship."[143]

After spending some time at Gibraltar, they eventually set sail for Georgia. Whitefield, who made seven trips to America and adapted very well to both places, was the first evangelist to have a ministry on both continents.

Dallimore shared the kindness of the captain to Whitefield in his accommodations aboard the ship:

---

139 Dallimore, vol. 1, 143.
140 Ibid., 143.
141 Ibid., 143.
142 Ibid., 143.
143 Gillies ed., *George Whitefield's Journals*, 136.

Then the ship's Master, Captain Whiting, began to show favor. Noticing that Whitefield had no place of privacy for study and prayer, he offered him the use of his cabin.

Whitefield's practice of discipline and industry made such a place a boon, and in using it he reported, "I fancied myself in my little cell at Oxford; for I have not spent so many hours in sweet retirement since I left the university."[144]

Whitefield's interaction with the crew and soldiers was interesting. He related a strategy of sharing the gospel with them:

About twelve, I came on board, being unwilling to be absent from my proper charge long together. I was received kindly, visited the sick and catechized the soldiers, some of whom answered most aptly, for which I distributed amongst them all something I knew would be agreeable. Oh, that I may catch them by a holy guile! But that power belongeth only unto God.[145]

Whitefield was familiar with the rough nature of those on the ship. They ridiculed him at first, but eventually, his time with them was pleasant. He prayed for them, was sincere in his efforts to minister to them, took an interest in them and he spoke directly to their heart in vespers.[146]

The effects of the gospel Whitefield represented and preached became increasingly evident as the journey continued on the open sea. "The captains made it their practice to stand, one on each side of Whitefield as he preached, and Captain Mackay ordered a drum to beat, calling the soldiers to Divine service every morning. There were occasions when the other ships' heard him too, "for being in the trade winds, the other two ships' companies drew near and joined in the worship of God."[147]

Dallimore imagined the sight of Whitefield preaching on the ship:

What a sight it must have been! The calm sea, the three vessels clustered together, the crowded decks ablaze with the red coats of soldiers, and one deck serving as an open-air chapel, replete with make-shift benches and, possibly, a male choir. Before them stands the young chaplain, a Captain on each side and officers round about. In a voice which can be clearly heard on each of the three vessels, he leads a service which includes the singing of Psalms and the prayers of the Church of England liturgy. Many who recently cursed God join in the words of petition and praise.[148]

---

144   Dallimore, vol. 1, 153.
145   Gillies, ed., *George Whitefield's Journals*, 116.
146   Dallimore, vol. 1, 152.
147   Ibid., 158.
148   Ibid., 158.

The preacher's influence was realized through the improvement of the men's speech and the reported conversions. Whitefield's fearlessness in the face of hardship was a powerful witness to the crew. [149]

Whitefield probably used the time wisely to remind the soldiers and crew of the inevitability of their death and the full accounting of their lives they would all give to God for their immortal souls. What an opportunity they had with the young evangelist, calling them to Christ! Whitefield's influence on the voyage was substantial. Evidence of the change in the crew was seen through the change in their reading. He recounted, "...dispersed Bibles, Testaments. Soldiers' Monitors amongst the men; exchanged some books for some cards, which I threw overboard; preached a sermon against drunkenness, which God enabled me to finish yesterday; and returned in the evening, delighted with seeing the porpoises roll about the great deep."[150]

Whitefield took the books of sordid details and threw them overboard because the crew had no more use for them, since they were engaged in the study of God's word and the literature Whitefield was distributing.[151]

There were other ministries aboard the ship. Habersham taught the children, "the lambs of his flock," according to Whitefield. He conducted a school aboard the ship and the children attended during regular school hours. Several of the soldiers were taught to write and read, "... my friend is likely to make a useful man" said Whitefield, (referring to Habersham) as recorded in his journal March 15.[152]

Evidently, Whitefield conducted funerals aboard the ship because there is a record of a service for a young slave in his journal.[153]

He also performed weddings on the ship. One notable wedding is recorded by Wakeley when he revealed some of Whitefield's youthful impulsiveness:

> During the voyage a marriage took place on board the vessel, the ceremony being performed on the deck. The bridegroom exhibited great levity while Mr. Whitefield was going through the service. He thereupon closed the prayer book, and refused to proceed further until a more serious appreciation of the

149 Ibid., 152.
150 Gilles, ed., *George Whitefield's Journals*, 141.
151 Dallimore, vol. 1, 156.
152 Gilles, ed., *George Whitefield's Journals*, 140.
153 Ibid., 144.

obligations they were taking upon themselves had been evidenced, when he finished the ceremony, and on closing gave the bride a Bible.[154]

Many suffered severe sickness through an epidemic of fever that swept throughout the ship before they reached America:

> For many days and nights Whitefield visited between twenty and thirty sick persons, and, as was to be expected, he contracted the disease himself. The foolish medical practices of the times were used on him; he was blistered and vomited once, and blooded thrice, but he became worse and lay at the doors of death for some days. Yet from this extremity he was brought back and later testified: "I earnestly desired to be dissolved and go to Christ; but God was pleased to order it otherwise, and I am resigned, though I can scarce be reconciled to come back again into this vale of misery. I had the Heavenly Canaan in full view and hoped I was going to take possession of it, but God saw I was not yet ripe for glory, and therefore in mercy spared me."[155]

One soldier who branded Whitefield as an imposter was a cadet and former university student. He had a change of heart (according to Whitefield in describing his experience), "...who was so moved upon by the Holy Spirit that he asked Captain McKay for release from the military in order that he might devote his life to the service of Christ."[156] Whitefield's influence was definitely positive on the ship. His leadership, in spite of his youth, was impressive.

His first visit to Georgia featured the discovery of disorganization and chaos in the colony. Dallimore illustrated the state of Georgia:

> The colonists in Georgia were for the most part a shiftless sort in poor health inexperienced in farming and physically incapable of pioneering a wilderness land.
>
> But others came who were of a better class. Among these were additional Englishmen, a group of pious Germans known as Saltzburgers, a few French-speaking Swiss, a party of Scottish Highlanders and two small companies of Moravians.[157]

Whitefield ministered in Frederica en route to Savannah. He and his young men lived together at the parsonage, keeping with their intention to have no female help. The two menservants assumed the domestic duties. The young preacher set up his system of living by rule, and matters worked out well. He said, "I find it possible to

---

154 Wakeley, 86.
155 Gillies, 23.
156 Ibid., 160.
157 Ibid., 201.

manage the house without distraction."[158]

It is interesting to note Whitefield's first impression of America: "America is not so horrid a place as it is represented to be. The heat of the weather, lying on the ground, etc., are mere painted lions in the way, and to a soul filled with divine love are not worth mentioning…"[159]

The colonial missionary's ministry was one of visiting from house to house, catechizing children, and reading prayers twice daily, while expounding two lessons daily. He would read to a houseful of people three times a week; expound the two lessons at five in the morning, read prayers and preached twice, and expound the catechism to servants at seven in the evening every Sunday.[160] He had a full schedule and threw himself wholeheartedly into the ministry with the people of Georgia, whom he attended constantly.

Whitefield was not immune to trials and tests in Georgia, but he handled them differently than Wesley did. Unfortunately, Whitefield's fever that attacked him on his voyage returned, but, undaunted, he was in the pulpit that following Sunday. He became ill in the midst of worship and had to retire before he began the second service.[161]

The young missionary visited the villages of Thunderbolt, Highgate, and Hampton as soon as he recovered. Meanwhile, he called on Thomas Causton, chief magistrate of the colony, and visited with Tomo Chachi, the famous Native American who previously visited the royal court in England. Communication with Whitefield and the old chief was difficult, hampering the evangelist's effort to declare the gospel. The young missionary managed, at least, to speak of hell to the old man—a hell he described by pointing to the fire. The chief explained he would not become a Christian because of the inconsistencies in some of Christ's followers and excused his lack of conversion because of these hypocrisies.[162]

Wherever he went, Whitefield preached the gospel. In Savannah, the same yearning came to him as in England to preach to people in all places. The gathering to hear him preach was not as vast as in England

---

158   Ibid., 202.
159   Ibid., 202.
160   Ibid., 202.
161   Ibid., 202.
162   Henry, 37.

because of the sparse population, so Whitefield preached mainly to smaller groups of people.

The social conditions of the primitive colony moved Whitefield through the orphans he met. He felt there must be a place of safety for them, a house of refuge where these little ones would be taught the riches of Christ and learn spiritual truths to pull them out of their hopelessness.

Whitefield's trip to an orphanage in Ebenezer administered by the Saltzburgers sealed his decision to begin an orphanage. Belcher reveals, "The Saltzburgers were exiles for conscience' sake, and were eminent for piety and industry. Their ministers, the Rev. Messrs. Grenaw and Boltzius, were eminently evangelical, and their asylum, which they had been enabled to found by British benevolence, for widows and orphans, was flourishing."[163]

Whitefield was delighted with the order and harmony of Ebenezer, and he gave a share of his own "poor's store" to Boltzius, the headmaster for his orphanage. A scene was etched in Whitefield's mind completing his purpose for his visit as he described: "Boltzius called all the children before him, catechized and exhorted them to give God thanks for his good providence towards them. He prayed with them, and made them pray after him; they then sang psalms. Afterwards, the little lambs came and shook me by the hand, one by one, and so we parted."[164] Whitefield was now pledged to this cause for life. He shared how he must have "little lambs" to minister to.[165] The potential school would mean Whitefield would go back to England and raise funds for an orphan house.

Whitefield's travels continued during August when he ventured south. Cashin described the visit: "He went to Frederica, a town greatly swelled in population by the five hundred men of Oglethorpe's regiment and their families. Then, he called on the Highlanders at Darien and the Reverend Mr. McLeod, their minister. Many of the Scots talked openly of quitting their frontier outpost in favor of Charlestown, where they had relatives."[166]

---

163 Belcher, 62.

164 Ibid., 62.

165 Sarah Coleman Temple, *Georgia's Journeys*, (University of Georgia Press: Athens, GA), 220.

166 Cashin, 10.

After three months' time in Georgia, Whitefield was surprisingly generous in his opinion of the colony and Georgians. He thought that despite appearances, the infant colony might succeed. Because the Georgia experiment was still popular in England, Whitefield thought he could easily raise money for an orphanage.[167]

Whitefield's time in Georgia was short. The weather was hot and humid; the crowds hearing him preach were smaller, but the opportunities for a life's work abounded. He would go back to England and disclose his plans. With a heavy but hopeful heart, the aspiring missionary left after several brief months in the backward colony. After raising support in the colony, he hoped to use his preaching back in England to present the burden for an orphanage to people who would support his dream.

Cashin recalled the young evangelist departure: "Whitefield departed from Georgia on August 28, 1738, to the tearful good-byes by some of his flock. He left to James Habersham the responsibility of keeping the prayer meetings going, taking in orphans at his Savannah school, and preparing to build a proper orphan house."[168] Habersham also eventually returned to England before the orphanage began.

As Whitefield came to Charleston, Cashin noted, "Alexander Garden, commissary of the Church of England in Charlestown, greeted Whitefield warmly, sympathized with him about how badly John Wesley had been treated, and assured his guest of his support should Whitefield suffer the same treatment Wesley endured."[169] Unfortunately, this sympathy would not continue in future encounters with Garden; the tensions got worse between these two, and these were the last pleasant words between them. Whitefield sailed for England on September 8, 1738, and after a perilous crossing, landed in Ireland, where the ship was diverted there. The voyage back featured a total diminishment of supplies on board as they were blown off their course.[170]

Landing in Kilrush, Ireland, Whitefield began to be aware of Ireland's Catholic influence. He referred to the residents and priests there as "blind guides."[171] He said, "I can think of no likelier means to convert

---

167   Ibid., 11.
168   Ibid., 11.
169   Ibid., 11.
170   Gillies, ed., *George Whitefield's Journals*, 181.
171   Ibid., 181.

them from their erroneous principles, than to get the Bible translated into their own native language, to have it put in their houses, and start charity schools erected for their children, as Mr. Jones has done in Wales, which would insensibly weaken the Romish interest."[172]

Whitefield dined with the mayor of Limerick after he fully recovered from the exhausting off-course voyage. He spoke to several groups there, in various places. The young preacher's stay in Ireland was sufficient time to recover, and soon he was back in England. [173] Whitefield would raise support for the colony while using his preaching in England to take the burden of the orphanage to people who would support it. It would be a place to rescue orphans from their perilous plight. He made his way to London, arriving on December 8, 1738.

---

172   Ibid., 181.
173   Ibid., 182.

5

To the Open Fields

with the Gospel

(1738-1739)

W HITEFIELD PLANNED TO GO BACK TO Georgia as soon as he received sponsorship from Parliament to start an orphanage there. He would present the need to Parliament to raise support for the work; he would also be appointed Chaplain to Georgia.

The process took several months, while he assembled a team of workers and children to go back with him to birth this needed ministry.

Cashin described the process of the sponsorship for the orphanage from the trustees:

> All inconveniences aside, Whitefield was willing to return to Georgia if only the trustees would agree to certain conditions. He wanted a house and garden plot, and asked the trustees to reimburse him and a friend Delamotte for the cost of their travel. He also requested a letter from the trustees to the Bishop of London endorsing his ordination to the priesthood and his assignment to Savannah. Finally and most importantly, he wanted the trustees to commission him to go about the country to collect money for his favorite project: the orphan house. He made it clear that if he could solicit money, he would bear the full costs of the orphan house and its upkeep; in other words, the trustees would not need to pay so much as a shilling.
>
> As the weeks passed, the trustees must have felt that they were losing control of this particular Georgia clergyman. The trustees did as Whitefield wished, writing letters to the bishops, making out the commission for him to

collect for the orphan house, and in due course, deeding him 500 acres for the precious orphan house.[174]

Parliament deliberated and heard Whitefield's plea. The support of the orphanage in Georgia would be tied to General Oglethorpe's support of the colony and his raising an army and additional party leaders to venture to the needy region. Oglethorpe needed an army, not only for stability in the colony, but also for protection of the settlers threatened by the rumblings of the Spanish in Florida.[175]

Whitefield raised support for the orphanage during the delay of departing to Georgia. He was busy preaching the gospel during this waiting period. His name was famous in England, and invitations came from many places to speak.

A battle ensued with Whitefield's friends and enemies because many were opposed to the awakening. He was shut out of some churches that forbade him to use their pulpit because of this new form of preaching. Several times he would arrive to speak at a church only to have the invitation rescinded because the parish minister succumbed to the pressure and wouldn't allow him to speak. Others did not wish to enjoin the controversy either with the skeptics of the movement or those supporting Whitefield's ministry. He knew this opposition was coming, but he saw it intensify rapidly as he returned to England. The division concerning his ministry led to other options.

Cashin shared an ugly incident illustrating the tension toward Whitefield from the established clergy:

> In the process of collecting money for the orphans, Whitefield caused a religious revolution. Rather, he first created a sensation, then a revolution. There was the affair of St. Margaret's Church in Westminster on a Sunday in early February 1739. The affair highlighted the opposing forces at play in the Church of England at that time. Whitefield attended the service in the old church adjacent to Westminster Abbey, expecting to be called on to preach. However, the resident minister refused to allow the visitor in the pulpit. Then, some unruly members of the congregation locked the pastor in his pew and triumphantly conducted Whitefield to the pulpit. The publicity did little more than make Whitefield look like a bully.[176]

---

174 Cashin, 12.
175 Ibid., 12.
176 Ibid., 14.

The controversy was divided between the established clergy and Whitefield's brand of religious enthusiasm, as they called it. One example was the Bishop of Bristol, who denied him access to pulpits in the city.[177] The controversial preacher was on the outside of churches looking in, for all practical purposes.

Whitefield began to preach in the Bristol area, although he was still smarting from not being allowed to preach in London. He had said publicly he "could produce two cobblers who knew more of true Christianity than all the clergy in the city of Bristol."[178] Cashin shared how "Whitefield complained to the dean of the Bristol clergy, yet received the equivalent of the modern 'Don't call us, we'll call you.'"[179] This prohibition added insult to injury.

Next, the revolution came in England because of the young preacher. With the pulpits denied to him, Whitefield did the unprecedented: he preached freely in the fields! On February 17, 1739, he went out to the fields with a friend, William Seward, preaching to a gathering of roughly two hundred coal miners. Many of them had never heard a sermon before in their lives. It was an invigorating event. This initial effort took place in Kingswood Colliers near Bristol, making it a historic place.[180]

Whitefield longed to go to the unchurched of England. He believed he would have a greater hearing and response to the gospel there. He made a monumental decision that shaped his ministry. He would go to the lower classes with the gospel, to those outside the church building.[181] He had been heavily influenced by his upbringing as a pot boy at the Bell Inn and he knew these people; he was at home around them. Whitefield had a "burden of the Lord" on his life, as Jeremiah had in his ministry (Jer. 23:33). He would go to those not attending established churches and still remain loyal to the Church of England.

Whitefield shared his vision with others. He wanted them to understand how he wanted to preach to those who were similar to the Native Americans in Georgia. One remarked, "What need of going abroad for this? Have we not Indians enough at home? If you have a

---

177 Ibid., 14.
178 Ibid., 14.
179 Ibid., 14.
180 Ibid., 14.
181 Hardy, 127.

mind to convert Indians, there are colliers enough in Kingswood."[182]

Whitefield was burdened for the people, although Kingswood was a place inhabited by roughhewn individuals. Working in the mines seven days a week, they knew nothing of the upper class and their customs. Here were people who needed the gospel but could not attend a building. Since they could not come to a church, the hopeful preacher went to them with the offensive weapon of the sword of the Spirit. He knew the best time to speak to them was during their coming and going from work in their shifts.[183] As John Wesley returned from Georgia trying to find himself and salvation, Whitefield was in Kingswood preaching to the poor miners.

Belcher wrote of the importance of Kingswood:

> We scarcely need to remark here, that Kingswood has ever since been regarded as a sacred spot in ecclesiastical history. Here houses for Wesleyan Methodists and Independents were soon erected, and in them, thousands have been converted to God. Here was placed the first school for the songs of Methodist preachers, and on Hanham Mount, besides the voice of Whitefield, those of the Wesleys, Coke and Mathes, Pawson, Benson, and Bradburn, accomplished some of the mightiest effects which attended their powerful preaching.[184]

On the afternoon of Saturday, Feb. 17, 1739, Whitefield stood to preach upon a mound in a place, called Rose Green. This was his "first field pulpit," where he preached to as many who came to hear, attracted by the novelty of his first address.[185] He also approached the miners in subsequent times who were headed to the mines. What would their response be to Whitefield? He did not know, although he hoped for the best. He was concerned about giving them the gospel and having them commit themselves to God. There they stood, arrested by the young parson speaking with eloquence and passion. He spoke to a small crowd, but they brought others and the crowd expanded. Daily the crowd grew. Some came for novelty, while others were sincerely interested by what they heard. England's spiritual condition was exemplified in these people. They had never heard the Bible preached the way Whitefield proclaimed

---

182   Wakeley, 92-93.

183   Dallimore, *George Whitefield: God's Anointed Servant in the Great Revival of the Eighteenth Century*, 46.

184   Belcher, 74.

185   Johnston, vol. 1, 131.

it. In a few short weeks, Whitefield gave a moderate estimate of twenty thousand people hearing his sermons.[186] "The trees and hedges were full. All was hush when I began; the sun shone bright, and God enabled me to preach an hour with great power…The fire is kindled in the country and I know, all the devils in hell shall not be able to quench it."[187]

The miners stopped, paused to contemplate and immediately were brought under the authority of God's Word. The burning flame in Whitefield's heart was clear and ignited spontaneous combustion. Through this movement of God, the convicting power of God's Word came upon these unsuspecting hearers. Dallimore described the emotional response:

> Having no righteousness of their own to renounce they were glad to hear of a Jesus who was a friend of publicans, and came not to call the righteous, but sinners to repentance. The first discovery of their being affected was to see the white gutters made by their tears which plentifully fell down their black cheeks, as they came out of their coal pits. Hundreds and hundreds of them were soon brought under deep convictions, which as the event proved, happily ended in a sound and thorough conversion. The change was visible to all, though numbers chose to impute it to anything, rather than the finger of God.[188]

The deep realization of their condition and response to God's free grace in Christ was the key to the rapid spread of revival. Later, Sunday services were planned and Whitefield established a daily preaching schedule. He worked tirelessly visiting in homes and ministering to the poor. He was immersed in the lives of this unlikely congregation so that he became their unofficial pastor.[189]

One place did not contain Whitefield for long. He was preaching in churches still open to him, to crowds hearing him gladly. He again preached in London, as England was soon ablaze with a revival of the heart. Congregations were awakened by the Spirit. The churched, as well as the unchurched, came to hear him preach, as he challenged their spiritual complacency. His powerful preaching and thought provoking concepts caused hearers to see their condition, and they saw the fallacy of their unconverted membership. This was visualized in one of Whitefield's early sermons, "The Almost Christian.":

---

186   Ibid., 131.
187   Dallimore, vol. 1, 263.
188   Ibid., 263-264.
189   Gledstone, 74, 76.

> An almost Christian is one of the most hurtful creatures in the world. He is
> a wolf in sheep's clothing. He is one of those false prophets of whom our Lord
> bids us beware, who would persuade men that the way to heaven is broader
> than it really is, and thereby enter not into the kingdom of God themselves,
> and those that are entering in they hinder. These are the men who turn the
> world into a lukewarm Laodicean spirit; who hang out false lights, and so
> shipwreck unthinking benighted souls in their voyage to the haven where
> they would be. These are they that are greater enemies of the cross of Christ
> than infidels themselves; for, of an unbeliever everyone will be aware; but an
> almost Christian, through his subtle hypocrisy, draws away many after him,
> and therefore must expect to receive the greater damnation.[190]

Even members of the clergy were confronted with their spiritual
condition. One affected clergyman, Rev. Robert Robinson of
Cambridge, described his awakening upon hearing Whitefield's
preaching. He told the celebrated Rev. Andrew Fuller that he went
to hear Whitefield preach. That evening his text was, "But when he
saw many of the Pharisees and Sadducees come to his baptism, he
said unto them, "O generation of vipers who hath warned you to flee
from the wrath to come." (Matt. 3:7).

Robinson confirmed that Whitefield's preaching convicted him of
his false assurance of salvation:

> Mr. Whitefield…described the Sadducees' character; this did not touch
> me; I thought myself as good a Christian as any man in England. From this,
> he went to that of the Pharisees. He described their exterior decency, but
> observed that the poison of the viper rankled in their hearts. This rather shook
> me. At length, in the course of his sermon, he abruptly broke off; paused for
> a few moments; then burst into a flood of tears, lifted up his hands and eyes,
> and exclaimed, "Oh, my hearers, the wrath's to come! The wrath's to come!"
> These words sunk into my heart like lead in the water; I wept, and when the
> sermon was ended retired alone. For days and weeks, I could think of little else.
> Those awful words would follow me wherever I went: "The wrath's to come! The
> wrath's to come!"[191]

John Wesley's conversion brought greater possibilities for revival in
England. Whitefield was excited about Georgia, but also thrilled about
the expansion of gospel preaching in his homeland. The atmosphere
was ripe for the Great Awakening; England was poised to come out of
the throes of their spiritual darkness. God began to work in Wesley, and
Whitefield came back as a welcomed messenger.

---

190   Dallimore, vol. 1, 120.
191   Belcher, 92.

A golden era of the preaching of the gospel was commencing. George Whitefield and John Wesley would be at the forefront of this period. Whitefield wasted no time introducing Wesley to field preaching, as churches began to be shut to Wesley also. The local pastors of a parish church demanded Whitefield seek permission to preach in a congregation or use another building.[192] Their seething hatred of him and his rebuke of them because they were missing the mark in preaching the gospel were leading reasons why they denied him their pulpits.

In some instances, Whitefield followers tried to force the issue, resulting in civil authorities stepping in and forbidding use of a building, although the people wanted to hear him.[193]

Whitefield first preached at Kingswood in Bristol, then returned and continued his labors there. He was not bound to one place. He preached at a cemetery in Islington and at Kennington Common. He would soon preach at Moorfields in London.[194]

The practice of field preaching caused early Methodism to thrive. It offered an alternative to the established churches' traditional ministry. Although being shut out of churches could be viewed as a setback, Whitefield viewed it as an open door, giving him more access to the world. He had seen the results at Kingswood. He was convinced this type of "new preaching" would get the gospel to more people, providing greater coverage. These open doors were a respite to the denial of pulpits in established churches. The evangelist did not have to beg for opportunities to go to the open fields. He shared with joy: "Now I know that the Lord calls me to the fields for no house or street is large enough to contain the people who come to hear the Word."[195]

Whitefield preached in a new district of Marylebone Fields on August 1, 1739 to a crowd estimated at more than thirty thousand, adding to his joy.[196] Just as the apostle Paul turned to the Gentiles after the Jewish rejection of the gospel in Acts 13:45-48, Whitefield turned to the masses with great joy and excitement for the open doors God gave him in the preaching of the gospel.

---

192 Cashin, 14-15.
193 Dallimore, vol. 1, 219.
194 Hardy, 126.
195 Ibid, 127.
196 Ibid., 127.

The situation was different with Wesley. Whitefield invited him to preach at Kingswood after hearing of his conversion. Wesley was more formal than Whitefield and felt uncomfortable going outside the church building to preach. He had been heavily influenced by the Moravians, who put emphasis on deciding matters by lots, opening the Bible, believing the first place they turned was a message from God. He decided to use this method in determining if it was God's will to preach in the fields.[197]

Belden shared John Wesley's struggle in becoming a field preacher:

> The first Scripture he obtained in this way was: "Get thee up into this mountain, and die in the mount whither thou goest up." Not liking this, he appealed to the Fetter Lane meeting to take up the inquiry. They tried, and turned up: "Son of man, behold I take from thee the desire of thine eyes at a stroke; yet thou shalt not mourn nor weep, neither shall thy tears run down."
>
> Not satisfied even yet, the brethren tried once more, only to learn: "And Ahaz slept with his fathers, and they buried him in the city, even in Jerusalem." In spite of this, to Wesley's credit be it said, he went to Bristol. We notice the struggles of the donnish little Oxonian to reconcile himself to Whitefield's new practice of open-air preaching. Wesley revealed his reluctance saying, "I could scarce reconcile myself at first to this strange way of preaching in the fields, of which he set me an example on the Sunday, having been all my life (till very lately) so tenacious of every point relating to decency and order, that I should have thought the saving of souls almost a sin if it had not been done in church."[198]

Commenting on John Wesley's attitude toward field preaching, Gledstone penned a shrewd note:

> True to his cautious, practical mind, Wesley adopted field preaching only when he had seen its worth, just as he took up the class-meeting idea from others, and only consented to lay preaching because it had been started by men more headlong than himself, and these supported by the wisdom and piety of his mother, who warned him not to hinder a work of God. Others moved, he quietly followed, and if it was found practicable, passed on and took the lead.[199]

Whitefield conducted Wesley on a tour of his constituency from meeting to meeting, at the bowling green, in the Kingswood fields and elsewhere. He introduced Wesley to the great audiences gathered, and he himself left quietly. That evening, when he was going to say good-bye

---

197 Tyerman, vol. 1, 192.
198 Belcher, 66.
199 Gledstone, 85.

to one his societies, he found the way crowded and had to get to it by using a ladder, climbing the tilling of the adjoining house![200]

Wesley did pursue the calling to field preaching and took over where Whitefield had left off despite his initial reluctance. Belden commented:

> "Before Whitefield had been gone from Bristol three hours, Wesley had proved himself a worthy successor by submitting, as he put it, to "make myself more vile," and preaching in the streets to roughly three thousand people. The good work of aerating religion went on, whilst Whitefield sped to the metropolis.[201]

It is very evident that Whitefield introduced Wesley to field preaching and relinquished his work at Bristol to him. One could speculate what would have happened to Wesley's ministry if his friend had not encouraged him in this way. Whitefield knew the opportunity for expansion of the itinerant ministry to the world was greater if he shared the work with his friend. Wesley inheriting Whitefield's work opened the door for the evangelist to go back to America and other places in England, knowing gospel preaching continued in his home country to the masses. This referral of the work at Bristol to Wesley was a wise move, but also illustrated the perceptiveness Whitefield had in understanding his world-wide task.[202]

Whitefield was ordained as a priest in the Church of England in Oxford on January 11, 1739, without fanfare, in a ceremony conducted by his good friend Bishop Benson. The evangelist stayed there a few days ministering in the area.[203] There were still many friends and supporters in the church who were thrilled with the response his ministry had received. Whitefield maintained his support for the church and its Thirty-Nine Articles, believing they were scriptural doctrines and principles.[204] While many of the churches were closed to him, but support was rising in England, building to an insurmountable tidal wave of excitement. The lower class support was very important to the response and acceptance Whitefield was receiving.

Whitefield won the life-long support from Selina, the Countess of

---

200   Ibid., 85-86.
201   Belcher, 67.
202   Belden, 66-67.
203   Gillies, 35.
204   Dallimore, vol. 1, 218-219.

Huntingdon, a woman of enormous wealth, who had been widowed at thirty-nine. Her second husband dying shortly after their marriage and her inheritance made her one of the wealthiest women in England. She was awakened to her condition after hearing Whitefield.[205] Here was a young man that God was using to touch her, seeing true religion for what it was. She was impressed with the simplicity of the gospel and Whitefield's dramatic presentation of it to the masses. She was won to Whitefield's side through his getting to the heart of the Scripture and seeing his control over the audiences by God's anointing in his preaching.

After correspondence and meeting, Lady Huntingdon pledged what she could of her vast resources to support the Methodist movement in furthering the gospel led by Whitefield. Henry disclosed, "By this time Lady Selina, Countess of Huntingdon, (destined to become Whitefield's staunch patroness), was already looking with favor on the young celebrity. Eventually the list of guests assembled by her ladyship to hear the Methodist preachers whom she sponsored read like a roster of the peerage."[206]

Whitefield's pleading to help establish an orphanage in Georgia caught the lady's eye. She had long been a benevolent benefactor of similar causes. He, in fact, bequeathed the orphanage to her after his death since she had been a continual sponsor.[207] The orphanage offered an opportunity to start something in the New World, turning the direction of the debtor colony toward a strong Christian foundation in spite of all its hindrances to endure. Whitefield began to meet with the trustees in Parliament, offering his services to help remedy the situation. He had seen firsthand the children's lack of parental care. His intention was to return soon to Georgia after he had raised support for this venture.[208]

The idea of field preaching was not original to Whitefield. He was influenced by Howell Harris, a Welsh evangelist, to whom he had begun to correspond. He was in awe of Harris, an Oxford graduate and fellow member of the Holy Club. Although Whitefield popularized field preaching, he knew of it through Harris and later accompanied

---

205 Dallimore, vol. 2, 262.
206 Henry, 44.
207 Dallimore, vol. 2, 547.
208 Cashin, 12-13.

Whitefield to Wales, preaching jointly with him.[209] Harris became one of his loyal supporters and was particularly supportive of the Calvinistic doctrines that he had adopted as a standard of his ministry. The Welsh evangelist carried on the work in places Whitefield was unable to go. He became a loyal associate, spreading the gospel in the same way Whitefield did.[210]

Whitefield developed a circuit and became a popular figure in England. When one of his converts, Joseph Periam, was deemed to be mad by his parents, they had him admitted to Bethlehem Hospital (Bedlam), the home for mentally ill in London. Because Whitefield knew that Periam was suffering from opposition to his newfound zeal for Christ, he secured his release, and Periam accompanied him on his next trip to Georgia to establish the orphanage.[211]

Tyerman revealed the difference conversion made in Periam:

> The change in him was so great that his father and friends thought him mad. The "symptoms," proofs of his madness were three-fold: 1. He had fasted for a fortnight. 2. He had prayed loud enough to be heard all over a house four stories high. 3. He had sold his clothes and given the money to the poor. The first of these allegations was probably a fact exaggerated. The second in all likelihood was perfectly correct. The third was literally true. [212]

For these false-conclusions of supposed madness, "Joseph Periam was put into the general receptacle of all London lunatics—Bethlehem Hospital, an old edifice founded in 1547, and standing in St. George's Fields, Lambeth. The institution was a disgrace to all connected with it. The miserable inmates were treated most brutally."[213]

Periam was delivered from Bedlam on one condition: Whitefield would take him to Georgia. At one time during the negotiations to have him released, the authorities speculated about the possibility of Whitefield's sanity.[214] Because they misunderstood his ministry, they speculated about his mental health.

Whitefield was soon to depart for Georgia but delays hindered his voyage. Henry disclosed the reason for the delay in sailing to America:

---

209 Dallimore, vol. 1, 264-266.
210 Ibid., 233-234, 246.
211 Tyerman, vol. 1, 227-230.
212 Ibid., 227.
213 Ibid., 227.
214 Ibid., 228-230.

The record of the summer of 1739 tells of throngs of people who continued to attend Whitefield while he was detained in England, because the Elizabeth, on which he had booked passage for America, had no crew. A time of waiting was imposed for the purpose of finding a crew. Her seamen had been forced into his majesty's service through an eighteenth-century practice of "the Press," and it was necessary to wait until other sailors could be secured. In the meantime, as might have been expected, Whitefield preached often.[215]

Although Whitefield had gained popularity, he now had Georgia on his heart by hoping to establish an orphanage there. He had raised support for the mission, looking toward his second trip to America and had negotiated his trip with the trustees of Parliament, who generally gave him control of the enterprise.

Whitefield again brought James Habersham with him to be the superintendent of the orphanage. He was given a land deed of 500 acres out of Savannah to establish the work. Provisions were given for a staff and any companions accompanying him on the trip. Whitefield was excited to go back to the New World. All that remained now was the timing of General Oglethorpe to enlist soldiers, and to find a vessel for the journey.[216]

In the meantime, Whitefield continued to preach to bigger crowds. Some tried to reason with him to stay in England, explaining that he needed to continue his ministry there. He had his sights set on America, and the greater the response in England, the more he looked to what awaited him in America, even as the crowds grew phenomenally at Bristol. Whitefield shared his burden for Georgia with his makeshift congregation, who were saddened at the thought of losing their preacher. Some begged him more intensely to stay with them. Others were disheartened by the prospect of Whitefield going to the New World.[217] As he waited, he preached and was encouraged that the movement would continue under the leadership of Wesley, Harris and others.

---

215 Henry, 50.
216 Cashin, 13.
217 Gillies, ed., *George Whitefield's Journals*, 278.

6

TO AMERICA

AND THE FOUNDING OF BETHESDA

(1739-1740)

WHITEFIELD DID NOT GO IMMEDIATELY TO Georgia. Instead, he landed in Pennsylvania on the Elizabeth.[218] He wanted to meet other like-minded brethren in New England and garner support and materials for the orphanage, although it was only a concept at the time.[219] This strategy was perfectly natural since New England initially constituted the highest concentration of people in the colonies. Benjamin Franklin questioned the location of the orphanage in faraway Georgia, removed from the center of colonial life.[220]

Whitefield's notoriety had been observed by Benjamin Franklin, the great American statesman who was not a professed believer, but did develop a peculiar friendship with Whitefield. Their friendship continued throughout the evangelist's life.[221]

Whitefield was happy to be in New England, not only to find support for the orphanage, but also to be encouraged by mutual fellowship with like-minded brethren. He explained how he went there, "…not to spy out the nakedness of the land, nor to search for declensions; but to

---

218 Gledstone, 118.
219 Dallimore, vol. 1, 431.
220 Ibid., 453.
221 Johnston, vol. 1, 309-310.

be refreshed amongst the descendants of the good old Puritans."[222] The theology of many of the pastors and leaders he would encounter was more strongly suited to Whitefield's rapidly developing Calvinistic thought.

Ninde assessed the difference in England and what Whitefield found in America:

> Whitefield soon discovered on the whole, morals in America were higher than in England. There were less crime, highway robbery and murder. Corruption in government was infrequent. Lawbreakers were treated with greater kindness than in his native country. At the very period when the statute books of England specified more than two hundred crimes punishable with death, Massachusetts named twenty and Pennsylvania only two.[223]

The timing of God's working by scattering members of the Holy Club into the world and to preach the gospel after their conversion is quite impressive. Ninde asked this question reflecting on scattering these men:

> Was there not a heavenly coincidence in the fact that at the very time when the Holy Club at Oxford was sending out the leaders of the Evangelical Revival which spread over Britain and beyond, the Great Awakening in America was getting under way? And George Whitefield, born again in the Holy Club, was the chosen Apostle of the Lord in linking together these two awakenings that finally merged into the vast movement which changed the religious face of the English-speaking world. He came to America just in time to infuse new energy into the languishing work begun under Edwards, and to thrust it forward like a flaming torch into all the Colonies.[224]

New England was not without a movement of God happening in their midst. The awakening had first appeared at Northampton, Massachusetts. Under the leadership of Jonathan Edwards, the pastor of the Congregational church, the town had seen a virtual wholesale conversion of the Northampton residents. The esteemed pastor did not meet Whitefield his first trip to New England because Whitefield visited the main cities and was going to Georgia as his eventual destination.[225] New England seemed ready for an even greater awakening to spread

---

222 Philip, 151.
223 Ninde, 131.
224 Ibid., 137-138.
225 Ibid., 146.

through the whole region. The excitement was building, and Whitefield was strongly impressed at the hunger for revival and the preaching of the gospel in the region.

Whitefield met with William Tennent and his son Gilbert before beginning his preaching tour. They were instrumental in the awakening movement. William established the Log College, a school which became the forerunner for theological education in West Pennsylvania-New Jersey area, leading to the eventual evolution of what became Princeton University. The Tennent's school, patterned after "The School of the Prophets" under Elisha (II Kings 6:1-4), was devoted to raising ministers who were pursuing an itinerant ministry. Whitefield liked the elder Tennent and learned from his leadership in the movement and his many years of pastoral experience.

Dallimore shared the history of the Tennents' ministry and Whitefield's discovery of them:

> During the years following 1720, however, a voice began to be raised in protest against these conditions. This was the voice of the Rev. William Tennent (1673-1745) minister of the Presbyterian Church at Neshaminy in Pennsylvania. Tennent was a man of extensive learning and his ministry was marked by vital evangelism and spiritual power.
>
> Tennent had four sons, all of whom experienced the call of God to the ministry, and fearing the baneful influences of the usual places of education, he trained them in his own home. Other young men asked for the same training, and in order to train them, Tennent built a one-room schoolhouse, which, in contempt, was termed The Log College by its detractors.
>
> As William Tennent aged, the leadership of this work passed into the hands of his son Gilbert (1703-64). In 1726, Gilbert was settled at New Brunswick in New Jersey, and eighteen years later, in response to a request for a report of the blessing experienced there, he wrote:
>
> "The labours of the Rev. Mr. Frelinghuysen, a Dutch Calvinist minister, were much blessed to the people of New Brunswick and places adjacent, especially about the time of his coming among them.
>
> When I came there, which was about seven years after, I had the pleasure of seeing much of the fruits of his ministry; divers of his hearers, with whom I had opportunity of conversing, appeared to be converted persons by their soundness in principle, Christian experience and pious practice: and these persons declared that the ministrations of the aforesaid gentleman were the means thereof."[226]

---

226   Dallimore, vol. 1, 415-416.

Whitefield gave fatherly respect to the elderly Tennent and brotherly encouragement to his son Gilbert, who had developed a similar pattern of preaching as Whitefield had in England. When Whitefield heard Gilbert Tennent preach at an open-air meeting in New York, he was strongly impressed and challenged.[227] Not only would his style of ministry be effective in New England, but it would also be well received. One is struck by the camaraderie and respect each man had for the other, as they supported each other's ministry. Whitefield was helped immensely by Tennent and his introduction to the spiritual climate of New England.

Whitefield's first public open air meeting was in Philadelphia at the invitation of several "New Light" ministers there. Lambert explained their beliefs and practices:

> Although all embraced Calvinism with its emphasis on election, original sin, and the covenant of grace, they differed over the clergy's role and authority. So-called Old Lights favored a "highly skilled, academically trained ministry" presiding over a "formal, hierarchical structure of Presbyterian government." New Lights advocated an actively personal piety, demanding that individuals "participate actively in their own conversion." Through their diverse reactions to Whitefield's preaching, contending factions widened their rift.[228]

The first series of meetings Whitefield conducted were very visible. He preached in front of the old courthouse in Philadelphia, and the crowds began to grow each night.[229] They flooded the meeting area to hear the dramatic style of his preaching that they had heard of in England. They were moved by his dramatic presentations and powerful voice as they now heard him in person.

One of his interested listeners was Benjamin Franklin, who calculated how far away Whitefield's voice could be heard while the evangelist preached. He stepped it off and realized he could hear Whitefield from far away. Franklin recounts his voice in the distance:

> ...He had a loud and clear voice, and articulated his words and sentences so perfectly, that he might be heard and understood at a great distance, especially was his audiences, however numerous, observed the most exact silence. He preached one evening from the top of the Court House steps, which are in the middle of Market-street, and on the west side of Second-street,

---

227 Gillies ed., *George Whitefield's Journals*, 347-348.
228 Lambert, 150.
229 Dallimore, vol.1, 432.

which crosses it at right angles. Both streets were filled with his hearers to a considerable distance. Being among the hindmost in Market-street, I had the curiosity to learn how far he could be heard, by retiring backwards down the street towards the river; and I found his voice distinct till I came near Front-street, when some noise in that street obscured it...[230]

Franklin supported Whitefield's efforts to begin an orphanage in Georgia, seeing it as a worthy project. He realized it represented the betterment of society in the American colonies. The evangelist gave a plea for the orphanage and took an offering for it in almost every meeting. Although Franklin had determined not to give to the offering in a meeting he attended because of another benevolent project, Whitefield's plea for the orphanage's plight was so powerful that Franklin emptied his pockets during the offering and borrowed from a friend to give more.[231]

Jerome Mahaffey, in writing a recent biography on Whitefield, concludes that his widespread coverage of the colonies in his preaching tours made him an "Accidental Revolutionary." He describes this maximum exposure to his message in this first initial visit of the colonies:

In November of 1739, George Whitefield, now twenty-five, arrived in Philadelphia to begin his tour. His challenge was to reach as many colonists as possible....On the tour Whitefield preached over 350 times while traveling some 2,000 miles on horseback and 3,000 miles by boat, visiting over seventy-five cities and towns. He was constantly on the move, never staying put for more than a week. Under the impact of this tour, Americans were exposed to his message. A large number participated in a religious revival, if not led by Whitefield, then by one of the copycats, who quickly followed, inspired by his successes. As Whitefield addressed each township, he attempted to lead them to the new birth... His message was consistent in every colony and town that he visited. For the first time in American history, a specific and powerful message spread throughout every colony, inviting everyone who listened to adopt a new identity and join the community of believers.[232]

It was difficult for Whitefield to consider pulling away, leaving New England for Georgia, because the response was great and the spirit warm in these initial early meetings.

---

230   Ibid., 439.
231   Ninde, 153.
232   Jerome Dean Mahaffey, *The Accidental Revolutionary: George Whitefield and the Creation of America* (Baylor Press: Waco TX, 2011), 41.

The plan had been to get acquainted with churches and ministers who supported his ministry. He knew he would have many other opportunities to preach in New England because of the warm welcome he had received.

Georgia did call, and in the fall, Whitefield embarked for the southern colony. He preached in colonies on his way with the intent of getting to Savannah by the first of the year. Traveling great distances in the remotely populated land was a challenge, but the hope of what awaited him there drove him to travel in the harsh winter climate. It was warmer when he did get to the Carolinas and Georgia.[233]

Whitefield had sent James Habersham and his party ahead to survey the land and find a suitable location for the orphanage. A place ten miles southwest of Savannah was deemed sufficient distance to be away from the city's influence, though it would be close enough to fulfill needs and provisions they would require.[234]

The 500-acre site offered possibilities to be self-supporting through the development of a farming economy. Orphans who had gone with Habersham were housed temporarily in the David Douglas home. The orphanage's ministry began immediately, with efforts to find displaced children throughout the colony.[235]

Whitefield was also made the minister of the church in Savannah by the trustees. The previous minister, William Norris, relocated to Frederica.[236] With his preaching ministry, Whitefield could keep the residents abreast of the work going on for the homeless in Savannah.

On March 25, 1740, an important event took place in Whitefield's life and the colony of Georgia when the first stone was laid for the orphanage. It was to be the most famous orphanage in America and possibly England.[237] It was named "Bethesda" because so many deeds of mercy could be accomplished there.[238]

Wherever Whitefield traveled, Bethesda would always be close to his heart and known abroad wherever he ministered.

---

233 Gledstone, 128-130.
234 Cashin, 20.
235 Temple, 220.
236 Ibid., 220.
237 Gledstone, 133.
238 Temple, 220.

The dedication is described by Gledstone:

> The foundation-brick of the "great house," as he called the orphanage, was laid by himself on Tuesday, March 25, 1740, without any parade—even without a silver trowel or a mahogany mallet—but with full assurance of faith. The workmen were the spectators, and knelt down with him to offer the dedication prayer. They sang a hymn together, and he gave them a word of exhortation, bidding them remember to work heartily, knowing that they worked for God. Forty children were then under his care, and nearly a hundred mouths had to be supplied with food.[239]

Peter Hoffer shared this insight, "The orphanage was the joy and travail of Whitefield's life. Its children were his surrogate family." [240] He devoted his life to its success and it was a lifelong burden to him wherever he traveled.

Whitefield also worked with Habersham to develop a schedule for the school. It was filled with devotions, instruction, catechism, work and involvement in church services on Sunday. It was both Habersham and Whitefield's belief that the children must have a steady regime of work and instruction to keep them occupied and not idle, leaving them open to temptation. A rigid schedule kept them busy constantly.

Dallimore elaborated on the plan for the orphanage at its beginning:

> Of course, Bethesda was to be primarily a home for orphaned children. But Whitefield intended that it should also supply them with a goodly education; not only were the usual subjects to be taught, but he made a list of books on religion, history and literature which he wished the children to read, and in a few months' time he added a Latin Master to the staff. We have noticed the spinning operations, and while the girls learned this employment, for the boys the institution was to be "a nursery for mechanics and planters."[241]

The children's conversions were reported, and proper instruction was standard fare. Amazing reports of a full understanding of their condition before God are seen in the school's early records. One ten-year-old girl wrote to Whitefield: "God has shown me the hardness and wretchedness of my wicked heart. Oh, it fills me with wonder to think God has not cut me off."[242]

---

239 Gledstone, 133.

240 Peter James Hoffer, *When Benjamin Franklin Met The Reverend Whitefield: Enlightenment, Revival and the Power of the Printed Word* (John Hopkins University Press: Baltimore 2011), 96.

241 Dallimore, vol. 1, 448.

242 Temple, 231.

Sarah Coleman Temple, in describing Georgia's early history, shared the founder's early instruction with the children: "Whitefield examined the children in a question and answer period. He tried to ground children in the belief of original sin and to impart the necessity of a change wrought by God in their souls. Residents quite often attended these sessions."[243] What sessions these must have been, attracting adults to hear the evangelist instruct the children. The main building completed in November, resulted in the orphanage moving to its permanent location outside Savannah.[244] The move was more conducive for supervising children and having more activities to occupy their time. The early days were crucial in the establishment of the home and enabled it to be on a stable footing.

Invitations to preach in New England came sooner than Whitefield expected. He was encouraged by the start of the school, he trusted in Habersham's leadership of Bethesda and he felt safe to go on another preaching tour.[245] He took the swoop, "Savannah," sailing north and embarked for New England.[246]

Whitefield was beginning to realize his need for companionship, and at the age of twenty-five, he was considering marriage. On board the Savannah, he wrote a letter of proposal to Elizabeth Delamotte, who came from a respected family he was acquainted with at Belden Hall, England. Although Elizabeth may have been interested in Whitefield, her hopes were quickly dashed by his proposal letter. It appeared that he who eloquently presented the gospel and the truth of God's word was inept at expressing his deepest feelings of romantic love. He instead proposed by calling for his future wife to be a woman of self-sacrifice and courage. He appeared to be looking more for a caretaker of the orphanage who could serve as its matron than a wife to him.[247]

Portions of Whitefield's proposal letter read:

> **Can you bear to leave your father and kindred's house, and to trust in him (who feedeth the young ravens that call upon him) for your own and children's support, supposing it should please him to bless you with any? Can you bear**

---

243   Ibid., 228.
244   Ibid., 222.
245   Ibid, 228.
246   Tyerman, vol. 1, 371.
247   Ibid., 367-368.

the inclemencies of the air, both as to cold and heat, in a foreign climate? Can you, when you have a husband, be as though you had none, and willingly part with him, even for a long season, when his Lord and Master shall call him forth to preach the gospel, and command him to leave you behind? If after seeking to God for direction, and searching your heart, can you say, "I can do all those things through Christ strengthening me," what if you and I were joined together in the Lord, and you came with me at my return from England, to be a help meet for me in the management of the orphan-house? I have great reason to believe it is the divine will that I should alter my condition, and have often thought you were the person appointed for me... to keep my matrimonial vow, and to do what I can towards helping you forward in the great work of your salvation. If you think marriage will be any way prejudicial to your better part, be so kind as to send me a denial. [248]

The challenge was too enormous and Miss Delamotte spurned his proposal, leaving Whitefield disillusioned with matrimony for one of his position.[249]

Whitefield had no time to fret, for he soon was in New England again, preaching to even greater crowds in New York and Philadelphia, where he stayed with respected families in the area. The response to his preaching was even more encouraging than his first preaching tour. After he had fulfilled his obligations, he set sail for Savannah again, on the Savannah.[250]

The orphanage was becoming a promising place for the orphan problem in the colony. Whitefield, however, went to Charleston to answer a summons from Alexander Garden, the minister of the church there, for preaching in his unorthodox way and his criticism of the established clergy. Whitefield affirmed his support for the Church of England and when told to restrict what he said and where he preached, he told Garden that his authority to preach came from Christ. He said the summons had as much authority to him as a "Pope's bull."[251] This response left Garden infuriated and a bitter enemy of Whitefield's ministry, as evidenced by his future opposition to him. By their continual support, the trustees of Georgia obviously asserted his right to the ministry God had given the evangelist. They saw him as a strong leader in the burgeoning colony, especially with his initial success at Bethesda.

248   Philip, 179-180.
249   Tyerman, vol. 1, 369.
250   Ibid., 371.
251   Kidd, 102.

In the second trip that year to Savannah, Whitefield saw what he had hoped for Bethesda begin to materialize. He tried to move out of direct responsibilities, assuming the role of a chancellor and public relations representative. Even though the orphanage was always on his heart and was always associated with him as its founder, he knew the school was too confining for him to be directly involved in its maintenance. The Reverend Jonathan Barber had arrived to become the Superintendent of Spiritual Affairs for the school. He and Habersham worked in the growing ministry of Bethesda. Christopher Orton became the new minister of the Savannah church, while Whitefield pre-occupied himself with an itinerant ministry.[252] He realized serving as a regular minister in Savannah would not work (having been there briefly), because of his obligations to preach elsewhere.

Whitefield was off to a glorious tour of New England again. He would go this time to Massachusetts where he would have a warm reception, for the region was stirring with the word he would be returning. As autumn leaves turned all shades of beautiful colors in the fall, Whitefield began a stay of several months before he returned to England. He would not be disappointed at the response in his next New England tour.[253]

---

252 Temple, 229.
253 Tyerman, vol. 1, 389.

7

PREACHING IN NEW ENGLAND

AND ENCOUNTERING LIKE-MINDED BRETHREN

(1740-1741)

WHITEFIELD'S RETURN TO NEW ENGLAND WAS greeted with great anticipation. His two previous trips had sparked a keen interest and resulted in opportunities to have an even greater influence as he approached this welcome region. The result of his preaching was an avalanche, a golden era, in his ministry that he would never forget. The vibrant evangelist was in the prime of his life and still in good health. God had done great things during his time in America, and he knew it had been the right decision to come to America and preach the gospel in all the open doors God gave him.

Whitefield landed in Newport, Rhode Island, although his primary focus was in Massachusetts and the places open to him there. He was welcomed by Nathanial Clap, a famous minister and new friend he joined for breakfast. He described Clap as "a dissenting minister and the most venerable man I ever saw in my life. He looked like a good old Puritan."[254] After preaching there to several groups he went to Boston and preached for the first time in this great Puritan city. The response was overwhelming as he preached in the open air for several nights, with his final service at the Boston Common on a Sunday afternoon. It seemed

---

254   Gillies, ed., *George Whitefield's Journals,* 451-452.

the whole town came out to hear him. Approximately 20,000 persons attended his farewell sermon.[255] The evangelist possibly reminded them of the godly heritage in the city and its vicinity, an influence that they should not forget. He most certainly warned them of false assurance, thinking they were true Christians because of their association with the first permanent English settlers who had come seeking religious liberty. They had established a city set on a hill, founded on biblical principles. The result of Whitefield's preaching on the town was one of serious introspection in response to his preaching. He caused them to evaluate their spiritual condition, and they were moved to strong self-examination. The evangelist remembered, "Most wept for a considerable time."[256]

Whitefield's recollection of the event was near and dear to him as a highlight of his ministry. He recounted, "Oh how the Word did run! It rejoiced me to see such great numbers affected, so that some, I believe, could scarcely abstain from crying out, that place was no other than Bethel the gate of heaven!"[257] Whitefield found joy in the people's response, as Boston was always a special place for him to preach.

The evangelist visited Harvard in Cambridge, which at this time was the oldest school in America, strongly emphasizing theological education. The school had not forsaken biblical teaching, but took a long look at one in their midst who was noted on both continents for his persuasive preaching. The thought of itinerant preaching was a foreign ministry concept to the faculty and students. Some of the administrators were possibly troubled by the great fanfare associated with Whitefield's ministry, which was overwhelming at first. The negative factor against Whitefield was the stand some ministers had taken against him in New England. Although the majority of ministers and people had followed his preaching and welcomed him, some established ministers had dismissed him as eccentric.[258]

One minister who opposed Whitefield from the outset stated, "I am sorry to see you here." His quick retort was, "So is the devil."[259]

---

255   Philip, 152.
256   Mahaffey, 61.
257   Belcher, 163.
258   Dallimore, *George Whitefield: God's Anointed Servant in the Great Revival of the Eighteenth Century*, 92.
259   Gledstone, 149-150.

Whitefield's opponents felt his type of ministry was out of place for a Church of England minister. He received a mixed reaction from Harvard because of these reasons.

Whitefield preached on the necessity of being converted, staying away from harmful books and the value of a devoted spiritual life in school. He probably reflected on his own experience at Oxford as an unconverted student.[260] He was politely treated, although his reception was not as exciting as the one he received from the general population. His impression of the school was unfavorable, because he believed the school was lacking in spirituality. His suspicion that some there were unconverted students did not bode well for a return visit soon, yet the evangelist would continue to have an association with Harvard in the future.

The end result of his preaching was that it bore fruit after he left the school. Dr. Colman, a local pastoral supporter revealed, "The college is entirely changed. The students are full of God. Many of them appear truly born-again. The voice of prayer and praise fill the chambers...I was told that not seven out of a hundred in attendance remain unaffected."[261]

Everywhere Whitefield went, he was treated royally. Governor Jonathan Belcher gave him the use of his coach as he departed Boston, en route to Concord, New Hampshire, to preach.[262] His stay was short, for he was off to a long anticipated visit to Northampton, Massachusetts, to conduct meetings with Jonathan Edwards, the minister there.

Whitefield wished to meet Edwards and his congregation. He was familiar with the ministry of Edwards because of the revival in Northampton, Massachusetts, and the works he had published: *A Narrative of the Surprising Conversions* and *A Treatise on Religious Affections*. Edwards had fired the first volley through his writings and experiences for revival and awakening in the area. He spoke out against the Half-Way Covenant and against his grandfather Solomon Stoddard's practice of admitting everyone to the Lord's Table. He served as associate until Stoddard's death, but opposed this practice. Edwards had been very resolute against the immorality practiced in the town. Above all, he

---

260 Dallimore, *George Whitefield: God's Anointed Servant in the Great Revival of the Eighteenth Century*, 92.
261 Ibid., 92.
262 Dallimore, vol. 1, 536-537.

was a man of deep piety known to bury himself in study for more than thirteen hours a day. He had a godly wife, Sarah, who was a wonderful mother of ten.[263]

The whole town had been touched by the results of the awakening, but the atmosphere had cooled when Whitefield came. The evangelist viewed his task as simple: he was to be the spark of the flame that would rekindle the fire of revival in the congregation. His preaching was direct and forthright, and he strongly encouraged the church where he preached several days and on Sunday. Kidd shared how he "hoped that he could help the people of Northampton recover their first love."[264]

The Sunday service was well-remembered as Whitefield preached on "The Consolations and Privileges of the Saints and the Plentiful Effusion of the Spirit upon Believers." He reminded the church of the glorious days of revival. In the meeting, he commended Pastor Edwards' strong leadership. The direct inference was clear: where was the "flame of God" now? The persuasive message recalled the fame of the church and the lives changed. The noted evangelist called for the people to humbly seek God and for Him to restore a spirit of revival to the community and church. Pastor Edwards was moved deeply and he, uncharacteristically began to weep as he recalled the initial days of the revival. Edwards' response was very rare for him because he was not emotional.[265] The spirit of the services was deeply moving, and Whitefield's message was well received.

The time spent with Edwards, his family, and his church left a lasting impression on Whitefield. The character of Edward's wife Sarah and her support as a helpmate to her husband, the management of the home, and deep piety along with the deportment of the children moved the observant preacher. Fresh from the rejection of his marriage proposal by Elizabeth Delamotte, he longed to have a similar companion in life. He remarked, "...she caused me to renew prayers, which for some months, I have put to God, that he would be pleased to send me such a daughter of Abraham to be my wife."[266] The fact that the Edwards' home was a model of godliness was evident to all who visited there.

---

263 Ibid., 538.
264 Kidd, 128.
265 Wakeley, 275.
266 Stout, 168.

Sarah Edwards was moved by Whitefield's ministry. Her honest description of his ministry revealed that he was unlike other ministers who had spoken to the head, trying to stimulate the congregation's thinking. She said, "He aims at affecting the heart."[267] The personal appeal in his sermons touched many.

George Marsden gave this assessment of Whitefield's influence on the Northampton preacher in his biography of Jonathan Edwards, commemorating the 300th anniversary of his life:

> Whitefield's visit changed Edwards' life, as it changed New England and the American colonies generally. Awakenings were familiar in the Connecticut Valley, and Edwards played a key role in one that touched as many people there as did Whitefield. Yet there were some notable differences. Whitefield's tour was an international phenomenon. It was also the first inter-colonial phenomenon. It was also the first intercultural event, the beginning of common American church cultural identity. Moreover, like most else that succeeded in America, it was not so much on what was imposed from above as much as by the popular response generated from below.[268]

Whitefield journeyed from Northampton toward New York, dining with teachers and speaking at the New Haven College (presently Yale University), where he spoke to the students.[269] He spoke in a few gatherings in New Jersey at Staten Island, Newark, Baskinridge and Trenton.[270]

The evangelist's sermon at Baskinridge was greeted with great sadness because he would be departing to another continent and possibly not returning. Whitefield was aware of responses to his preaching here that he had not seen before in other places of America. These responses included emotional excesses. He did not wholly endorse these practices.[271]

Whitefield spoke in Philadelphia for a week at one of his favorite preaching spots. Tyerman reported that he "spent a successful and happy week among friends."[272]

It was almost time for Whitefield to return to England, but the same

---

267   Haykin, 39.

268   George M. Marsden, *Jonathan Edwards, A Life* (Yale University Press: New Haven, CT, 2003), 209.

269   Tyerman, vol. 1, 430.

270   Ibid., 433-434.

271   Ibid., 434.

272   Ibid., 436.

sensation confronted him as he left New England. He loved the New England area and was never more at home than in this region. Just as the people in England hadn't wanted him to leave, the people here didn't want him to go either, but he knew he must. The congregations appreciated his labor and were saddened by his departure. They would long remember the sermons and the response to them. Revival had truly come to America, and God worked the same way He did in England.

Whitefield went to Bethesda one more time, but stayed there only briefly before setting sail for his native country. He sailed from Charleston after speaking in several meetings with his friend Hugh Bryan, who had been opposed by the same clergy that opposed Whitefield.[273] When the clergy issued a summons and forbade the evangelist from preaching in the established parish boundaries under Alexander Garden, he realized the hostility toward him had not subsided.

Whitefield saw the need to go back to England and conclude his tour of America. He had to give the trustees in Parliament an accounting of the orphanage's progress and the work in Georgia since he was under their sponsorship. It would be a glowing report and confirm the fact that God was in the establishment of the orphanage in Georgia. The colony's need was great in spite of the sparse population. The ministry of the orphanage had been suited to meet the need of the rustic colony. Bethesda was on its feet with tests and hardships ahead of her. The orphanage was going to grow and prosper, and Whitefield gave all the glory to God.

Another reason why Whitefield needed to return to England was because the Methodist movement, which God had blessed so wonderfully at its inception, was now factionalizing. Whitefield had adopted Calvinism as the way to reconcile the sinfulness of man and Christ's righteousness, not our works, as the only source of salvation.[274]

Unfortunately, the Moravians had influenced John Wesley and his brother Charles. The Wesleys reacted strongly against predestination and believed it restricted many from coming to Christ. John Wesley even called it a "doctrine full of blasphemy... in the horrible decree

---

273 Ibid., 448-449.
274 Johnston, vol. 1, 26.

of predestination."[275] John, who believed more in man's free will and universal atonement, wrote a letter to Whitefield, urging him not to preach on predestination again.

Whitefield believed Calvinism highlighted salvation originating from God, through His grace and denied any human effort to bring about salvation. However, the Arminianism John Wesley and the Moravians taught opened the door to a works-type salvation by their efforts. Whitefield disagreed sharply with the belief that as easily as someone accepted salvation, he or she could reject it and not come to a full assurance of salvation. The belief of free will to accept or deny God's salvation was a major tenant of Arminianism. Whitefield saw this belief going against God's eternal decree of salvation.[276]

He wrote a response to John Wesley's plea, urging him to tear up his sermon on predestination, which he did not publish until he returned to England to state his position.[277] It seemed strange to Whitefield that the friendship he had with the Wesleys and his support of the unsure preacher in his early days of field preaching would be shunned because of doctrinal matters. Although the letter by Wesley attempted to delineate his differences with Whitefield, it stunned and surprised him. Even more troubling was news that Wesley was speaking against Whitefield and his ministry wherever he went. The evangelist had to prepare himself for his reception in England, and it was not the reception he was anticipating.

---

275 Dallimore, *George Whitefield: God's Anointed Servant in the Great Revival of the Eighteenth Century*, 63.

276 Dallimore, vol. 1, 307, 407-409.

277 Ibid., 580.

8

Theological Controversy

and Commitment to the Doctrines of Grace

(1741)

WHITEFIELD WAS SOON TO LEARN ABOUT THE disturbance caused through the theological controversy afflicting the Methodist movement. He was not in England to be an advocate for Calvinistic Methodism when the controversy began. In the meantime, John Wesley had done his best to launch a frontal assault on the Doctrines of Grace which highlighted believers saved by God's grace offered in Christ through His sovereign will to undeserving sinners.[278] Although his associates had stood firm against Arminianism, they were not the voice Whitefield had become. They supported him as the mouthpiece of the movement.[279]

Hardy got to the core of the doctrinal controversy as the source of the dispute between Wesley and Whitefield when he explained:

> It was simple in understanding the source of the controversy. Whitefield was a Calvinist, Wesley an Arminian, and both held to their opinions most tenaciously. Predestination was one of the chief bones of contention. Charles Wesley had preached and published a sermon against it, John Wesley preached and published a sermon against election and Whitefield was also making use of the press.[280]

---

278 See *Glossary of Terms* for further explanation of the Doctrines of Grace.
279 Dallimore, vol. 2, 157-158.
280 Hardy, 171.

Whitefield first learned of the divisive nature of the issue when he read Joseph Hutton's articles against him, while refusing to publish the evangelist's writings. Hutton, who had become a Moravian, refused to publish Whitefield's writings because of the latter's Calvinism. Whitefield told of how Hutton accused him of "dressing up the doctrine of election in such horrible colours."[281] Hutton learned that Whitefield's debts were mounting because the orphanage's expenses were exceeding the amount allotted by the trustees, making matters worse.[282] The vigor he felt by his warm reception in America was quickly replaced by growing concern for the state of Methodism. The accusations over mismanagement of the orphanage were certainly to come.

Dallimore explains how the opposition hurt the orphanage:

> Bereft thus of his congregation he was robbed not only of the means of reaching people with the Gospel, but also of the means of supporting the Orphan House. He had assured the institution's long-suffering manager, James Habersham, that upon his return to England the offerings from his congregations would enable him to send him money, and we can imagine his feelings when he wrote to Habersham telling him there was no money forthcoming and explaining why.[283]

Whitefield dealt with the theological controversy first. It was hard for him to believe the Doctrines of Grace were under attack. The Puritans fostered the evangelical spirit of England when they strongly asserted their belief in the sovereignty of God. Great leaders such as Richard Baxter, John Owen and Thomas Watson supported these doctrines. Whitefield praised Baxter, for instance, when he visited Kiddmaster and preached there. He declared, "I was greatly refreshed to find what a sweet savour of good Mr. Baxter's doctrine, works and discipline remained to this day."[284] Their writings and leadership of the movement had seen England through some dark times. The Church of England would have been similar to the Roman church without these leaders and their writings. Although the Puritans had strongly advanced their beliefs, many still were opposed to their views. Despite this struggle,

---

281 Dallimore, vol. 2, 46.
282 Tyerman, vol. 1, 465.
283 Dallimore, vol. 2, 45.
284 Andrews, 183.

their views were strongly maintained within the Church of England.[285]

Whitefield had reason to assert the Doctrines of Graces as his personal convictions since he had steadily and consistently preached them in the colonies. Countless lives changed through their proclamation were evidence of their power. The doctrines had been encouraged through Whitefield's association and support with Calvinistic thought in America.[286] It puzzled him that Wesley and his followers would attack them so vigorously.

Whitefield had developed a theology in line with Calvinistic thought. The influences in his life toward Calvinism were multiple. The first contemplation of this doctrine by the evangelist was due to Calvinism being part of the evangelical climate in England. Because the Puritans were prolific writers, they influenced him through their biblical thought.[287] The books Whitefield was familiar with at Oxford dealt with grace as an unearned gift, graciously given to men by God. William Law's *A Serious Call to a Devout and Holy Life* was an early favorite of the Holy Club.[288] This work was generally the only major exception to Whitefield's exposure to Calvinistic theology. Many other works influenced him. *The Life of God in the Soul of Man* was heavily Calvinistic and the book Whitefield credits with leading him to salvation. In it, Henry Scougal taught that salvation was graciously given by God, not earned by good works.[289]

Whitefield's daily meditations included Matthew Henry's Commentary of the Bible. He consulted Henry's work daily and used it as a companion to his own devotional life. He began each day at 5 a.m., when he prayed over the Scripture line by line. Not only did he employ

---

285   A general understanding of the break with Catholicism in practice is fully realized with the rise and influence of the Puritan movement and these leaders who led England and the monarchy to be Protestant, not a hybrid of Catholicism and Protestantism.

286   Ninde, 185.

287   Main theological works in the time of Whitefield and the century before dominated by Puritan thought proved very influential. Their works advanced the cause of Reformed theology.

288   William Law's work was a favorite of the Holy Club because it outlined steps to holiness and righteous that fit the early theme of fellow members. Law's writing's directed them to practice extraordinary spiritual exercises to earn God's favor.

289   A more detailed account of the reading of Scougal's book being a primary factor in Whitefield's conversion is discussed in chapter 2.

Henry for devotional reading, but he also consulted it for understanding on doctrinal matters.[290]

The current writers of the day influenced Whitefield and others as he read their writings and he corresponded with them. The contemporary Puritan motif of these men was heavily Calvinistic. Wesley read Edwards' *Narrative of Surprising Works* and heavily impressed by it, he exclaimed, "This is the Lord's doing and glorious in our midst!"[291] By contrast, Whitefield looked at the theological truths laid out in Edwards' works and marveled at his strong reliance on God's sovereignty. He was convinced its truth was a key component of the awakening in Northampton.[292]

Whitefield's past friendship with Ralph and Ebenezer Erskine, leaders of awakening in Scotland, a reformed country, influenced him. He read their messages and corresponded with them regularly.[293] The brothers formed the Associate Presbytery, breaking off from the established church. They were fearful of the betrayal of Reformation theology by the state church of Scotland and perceived Episcopal practices within the established churches, particularly in the matter of church governance. Their split with the established church caused problems for Whitefield on his first preaching tour in Scotland when he received invitations to preach from churches not affiliated with the Associate Presbytery.[294]

Gilbert Tennent and his father William were Presbyterians who influenced Whitefield. Their school, The Log College, which William founded, trained itinerant preachers and was committed to God's sovereignty in salvation. The school was at the center of the awakening movement, believing that through it, God was awakening people to their condition without Christ. Salvation experienced by those awakened was a result of the gracious gift of God conferred on those believing

---

290 Dallimore, *George Whitefield: God's Anointed Servant in the Great Revival of the Eighteenth Century*, 22.

291 Richard Steel, *John Wesley's Synthesis of the Revival Practices of Jonathan Edwards, George Whitefield, Nicholas Von Zinzendorf*, Wesley Theological Journal, November 4, 2002, (accessed September 23, 2015). http://www.freerepublic.com/focus/religion.

292 Whitefield's time spent with Edwards at Northampton indicates this truth through his sermon titles, remarks, praise of Edwards leadership and preaching concerning the cause of the awakening there. He believed Reformed theology was a distinctive feature of that movement of God.

293 Dallimore, vol. 1, 384-385.

294 Ibid., 405.

the gospel of Christ. The successful itinerant ministry of Tennent and those he trained confirmed the Doctrines of Grace were not hindering evangelism. They rather awakened hearers who looked to God for salvation instead of themselves.[295]

Whitefield believed that the Doctrines of Grace were strongly consistent with the Church of England's "Thirty-Nine Articles of Faith." Article 9 taught that man is born with original sin. It specifically states it is against the Pelagian theory that man becomes a sinner when he chooses to sin. Article 10 taught that because of mankind's fall, he has no strength in himself to secure salvation. Article 17 boldly proclaimed predestination as the way God saw the elect in Christ before the foundation of the world and that our coming to Him is according to His gracious choice. Article 18 asserts that man is not saved or kept by the works of the law but through the sole sacrifice of Christ for man's sins, inferring that God gives eternal salvation.[296] Other notable reformed influences were included in the document. As a loyal churchman, Whitefield was only preaching what the church confirmed. Wesley and his followers, however, were the ones pulling away from church teaching in this matter. Henry explained how these doctrines were a source of difference with Whitefield and the established clergy. He believed Wesley had departed from the church's teaching. Henry revealed:

> Indeed, it was the basis of Whitefield's quarrel with the established clergy that they fostered the belief that man could by his own good works help to effect his salvation. Too often, thought Whitefield, clergymen were "blind unregenerate, carnal, lukewarm, and unskillful guides," who encouraged men in the delusion that they could lift themselves by their own boot straps....
>
> So passionately did Whitefield disbelieve in the efficacy of man's righteousness that he openly denounced Archbishop Tillotson (who did not see man's role in the drama of salvation as "merely passive") and said that his grace "knew no more of Christianity than Mohamet."[297]

Whitefield believed the doctrines of the Reformation defined by Calvin are fully represented by the Doctrines of Grace. Similar

---

295 Ibid., 437.

296 Charles Mortimer Guilbert, ed., *The Book of Common Prayer and Administration of the Sacraments and Other Rites and Ceremonies of the Church, Together with The Psalter or Psalms of David: According to use of The Episcopal Church* (Oxford University Press: New York, 1977), 869-871.

297 Henry, 107.

to Calvin's belief, Whitefield wanted people to know what the Bible taught.[298] He believed the Doctrines of Grace not only enlightened those awakened, but also motivated the forceful preaching of the gospel. Calvin's explanations of the Bible put these truths concerning salvation in the hands of the people. The preaching of the Reformation teaching on salvation had liberated the people and helped them experience the gospel message. The major truth to understanding these doctrines was the explanation that God was convicting people to come to Christ; He was calling the elect to Christ. Freely and openly, Whitefield called people to salvation whenever he preached, declaring the truths of what he preached to be the Holy Scripture.[299]

Whitefield stated, "I embrace the Calvinistic scheme, not because of Calvin, but Jesus Christ has taught it to me."[300] He counseled his friend James Hervey: "Let me advise Dear Mr. Hervey, laying aside all prejudice, to read and pray over St. Paul's epistles to the Romans and Galatians, and then let him tell me what he thinks of this doctrine."[301]

Whitefield declared these truths were the source of his zeal. He confessed, "I love the doctrines of our election and free justification in Christ Jesus. They fill my soul with a holy fire and afford me great confidence in God my Saviour."[302]

Steve Lawson, a recent biographer of Whitefield, clarified a popular misunderstanding of Calvinism:

> **Contrary to the popular Calvinistic stereotype, Whitefield was not a stale, stoic intellectual with a dour approach to Christianity. He was fervently enlivened by the sovereign grace of God, which sparked an intense urgency in his gospel preaching. It was his belief in the Doctrines of Grace that propelled his gospel proclamation far and wide. The deeper Whitefield plunged into these sacred truths, the higher he ascended in his declaration of them.[303]**

The Doctrines of Grace gave him a sense of urgency and obligation to share the gospel. E. A. Johnston said, "To understand George

---

298   The purpose of Calvin writing his *Institutes of the Christian Religion* was to teach the meaning of the central doctrines of the Bible.

299   Steve Lawson, *The Evangelistic Zeal of George Whitefield* (Samford, FL: Reformation Trust 2013), 58.

300   Dallimore, vol. 1, 406.

301   Dallimore, *George Whitefield: God's Anointed Servant in the Great Revival of the Eighteenth Century*, 69.

302   Ibid., 69.

303   Lawson, 51.

Whitefield and what made him tick, we need to know his theology. It is the motive which moved him... The Doctrines of Grace gave him fire in the pulpit to cry out and warn men of the wrath to come and to flee from it into the loving arms of a wonderful Savior."[304]

Both Johnston and Lawson concur that the doctrines motivated Whitefield to preach the gospel with great energy. He had to preach the gospel because he clung to these truths.

Whitefield's first rude awakening to this controversy came in the response to his preaching. The crowds were nothing compared to the ones he had experienced in America. Massive crowds from all over America had attended is meetings. His absence from England left a void for Wesley to fill with teaching that was contrary to Reformed theology. Those who came to hear him were only a shadow of those who had attended his meetings before he had left for America. Some who supported Wesley came to heckle Whitefield while he preached by putting their fingers in their ears and showing that they refused to listen to what he had to say.[305] Whitefield continued and saw a limited response to the gospel in places where he had seen great response only two years before. The issue of predestination, election, and salvation was central in the doctrinal crisis in which the evangelist found himself immersed with Wesley.

Wesley greatly accelerated the crisis when he ripped Predestination declaring:

> **Such blasphemy this, as one would think might make the ears of a Christian to tingle! But there is yet more behind; for just as it honours the Son, so doth this doctrine honour the Father. It destroys all his attributes at once: it overturns both his justice, mercy and truth; yea, it represents the most holy God as worse than the devil; as both more false, more cruel, and more unjust.**[306]

Wesley even preached a sermon against the doctrine of election. Dallimore indicates how this message set him apart from Whitefield:

> **This sermon was of major importance in Wesley's career. It was his first declaration of a distinctive theological position, and, as such, it removed him**

---

304 Johnston, vol. 1, 498.
305 Dallimore, vol. 2, 47.
306 Dallimore, vol. 1, 311.

from standing in a secondary relationship to Whitefield. It won the allegiance of a number of the Bristol hearers, and gave them reason to consider themselves no longer Whitefield's people, but Wesley's.[307]

Whitefield decided to respond publicly to Wesley. It grieved him to do so in that context, but his position had to be addressed due to Wesley's fierce opposition. Wesley had gone public in his opposition to Whitefield. Now Whitefield published his letter to Wesley and read it to a crowd. He confessed his grief that Mr. Wesley had made this doctrine an issue.[308] Whitefield believed the Doctrines of Grace enhanced the cause of Christ, because they assign salvation rightly to Christ. Instead, the Arminianism Wesley was advocating led to spiritual pride, and later some of his followers developed a belief in sinless perfection.[309] Salvation by works became a goal to achieve salvation in this erroneous teaching. Whitefield believed salvation was according to the gracious choice of God when He saw the elect in Christ. Confirmation of that choice comes through trust in His finished work on the cross in man's behalf.[310]

Whitefield responded to Wesley. He declared that election was consistent with evangelism:

> O dear Sir, what kind of reasoning, or rather sophistry is this! Hath not God, who hath appointed salvation for a certain number, appointed also the preaching of the word, as a means to bring them to it? Does anyone hold election in any other sense? And if so, how is preaching needless to them that are elected; when the gospel is designed by God himself, to be the power of God unto their eternal salvation? And since we know not who are elect, and who are reprobate, we are to preach promiscuously to all. For the word may be useful, even to the non-elect, in restraining them from much wickedness and sin.[311]

Preaching God's sovereignty in salvation was consistent with evangelism, for all Whitefield was doing was calling out the called. He was not preventing people from coming to Christ.

Wesley reacted at a public meeting after reading Whitefield's defense of the reformed doctrines of salvation. His response was shocking. A grandstanding moment came when he held up Whitefield's letter and

---

307 Ibid., 313.
308 Kidd, 145.
309 Ibid., 145.
310 Lawson, 59.
311 Gillies, ed., *George Whitefield's Journals*, 575.

said, "I will do just what Mr. Whitefield would have were he here himself."[312] He tore the letter into pieces. Every person there followed Wesley's example.[313] The rift had been sealed in this act; the shame of these actions was great. These two had been good friends, but now went their separate ways because the issue had been forced on Whitefield.

There was, however, an interesting occurrence in the split with Wesley when Whitefield began to use a building close to Wesley's Foundery in London to conduct meetings. The building became "Whitefield's Tabernacle."[314] Here were two revival leaders divided on the same theological issue, preaching to separate congregations in close proximity to each other.

Whitefield met with Parliament and shared information concerning the beginning of the Bethesda orphanage. He also appealed charges made against him by Alexander Garden's Commissary Court.[315] After reporting to friends and supporters the debt for building and maintenance of the orphanage, Whitefield worked furiously to receive offerings to decrease that debt.[316] This debt for building and maintenance of the orphanage came at an untimely juncture. The controversy with Wesley was breaking out, and support for the evangelist's ministry was waning. Whitefield had pledged to raise support for the orphanage himself from the very beginning of his sponsorship by Parliament. The rumors of excitement in the establishment of the orphanage were probably very stimulating. Parliament had been supportive of the efforts in Georgia and its members were concerned for the colony's survival. With the orphanage, a measure of civility had come to families in the region, and a benevolent way of caring for desperate children was seen as a positive step. Whitefield's meeting with the trustees lent accountability to his position and served to quell some fears about the debts he had incurred. He had also been successful in collecting large amounts to decrease the debt of the orphanage, and he published a full accounting of the collections.[317] A meeting of this type was very beneficial.

---

312 Philip, 199.
313 Ibid., 199.
314 Dallimore, vol. 2, 49.
315 Tyerman, vol. 1, 477.
316 Ibid., 492.
317 Ibid., 493-494.

The crowds began to return as Whitefield preached in familiar places to those who had previously heard him. His physical presence helped his doctrinal position as opposed to his absence while in America. John Wesley's ministry took him in another direction, and his path with Whitefield would not cross again for a long time. As Paul and Barnabas disagreed and separated, Wesley and Whitefield realized the world was able to sustain them in separate ministries (Acts 15:36-39). Whitefield never looked back. He did not seek reconciliation or spend his time complaining of accusations hurled at him by the Wesley camp. The confrontation with his Oxford friend was over. He looked onward to expand the mission field God had given him by preaching the gospel. Whitefield would maintain his strong Calvinistic convictions as the spokesman for Calvinistic Methodism. Wesley meanwhile became the leader of Arminian Methodism because of his high visibility.[318] One of Whitefield's notable sermons, "The Lord our Righteousness," had deep roots in the Doctrines of Grace. In one of his famous portions, he preached:

> This, however, is my comfort, "Jesus Christ, the same yesterday, today and forever." He saw me from all eternity; He gave me being; He called me in time; He has freely justified me through faith in His blood; He has in part sanctified me by His Spirit; He will preserve me underneath His everlasting arms till time shall be no more…Satan will accuse me; my answer shall be, The Lord Jesus is my righteousness; how darest thou to lay anything to the charge of God's elect? I stand here, not in my own, but in His robes; and though I deserve nothing as a debt, yet I know He will give me a reward of grace, and recompense me for what He has done in me and by me, as though I had done it by my own power. Oh, how ought this to excite our zeal and love for the holy Jesus![319]

Now the evangelist was on to new fields "white unto harvest." The movement was beginning anew. Word spread that Whitefield's preaching was as sharp and fresh as ever. People suspended judgment, and Whitefield found the same results he had before he left for America.[320] A band of leaders stood around him and took the reproach heaped on him. They began the construction of the Tabernacle for him to preach in and later formed the first Calvinistic Methodist Association.[321] Both

---

318 Dalimore, vol. 2, 40.
319 Ibid., 406.
320 Belcher, 218-219.
321 Dallimore, vol. 1, 467.

Wesley and Whitefield knew they were still not in the mainstream of religious life. Methodism was still persecuted and would continue to suffer reproach as the clear gospel of Christ was preached.[322] Its message confronted people with their need to repent and come to Christ for salvation.

Whitefield looked north toward Scotland, having been acquainted with the Erskine brothers through correspondence. They were for revival and supported him as a champion of the Doctrines of Grace. They were also embroiled in a separation issue with the Presbyterian Church in Scotland. The question was, "Would Whitefield preach to these congregations if the Erskine brothers were separating from them?" Other ministers, William McCulloch of Cambuslang and James Robe of Kilsyth were willing to sponsor him to preach in open meetings although they were part of the state church. Which group would sponsor Whitefield's preaching became a sticky issue for contemplation and prayer. Whitefield wanted to go to Scotland, meet with leaders and see what the prospects were of holding meetings there.

The dilemma Whitefield faced is seen in Ralph Erskine's response to his coming to Scotland:

> Come, if possible, dear Whitefield, come, and come to us also. There is no face on earth I would desire more earnestly to see. Yet I would desire it only in a way that, I think, would tend most to the advancing of our Lord's kingdom, and the reformation work, among our hands. Such is the Associate Presbytery, and to make your public appearances in the places especially of their concern,—I would dread the consequences of your coming, lest it should seem equal to countenance our persecutors.[323]

Whitefield sailed for Scotland and when he arrived, his first impression was that it was a land ripe for revival. Many believers were praying for God to work, and the rumblings of a movement of God was alive in the Cambuslang area. The impression of his ministry in Scotland was favorable, and the ministers extended an invitation to him to come and speak.[324] Whitefield was gracious in his camaraderie with the brethren as he was quickly picking up the trait of an encourager. He was more at home there when he was with like-minded brethren.

---

322   The bulk of the established clergy's opposition to the Methodist, despite their not leaving the Church of England, still contributed to this persecution.

323   Philip, 223.

324   Ibid., 246-247.

This encouraging trait and willingness to preach anywhere was spurring a spirit of cooperation with Bible-preaching ministers and churches. Whitefield was not going to let the theological controversy in Scotland keep him from preaching the gospel in the open air. He knew God was leading him to preach the gospel in Scotland. He began correspondence with the Erskines on the matter.[325] The stage was set for the first of many happy preaching tours he would be involved with in Scotland which was to be a place of great expectancy and blessing.

After traveling and preaching in only a few places, Whitefield traveled to Wales. He was soon to be twenty-seven and without a companion in life. The woman married to the roaming evangelist would have to be ready for a major adjustment in her life. Was there a woman able to make this type of commitment? Before the end of 1741, one of the greatest surprises in his life would stun his friends. He left Edinburgh and he traveled to Wales for a very eventful trip.

---

325   Ibid., 236-239.

9

MARRIAGE

AND THE CAMBUSLANG REVIVAL

(1742-1744)

WHITEFIELD CONTEMPLATED RETURNING to Scotland for a greater evangelistic thrust because he saw Scotland as an open opportunity to preach the gospel to crowds in a new venue. The Scots had a reputation for being ardent supporters of the Protestant Reformation and had bitterly fought for scriptural teaching, repelling Romanist practices from their churches.

Scotland had suffered from the same malady that was affecting America and England: a great disregard for true spiritual religion. This condition affected them in spite of the fact that their background had been one of support for the Doctrines of Grace.

Dallimore reveals the religious climate of Scotland:

> With the opening of the eighteenth century, however, there came much easier conditions and therewith the strong fervor of the militant years declined. Lip service continued to be paid to The Westminster Confession of Faith, but spiritual life was cold. The Calvinism that had been so meaningful to Reformers and Covenanters degenerated into little more than a form of fatalism, standards of conduct were lowered and evangelistic zeal withered away.[326]

---

326   Dallimore, vol. 2, 83.

Scotland's rich biblical heritage remained despite these losses and perhaps more than any other country on earth, its culture had deep roots in the Scripture. In the midst of the spiritual laxity, the Bible was still read in the majority of homes and was accepted almost everywhere as the Word of God. Whitefield wandered into this climate with great expectations.

Whitefield's first visit to Scotland came in the summer of 1741 and extended to the fall. He immediately confronted controversy within the established church because of a new movement and group in the church known as the Associate Presbytery. They disagreed with the Church of Scotland over the self-government of the church believing in appointments of the clergy by the congregation and not by wealthy landowners.[327] The leaders immediately tried to convince him to fellowship only with their group and not the established church.

Tyerman describes the Erskines' reception of Whitefield as he went directly to their fellowship, spending the first night in Scotland with Ralph Erskine at Dunfermline. Erskine wrote to his brother, Ebenezer in a letter dated, July 31, 1741:

> **Mr. Whitefield came to me yesternight about ten. I had conversation with him alone this forenoon. I only mention this one thing about his ordination; he owned he then knew no other way, but said he would not have it that way again for a thousand worlds. As to his preaching, he declares he can refuse no call to preach Christ, whoever gives it: Were it a Jesuit priest or a Mahomedan, he would embrace it for testifying against them. He preached in my meeting-house this afternoon. The Lord is evidently with him.[328]**

Tyerman dismissed Erskine's remark regretting Whitefield's Church of England ordination with skeptical questioning, "Was Ralph Erskine strictly correct in his statement that Whitefield said if he had life to begin again, he would not be ordained a minister of the Church of England for a thousand worlds?" Many will doubt this; others will raise the possibility considering Whitefield's openness to preach anywhere he had the invitation."[329] The expansion of preaching opportunities in churches not affiliated with the Associate Presbytery caused Whitefield

---

327   Roy Middleton, *Introduction to the Works of Ralph Erskine* Free Presbyterian Publications, 1991, (accessed Sept. 30, 2015). http://www.fpchurch.org.uk/2014/08/ralph-erskine-1685-1752.

328   Tyerman, vol. 1, 507.

329   Ibid., vol.1, 507-508.

to consider preaching wherever he had the invitation.

Whitefield's own estimation of his initial meeting with Ralph Erskine was different. On August 5th, he met the Associate Presbytery at Dunfermline. An idea of the debate following is gathered briefly from a letter Whitefield wrote afterwards to his friend, Mr. Noble of New York. He declared:

> The Associate Presbytery are so confined that they will not so much as hear me preach, unless I will join with them... I asked them seriously what they would have me to do? The answer was that I was not desired to subscribe immediately to the Solemn League and Covenant, but to preach only for them until I had further light. I asked, "why only for them?" Mr. Ralph Erskine said, 'they were the Lord's people.' I then asked whether there were no other Lord's people but themselves, and supposing others were the devil's people, they certainly had the more need to be preached to; and therefore I was the more determined to go out into the highways and hedges; and that if the Pope himself were to lend me his pulpit I would gladly proclaim the righteousness of Jesus Christ therein.[330]

Whitefield was clear in wanting to preach to as many people as possible and not be restricted by narrow sectarianism.

Ralph Erskine accompanied Whitefield as he preached in Edinburgh at the Orphan House Park. On the Sabbath evening he preached in the same place to upwards of fifteen thousand people and on Monday, Wednesday and Friday evening to nearly as many. On Tuesday he was in the Canongate church; on Wednesday and Thursday at Dunfermline and on Friday morning at Queensbury.[331] At Dunfermline, where Erskine lived, he told how surprised he was by "the rustling made by the opening of the Bibles all at once, a scene I never was witness to before."[332] The love of God's Word was a distinctive feature of believers in Scotland.

Whitefield said, "The auditories were large and very attentive. Great power accompanied the Word. Many have been brought under convictions, and I have already received invitations to different places." The reception in Scotland was very positive. Whitefield also was pleased that his printed sermons and journals "had been blessed in an uncommon manner."[333]

---

330 Ibid., 509.
331 Belcher, 228.
332 Belden, 124.
333 Belcher, 229.

Whitefield's first tour of Scotland kept a busy pace, ending in October with a whirlwind. Tyerman reported how hectic the pace was:

> Leaving Aberdeen on Wednesday, October 13, Whitefield began his journey back to Edinburgh. On October 14, he preached at Stonhithe and Benham; on the 15th, thrice at Montrose; on the 16th and 17th, five times at Brechin; on the 18th, twice at Forfar; on the 19th, twice at Coupar, near the residence of Earl Leven, whose guest he was; and on the 20th and 21st, four times at Dundee, where, he says, "the concern among the hearers was very remarkable." A week after this, he set out for Wales, but, before he went, he preached and lectured, in Edinburgh, in three days, not fewer than sixteen times.[334]

Whitefield's first tour of Scotland laid the foundation for his return the next year in Cambuslang. It would be a remarkable stretch because of several factors, not the least of which was his decision that when he returned to work with the established churches, he would not be restricted to the Erskine's Associate Presbytery.

The next monumental event in Whitefield's life was his marriage, which was originally unknown to the public and a secret to many. When he emerged as a married man, it was a shock to his friends. They had a hard time believing one with his boundless energy and who had crossed the ocean more than any other preacher had, would settle down. But settle down was hardly the word for his marriage. He believed it was time for him to have a companion in life, for despite his notoriety, he was often lonely.

Whitefield was anxious to be married. "Riding a gift horse he hastened on his way to Wales to be married. This happy event took place November 14, 1741. The bride was Mrs. Elizabeth James, a widow who came from a totally different background than Whitefield."[335]

Whitefield's search for a helpmate involved someone willing to sacrifice and willing to endure the frequent, extended times they would be apart from one another. She would also support him in the ministry and the orphanage when they were in Georgia. He did not visit the orphanage as frequently, as he would have desired because of his numerous other engagements. In choosing a wife, he was looking for someone who would assist him at Bethesda. In reality, the expectation of his wife, being a mainstay at Bethesda, was an

---

334 Tyerman, vol. 1, 523.
335 Hardy, 175.

unreachable goal. This presumed ministry at Bethesda was possibly the reason Miss Delmotte had refused his proposal.

Cashin confirmed how the search for a Bethesda helpmate weighed heavily on Whitefield, "Considerations regarding Bethesda influenced one of his most personal and important decisions: The choice of a wife."[336] Whitefield confided to a friend, "My poor family gives me more concern than everything else is put together. I want a gracious woman that is dead to everything but Jesus and is qualified to govern children and direct persons of her own sex."[337] This statement led Cashin to believe, "He seemed to suggest that although he did not need a wife, Bethesda required a mistress."[338]

Mrs. Elizabeth James was the unlikely prospect and Whitefield's eventual wife. She had a teenage daughter, Nancy, who lived with her at their cottage in Abergavenny, South Wales.[339] She was admired by Wesley and Howell Harris, having been an ardent supporter of the awakening and the Methodist movement. His search ended when he met and married Mrs. James at Caerphilly, Wales. He was twenty-six, she in her thirties. As his bride, Elizabeth James met the spiritual requirement he was looking for in a wife. John Wesley visited Mrs. James the month before she married Whitefield and enjoyed her hospitality and thought well of her as a "woman of candor and humanity."[340]

One is left to speculate on the friendship and the designs Howell Harris may have had with Elizabeth. He admired her greatly, and some felt he was deeply in love with her. However, the chance to introduce her to his friend was an opportunity he did not pass up.[341]

Whitefield decided Elizabeth was to be his life's companion in spite of the short time they had known each other. He proposed to her and she accepted recognizing something of a divine calling in the matter and probably knowing whatever feelings she or Howell Harris had for each were not going to materialize.

Dallimore indicates Elizabeth was faced with a decision between Harris and Whitefield. She had more in common with Harris, who was

---

336 Cashin, 52.
337 Ibid., 52.
338 Ibid., 52.
339 Dallimore, vol. 2, 110.
340 Cashin, 52.
341 Dallimore, vol. 2, 105.

Welsh and was from the same general area where she lived. Whitefield, whose life was one of adventure, was different from Harris, but Harris made his decision instantly. He let Mrs. James know the acceptance of Whitefield's proposal was up to her. She, apparently, sensed a duty to marry Whitefield.[342]

There did not appear to have been a courtship. The day before the wedding, Whitefield wrote to Earl Leven: "I find a restraint upon me now, so that I cannot write. God calls me to retirement, being to enter the marriage state tomorrow. I am persuaded your lordship will not fail to pray that we may, like Zacharias and Elisabeth, walk in all the ordinances and commandments of the Lord blameless."[343]

After Whitefield was united in matrimony to Mrs. James, he wrote to a friend: "The Lord has given me a daughter of Abraham." He speaks of her in the most endearing manner as his "dear partner," his "dear fellow-pilgrim," his "dear yoke-fellow."[344]

Whitefield was deeply impressed by Elizabeth James. She had a steady personality after enduring many trials herself. She was a woman of piety, soft-spoken and faithful in her admiration of him.[345] Although little is known of Elizabeth's feeling for him as a husband, his feelings for her were immediate and certain.

The couple was married at the old chapel: Capel Martin, in the village of Caerphilly, with the Reverend John Smith officiating. Howell Harris was the best man. The wedding party, which numbered only half a dozen people, met for the reception in the home of Thomas Price in the village of Watford.[346]

The register reads as follows, in the handwriting of the Rev. John Smith, Vicar of Eglwsilan:

GEORGE WHITEFIELD AND ELIZABETH JAMES, MARRIED, NOVEMBER 14, 1741.[347]

---

342   Ibid., 107-108.
343   Belden, 126.
344   Wakeley, 153.
345   Dallimore, vol. 2, 108.
346   Ibid., 109.
347   Belden, 126.

Whitefield's several sentences about his new wife to Gilbert Tennent are characteristic of him: "Once gay, but for three years past, a despised follower of the Lamb of God, neither rich in fortune nor beautiful as to her person, but I believe a true child of God, and one who would not think or attempt to hinder me in His work for the world."[348] It appears he was more concerned with the inner beauty of the heart, and he focused on her spiritual beauty. Elizabeth, strong and resolute, served him well as a wife, encouraging him to be determined as well.

Since obviously many young women and their mothers apparently had designs on Whitefield in the way of marriage, his having a wife put a stop to this problem.

The hardest course for the newly married Mrs. Whitefield was to endure her husband's frequent absences. Thomas Lewis courted Nancy, her daughter, eventually marrying her at the time her mother married Whitefield, settling in Bristol.[349] Elizabeth was at home by herself when her husband was preaching on his long trips. She endured many long periods by herself because when she tried to travel with Whitefield, her ill health prevented it. Elizabeth's introduction to the Tabernacle was a surprise to those attending, but it was evident that Whitefield had a wife.[350] The Whitefields' type of marriage was not uncommon for the time; those widowed and of marriageable age married quickly or did not remarry. They seemed to desire a wedding free from as much fanfare as possible..[351]

The only information on their married life suggests that they were not overwhelmingly in love, but they did care for each other. Cashin described a realistic picture of Whitefield's marriage: "The marriage was less than ideal." One of his closest associates, Cornelius Winter, said flatly, "He did not intentionally make his wife unhappy. He always preserved great decency and decorum in his conduct toward her."[352] Winter indicated Whitefield was somewhat of a fussy husband: "He was very exact to the time appointed for his stated meals: a few minutes' delay

---

348   Ibid., 126.
349   Information given by Digby James, October 22, 2014, at Whitefield and the Great Awakening Conference, held at Southern Baptist Theological Seminary, Louisville, KY, during a small group break out session he led on Elizabeth Whitefield.
350   Dallimore, vol. 2, 111, 113.
351   Ibid., 111.
352   Cashin, 52.

would be considered a great fault. He was irritable, but soon appeased... Not a paper must have been out of place, or put up irregularly. Each part of the furniture must have been likewise in its place before he retired."[353]

The couple had some debt because of Elizabeth's living situation. She could not sell her home in Abergavenny and had to leave it. Elizabeth vacated her home when they found a cottage in London. They borrowed furniture because they did not have money to buy it. Here was the great fundraiser for Bethesda, having to borrow furnishings for his first home, indicating Whitefield's self-denial.[354]

In the summer of 1742, Whitefield was off again to Scotland for a greater preaching tour with Elizabeth joining him. They left by ship on May 26, 1742. The evangelist had been inundated with letters since his initial visit, asking him to return. He concentrated on the villages around Glasgow, where revival had broken out in Cambuslang and Kilsyth.[355]

Whitefield arrived on June 3 in Scotland, on the Mary, expecting "great things" there and ready to preach. Five days later he wrote to William McCulloch, rejoicing at the continued progress of the work at Cambuslang: "I believe you will both see and hear of far greater things than these. I trust that not one corner of poor Scotland will be left unwatered by the dew of God's heavenly blessing. The cloud is now only rising as big as a man's hand; yet a little while, and we shall hear a sound of an abundance of gospel rain."[356]

Whitefield was again in Scotland, anticipating a great work of God. He had heard his friends, the Erskines, were greatly offended by what they considered his lax views of church government and failure to align only with the Associate Presbytery.[357]

Earlier, the mention of Whitefield going to Scotland for a preaching tour led him into the thick of controversy between the Erskine brothers' new Associate Presbytery and the established churches. Great Awakening had begun in the two churches where McCulloch and Robe served as pastors in the Cambuslang and Kilsyth areas. Because of Whitefield's interest in open air meetings, they issued an invitation for him to speak in

---

353 Ibid., 52-53.

354 Dallimore, vol. 2, 110-111.

355 Fish, 92.

356 Arthur Fawcett, *The Cambuslang Revival: The Scottish Evangelical Revival of the Eighteenth Century* (Banner of Truth: Carlisle, PA, 1996), 114.

357 Belcher, 238.

what they believed would be a good venue for his ministry. The Erskine brothers tried to persuade Whitefield to fellowship only with churches of their faction. When they pleaded with him to come, but to cooperate only with their churches, he responded that he would "go to Rome and preach in the Vatican to the Pope" if he ever got an invitation.[358] When he did go to Cambuslang to preach when he was invited, it was obviously the right decision because of the massive number of people who attended and the number who were converted to Christ.

Belcher describes Whitefield's amazing reception in Scotland as: "Notwithstanding the difference with the seceders, he was received by great numbers of persons of distinction, with cordiality and joy, and had the satisfaction of hearing more and more of the happy fruits of his ministry."[359]

Whitefield's pace was rapid and fruitful: "At Edinburgh he again preached twice a day, as before, in the Hospital-park, where the number of seats and shades, in the form of an amphitheater, were erected for the accommodation of his listeners."[360]

Whitefield's going to Cambuslang was met with great expectancy: "On the day of his arrival at Cambuslang, he preached three times to an immense body of people, although he had preached that same morning at Glasgow. The last service continued until eleven o'clock. People were so moved after Whitefield's sermon that they stayed till past one in the morning. Mr. McCulloch was scarcely able to persuade them to depart."[361]

The afterglow of Cambuslang spread to Glasgow: "Exactly one week later he was met at Glasgow and was welcomed by twenty thousand." Whitefield described his furious pace and the massive crowds: "By three o'clock this morning, 16 June, people were coming to hear the Word of God. At seven, I preached to many, many thousands."[362]

God had used the faithful preaching and preparation of William McCulloch in the Cambuslang parish church. James Robe, pastor in Kilsyth, also experienced great signs of revival in the neighboring town.

---

358 Ibid., 238.
359 Ibid., 238.
360 Ibid., 238.
361 Ibid., 238.
362 Ibid., 238.

The amazing reality of the Cambuslang revival was that it featured meetings in the open air, since no church was large enough to hold the massive amounts of people.

These meetings lasted for more than two months. The crowds numbered approximately 20,000 people with more than 40,000 on several Sundays, and Glasgow had a population of only 20,000 people in Whitefield's day. People walked and rode horses from great distances each day to hear the sermons and participate in the meetings.[363] Whitefield was the first to attest that he was not the cause of revival, but he was grateful to be a part of it and reap the results of the faithful labor of ministers McCulloch and Robe. The way God used different leaders to do His work was amazing, especially since McCulloch was not known for his pulpit skills. Arthur Fawcett, one of the leading students of the Cambuslang revival, correctly assesses McCulloch's speaking abilities:

> He was given the nickname of a yill or Ale-minister, for when he rose to speak, many of the audience left to quench their thirst in the public house… Despite his above-average scholarship, however, he had little gift for the pulpit. His own son writes that "he was not a very ready speaker; though eminent for learning and piety, he was not eloquent…his manner was slow and cautious, very different from that of popular orators."
>
> He was licensed to preach the gospel by the Presbytery of Wigtown in 1722 and lived mainly with Mr. Hamilton of Aitkenhead Cathcart, where he served as chaplain and tutor. This was a familiar and convenient arrangement whereby probationers supported themselves whilst waiting for a call.[364]

McCulloch, though, had a heart for his people and was devoted to God's work. He wanted to see revival in the "dry bones churches." On January 31, 1742, McCulloch preached to his own people on "The Abundance of Divine Consolation" with II Corinthians 1:3-4 as his text. In his closing paragraph, he declared:

> When I look around me, blessed be God, I see marks of more apparent concern about salvation than in times past among some of you. Beware of a noisy or ostentatious religion; and, at the same time, take heed that you run not to the opposite extreme, by endeavoring to stifle the convictions you may feel. "Follow on to know the Lord, and he shall come unto us as the rain, as the latter and former rain unto the earth."[365]

---

363 Ibid., 115.
364 Fawcett, 39.
365 Ibid., 104.

The turning point of the Cambuslang revival came through personal awakening and regeneration in the congregation. A woman in McCulloch's church, Mrs. Catherine Jackson, became extremely distressed and with her two sisters, were taken to the manse by Mr. Duncan, "a Preacher" and "another Person," an Elder Ingram More. It was in all probability, the incident that ignited the ensuing blaze.[366]

A full account of what happened that night was written down and drawn up from Duncan's memory. In the manse, Mrs. Jackson cried out three times, "What shall I do to be saved?" Weeping bitterly, she declared her sins were so many He would not receive her.[367] McCulloch's instruction to those under conviction of sin was as follows:

> **Whatever you have been, whatever you have done, come to Him, and he will not reject you. When there is a willingness on both sides He is willing... To each of her many semi-hysterical outbursts, McCulloch replied with some word of promise from the Scripture. "Come," said the Minister, "Shall we pray for a pull of God's almighty arm to draw you to Christ"... During a prayer, she told the person who was supporting her, "Christ says to me, He will never leave me or forsake me," repeating it over and over; ....and immediately after, she said, He is telling me, "He hath cast all my sins behind his back."[368]**

"There was a sound of weeping with others being heard at a considerable distance... McCulloch wrote out the story in full next morning and this was read by him to a General Meeting of the Societies for Prayer in the Parish meeting at his House that day; they were greatly affected in hearing it."[369]

The Rev. Mr. John Willison, one of Whitefield's correspondents, visited the place and wrote, "The work at Cambuslang is a most singular and marvelous outpouring of the Holy Spirit. I pray it may be a happy forerunner of a general revival of the work of God, a blessed means of union among all the lovers of Jesus."[370]

The revival at Kilsyth came after Cambuslang, and Robe was well aware of the objections noised abroad by opponents of the whole movement. The loud cries and bodily distresses to him "appeared unpleasant, yea even shocking," so he planned to have those behaving

---

366 Ibid., 106.
367 Ibid., 106.
368 Ibid., 107.
369 Ibid., 107.
370 Tyerman, vol. 2, 2.

in a disorderly way removed from his audiences to a place made ready for them. Elders were detailed to carry them off, but experience taught him more disturbances were made by removing them than by letting them stay. The evidences of God's work were everywhere. Their example of acute distress was a pointed reminder to others who were undisturbed. At first, Robe intended to have preaching only on Wednesdays, so the daily work would be unhindered, but eventually, he preached daily.[371]

John Willison of Dundee wrote from Glasgow on Thursday, April 15, after coming from the Cambuslang meetings. He had stayed with McCulloch for a few days, expressing his satisfaction with what he had observed at Cambuslang. He ended by regretting he could not stay to give any further help, explaining, "but my business and circumstances oblige me to return homewards."[372] He arrived at Kilsyth that evening with Robe prevailing upon Willison to preach the following morning when "a great multitude of people met though the warning was very short"[373] Many dated their first real interest concerning spiritual things to that specific sermon.

Fawcett continued chronicling the events leading to awakening at Kilsyth: "Robe preached sermons upon the Doctrine of Regeneration, just as McCulloch did. Robe gave a complete outline of his scheme, and wistfully remarks that his church listened attentively and approved, but no visible change was to be seen in their behavior."[374] His preaching was notably patient in anticipation of results. "Early in 1742, amazing news came from Cambuslang. Robe found fresh cause for hope and tried to interest his congregation but said, 'in spite of all my efforts, few of the people under my charge went to Cambuslang.' One encouraging result emerged; the societies for prayer, long abandoned, began afresh."[375]

Whitefield immediately began to enter into the labors of the godly pastors that God had used to prepare the way before him for a great work. Gillies said, "He preached no less than three times upon the very day of his arrival, to a vast body of people. Whitefield never before or after spoke to the Scots in such throngs, nor felt himself so elevated as during the season when the evangelist first visited Cambuslang on his

---

371   Fawcett, 126.
372   Ibid., 126.
373   Ibid., 126.
374   Ibid., 126.
375   Ibid., 126.

second trip to Scotland."[376] It was in July of 1742 when he wrote a letter with this excerpt:

> I am only afraid lest, people should idolize the instrument, cannot look enough to the glorious Jesus, in him alone I desire to glory. Congregations consist of many thousands. Never did I see so many Bibles, nor people looking into them, while I am expounding with so much attention. Plenty of tears flow from the hearers' eyes. Their emotions appear in various ways. I preach twice daily and expound at private houses at night, and am employed in speaking to souls under distress a great part of the day. I have just snatched a few moments to write to my dear brother. Oh, that God may enlarge my heart, pray for me. I walk continually in the comforts of the Holy Ghost and the love of Christ quite strikes me dumb. [377]

People came under a strong conviction of sin under Whitefield's preaching in Scotland. Whitefield was no mystic, despite accusations about emotional excesses at these meetings. He only wanted to see people converted to Christ. When he stood to preach, the conservative Scots were riveted by the realization of their lost condition under God. People were arrested and fainted as one shot by a gun under the weight of their sin.[378] Yet, the deep sorrow was momentary, for it gave way to the joy of salvation as multitudes professed faith in Christ. The meetings lasted for hours; no one really wanted to depart which was evidenced by those lingering after the services and the length of the services continuing into the mornings. Some even refused to leave the meeting place and stayed all night in fields where people gathered to hear the gospel. A specific scene described by Whitefield tells of these occurrences at the height of the Cambuslang meetings:

> On Tuesday, July 6, 1742, I came to Cambuslang at mid-day, and preached at two, six and nine o'clock at night. Such a commotion surely never was heard of. It far out-did all that I ever saw in America. For about an hour and a half, there were scenes of uncontrollable distress, like a field of battle. Many were being carried into the manse like wounded soldiers. Mr. McCulloch preached after I had ended, till past one in the morning, and then could scarce persuade them to depart. All night in the fields, the voice of prayer and praise could be heard.[379]

---

376 Gillies, 123.
377 Belcher, 229.
378 Tyerman, vol. 2, 6-7.
379 Fawcett, 114.

Writing to his steward in Georgia, Whitefield described the awakening as "unspeakable, akin to an experience they had once shared at Fagg's Manor in Pennsylvania: I never was enabled to preach so before."[380]

A deep seriousness for the future condition of their souls gripped the people as Whitefield preached to them. The criticism of frightening people through lurid descriptions of hell by Whitefield and the revival's leaders in these meetings were an exaggeration. These truths were preached as reality without apology. The preachers at Cambuslang believed in a literal hell, with all its torments, and because of their belief, they were earnest to warn their listeners of imminent danger. These pictures were understood by many. Vivid realizations of hell were given. A twenty-one-year-old man at Cambuslang one evening "thought I saw hell as it were at a distance from me, as a pit where the wicked were frying, and the devils going among them..." A boy of fifteen, before he fainted away, "thought I saw the flames of hell coming up to me." One young woman, with her breath almost taken away by the smell of brimstone, "took it to be the smell of the lake of fire and brimstone in the bottomless pit."[381]

Some young ladies were joined by a gentlewoman praising God till the break of day.[382] These incidences occurred because of the atmosphere in these heaven-sent meetings. As Whitefield preached, there was joy in the midst of the saddest and deep sorrow for the condition of unconverted souls.

The Cambuslang meetings included communion services. Andrews described the scene on the Sunday when it was administered and Whitefield's reaction to it:

> The next day being Sunday, upwards of twenty thousand persons assembled on the hillside, and the Lord's Supper was administered. Whitefield said, "Their joy was so great that, at the desire of both ministers and people, another communion was appointed to be held a few weeks later, when scarce ever was such a sight seen in Scotland. There were unquestionably twenty thousand persons: two tents were set up, and the Holy Sacrament was administered in the fields. When I began to serve a table the power of God was felt by numbers, but the people crowded so upon me that I was obliged to desist and go to the

---

380   Ibid., 114.
381   Ibid., 154.
382   Ibid., 154.

**tents, whilst the ministers served the rest of the tables: God was with them
and with his people. Upwards of twenty ministers assisted on this occasion."**[383]

Whitefield describes the aftermath of the communion services:
"Some at the same time wringing their hands, others almost swooning,
and with tears crying out, and mourning over a pierced Saviour. All
night in different companies, you might have heard persons praying to
and praising God. It was like the Passover in Josiah's time."[384]

The next Monday, Whitefield preached again, remarking, "Such a
universal stir I never saw before, the motion fled as swift as lightning
from one end of the auditory to the other."[385]

The aftermath of the Cambuslang meeting was continuous. The
revival was a topic of conversation for years to come and as with other
great revivals, had an effect on the moral climate of Scotland. Churches
were filled and court cases likely declined because of massive conversions
in the general populace. A great percentage of the population attended
and participated in the meetings.[386]

McCulloch continued to track the many lives changed in the revival
and the difference the Cambuslang revival had made in their lives. He
discovered "…in them was the evidence of ongoing revival. They found
in them the power to transform the individual, and thereby transmute
society. …there emerged a new sense of moral sufficiency and a warm,
genuine brotherliness, which reached out not only to those in the
fellowship but to those as yet outside."[387]

The revival was gripping the nation. One of the amazing occurrences
of this revival in Scotland, in 1742, indicated it was not localized but
spread across the region like a prairie fire.[388] Whitefield appropriately
summarized the atmosphere in the middle of the Cambuslang Revival
by declaring, "We have had several glorious days of the Son of man
since the work began. Last Lord's-day was a remarkable day of divine

---

383   Andrews, 163-164.
384   Henry, 78.
385   Philip, 295.
386   The assumption is that morality would change because of the Cambuslang
Revival. Other revivals have featured this change in the moral climate of an area or nation
such as in the Welsh Revival of the beginning of the 20th century.
387   Fawcett, 174-175.
388   Johnston, vol 2, 30-31.

power amongst us…. The Lord was with us of a truth."[389] Such were the glorious days of the Cambuslang Revival.

The meetings were successful enough for Whitefield to establish a life-long friendship with Scotland, resulting in many other meetings with his ministry. Scotland had been as open to the gospel and revival as New England had been. The Scottish people had longed for revival, and it became a reality. It was unlike any other they had ever seen in their history. It all came by expectation, faithfulness to God's Word, and people's availability to God. One of the greatest examples of this availability had been George Whitefield.

---

389   Ibid., 26.

10

DANGEROUS PREACHING,

THE BEGINNING OF A MOVEMENT, AND HEARTACHE

(1743-1744)

THE TRIP TO SCOTLAND WAS SUCCESSFUL for Whitefield and the cause of Christ. On his return to England, he rejoiced to find conditions had begun to change for him and the Wesleys. The hostility between the two parties had started to subside and would be finally healed later in Whitefield's life. The two parties in the old controversy were at least talking again as friends and the tempest of heated theological discussion soon spent itself. The Wesleys and Whitefield began correspondence, although they were ministering separately. Fish revealed the calming of the controversy between John Wesley and Whitefield:

> Whitefield began writing to John Wesley every couple of months. In early 1742, Whitefield finally received a reply to one of those letters and while in Scotland he actually met with John Wesley for about an hour. The differences between the two men were not healed but the relationship began to improve slightly.[390]

---

390 Fish, Bruce and Becky. George Whitefield, Pioneering Evangelist (Barbour Books: Uhrichsville, OH, 2000), 93.

These changed conditions gave Whitefield some of his greatest days in ministry. Back in England, Whitefield gloried in what God had done in Scotland. The revival still lingered and was to be the open door to many other meetings in the region. The return to England featured him speaking at The Tabernacle to growing crowds.[391] Dallimore shared about the evolution of the Tabernacle:

> Protestant Dissenters had started to build a huge wooden shed in the Moorfields district which they intended to serve as a place in which Whitefield's hearers, instead of meeting outdoors, might gather and be shielded from wind and rain. But since the location was not far from Wesley's Foundry, Whitefield disliked the idea and said it seemed erected as an altar against his will. Nevertheless, the people continued the construction, whereupon Whitefield, thinking of it as something temporary, termed it "The Tabernacle" and before long came around to a willingness to use it. It thence became the nerve center of his work and was the scene of some of his greatest evangelistic labours, and this it remained till replaced by a fine brick Tabernacle twelve years later.[392]

One advantage of the Tabernacle was that it confined Whitefield to one place, keeping him from his previous itinerate ministry. Seekers came there knowing he would preach and members of the upper class found a certain anonymity in going to the Tabernacle to hear him preach. Many who heard of Whitefield's fame and reports of his messages were able to judge his messages firsthand. A general acceptance of his ministry came from all quarters. Lady Huntingdon had tried to get her friends in the nobility to hear Whitefield, and when they heard him in the Tabernacle, they had the dignity of coming to a meeting place, rather than out in the open air. The crowds coming to hear were not disappointed.[393]

Whitefield did not entirely withdraw from preaching outdoors. In fact, more of a concerted effort was made to preach particularly at Moorfields in London. His preaching style gave an insight into God's presence in the services. As he announced a Psalm, his voice would become the organ leading the great host in the singing of it. After prayers of the Church of England, he would begin to preach.[394] This order of service was less formal and impromptu. It made his ministry versatile to all groups of people who were for or against his field preaching. There was

391 Ibid., 93.
392 Dallimore, vol. 2, 49.
393 Fish, 93.
394 Dallimore, vol. 1, 351.

a great hunger to hear Whitefield in the beginning of his field ministry. Those who initially heard him were supportive, but Whitefield's sojourn to Moorfields was to the unchurched at a very rough place in London. Moorfields, unlike Kingswood Colliers, featured people who were not only rough but hostile. Whitefield and his followers ventured forth in spite of the anticipated opposition.[395] The date of Whitefield's most extensive preaching at Moorfields was May 1742, after his marriage and before his trip to Scotland for the Cambuslang meetings.[396]

Tyerman exalted Whitefield's decision to preach to crowds in Moorfields, describing the desperate plight of his hearers. He announced:

> Seldom do the annals of the Christian church present a more remarkable example of the power of gospel truth. Here were assembled thousands, the very scum of London's teeming population, many of them clad in rags, and almost all of them labeled with the marks of vice and wretchedness; and yet, even in such a congregation, hundreds became penitent and began to call upon God for mercy. Whitefield's Eastertide services, in the midst of the Moorfields mobs, were not unworthy of the name he gave them, "a glorious Pentecost."[397]

Whitefield wrote of his "encounter with Satan" at Moorfields. He endured "cruel opposition" as did the Apostle Paul, when he "fought wild beasts at Ephesus" (I Cor. 15: 32). Quite an arsenal was arrayed against him. "The fields were frequented by drummers, trumpeters, Merry Andrews, Masters of Puppet shows, exhibitors of wild beasts, players, etc., and a crowd of some ten thousand stood waiting for the booths to open." His preaching featured supporters and detractors as he wrote, "I was attended by a large congregation of praying people. I ventured to lift up a standard among them in the name of Jesus of Nazareth." He records how the ten thousand waited for the amusements to begin: "Glad was I to find that I had for once, as it were, got the start on the Devil."[398]

Dallimore shared Whitefield's recollection of preaching in this dangerous environment: "I mounted my field pulpit, almost all flocked around it. I preached on these words, 'as Moses lifted up the serpent in

---

395 Dallimore, vol. 2, 115.
396 Ibid., 115.
397 Tyerman, vol. 1, 557-558.
398 Anthony Beaurepaire, *George Whitefield and the Great Evangelical Awakening: An Illustrated History* (London: Protestant Truth Society), 59-60.

the wilderness, so shall the Son of man be lifted up...' They gazed, they listened, they wept; and I believe that many felt themselves stung with deep conviction for past sins. All was hushed and solemn."[399]

The response was varied, for again at noon with everything in full swing he remarks, "What a scene! The whole field seemed all white, ready not for the Redeemer's but Beelzebub's harvest."[400]

On Monday, Whitefield shared the dangerous setting in which he was preaching:

> I opened with these words "I am not ashamed of the Gospel of Christ, for it is the power of God unto salvation to everyone that believeth." I preached in great jeopardy; for the pulpit being high, and supports not well fixed in the ground, it tottered every time I moved, and numbers of enemies strove to push my friends against the supporters in order to throw me down. But I was not much moved unless with compassion for those to whom I was delivering my Master's message, which I had reason to think was welcome to many.
>
> But Satan did not like to be attacked in his strong-holds, and I narrowly escaped with my life; for as I was passing from the pulpit to the coach, I felt my wig and hat to be almost off. I turned about, and observed a sword just touching my temples. A young rake was determined to stab me, but a gentleman, seeing the sword thrusting near me, struck it up with his cane. The enraged multitude soon seized him, and had it not been for one of my friends who received him into his house he must have undergone a severe discipline.
>
> The next day I renewed my attack on Moorfields. After they found that pelting, noise and threatening would not do, one of the Merry Andrews got up into a tree very near the pulpit, and shamefully exposed himself.[401]

Moorfields was a dangerous place to preach, but Whitefield felt this was the place where the gospel was needed most. He said, "With a heart bleeding with compassion for so many thousands led captive by the devil at his will." On Whit-Monday, he ventured forth in fearless fashion.[402]

Whitefield was not the only one receiving a pelting, as evidenced by a touching scene. The evangelist had always had a love for children as illustrated by his sponsoring the orphanage at Bethesda. He added how little boys and girls were fond of sitting around the pulpit, where he preached; "though they were often pelted with eggs, dirt, etc. thrown at me, never once gave way, but on the contrary, every time I was struck,

---

399   Dallimore, vol. 2, 115.
400   Ibid., 116.
401   Ibid., 117.
402   Ibid., 115.

turned up their little weeping eyes, and seemed to wish they could receive the blows for me."[403] Compelling stories such as this reveal the love Whitefield had for his ministry's children and his expansion out of the church to people far away from God who needed to hear the gospel message.

Whitefield never tired of preaching early and reading morning prayers. He continued this practice with his meetings in the colonies. The energetic preacher was a morning person, and this was his favorite time to preach, so many of the lower class heard him on the way to work or to the market. He influenced John Newton who said, "I bless God that I lived in the time of Mr. Whitefield. Many were the winter mornings in which I got up at four o'clock to attend his Tabernacle discourses at five, and I have seen Moorfields as full of lanterns at these times, as I suppose the Haymarket is full of flambeaux on an opera night."[404] Whitefield preached almost any time of day, seeking to reach as many people as he could for Christ.

John Wesley adopted the same methods of holding services as Whitefield, although he spent more time with small accountability groups, helping disciple new converts and train leaders for the burgeoning Methodist movement.[405] Wesley and Whitefield's paths did not seem to cross in the decade of controversy with each other. Wesley began his great trek throughout England and was familiar with almost every place in the country. Wesley's organizational ability influenced scores of Methodist ministers to ride on horseback throughout the country, sharing the gospel wherever they went.[406] Whitefield rejoiced in the furtherance of the gospel regardless of what his differences had been with his old friend.

It became apparent that Whitefield and his followers needed to organize because of the slings and arrows of the controversy. They preached as opportunities arose, leaving people to wonder what their association and theological orientations were. The rise of an organization

---

403 Ninde, 79.

404 Tyerman, vol. 2, 625.

405 Roland Q. Leavell, *Evangelism: Christ's Imperative Commission* (Nashville: Broadman Press, 1951), 70-71.

406 Harry Williams, *Vignette of John Wesley*, 9, Spiritual Awakenings Conference Notebook, G.W. Schweer ed. Golden Gate Baptist Theological Seminary, Mill Valley, CA, Sept. 18-20, 1980.

of strict societies fostered Arminianism under the Wesley brothers and gave rise to an organization representing Calvinistic Methodism. This association was the oldest and friendliest in its theological orientation to the dissenting groups in England, but the new society was not a new denomination.[407]

Dallimore revealed the reason for this association that Whitefield was instrumental in founding:

> He had, of course, not the slightest thought of forming a new denomination. "Methodism" was simply a term that designated an adherence to evangelical doctrine and a fervent manner of life, and was used then in much the same way a 'evangelical' is used today. Although the vast majority of the Methodist people were members of the Church of England, the public applied the term also to those others (Independents, Baptists and Presbyterians) who were noticeably evangelical and showed favour towards the work of the revival.[408]

Dallimore shared the extension of Whitefield's contact with the Church of England, by describing how he was a constant encourager to those sound in the evangelical faith:

> Whitefield saw this work extending to other denominations and other lands. He came into friendly relations with such as Isaac Watts and Philip Doddridge…he had begun to speak highly of certain Baptist pastors and people he met. His Presbyterian associations consisted chiefly of his correspondence with the Erskine brothers in Scotland, and, though there had long been bitterness between the English Church and the Scottish of his relation with Ralph Erskine, Whitefield said, "Some may be offended by my correspondence with him, but I dare not but confess one of my Lord's disciples."[409]

These associations broadened the scope of Whitefield's ministry. The evangelical spirit of England fostered by Whitefield and the formation of this society were great steps in this direction.

On January 5, 1743, Whitefield was elected moderator of the Calvinistic Methodist Association. It was only natural that one who was committed to the Doctrines of Grace and one who was using them effectively in his itinerant ministry should be the voice of the movement.[410] The association agreed to train more young preachers to

---

407   Tyerman, vol. 2, 47-49.
408   Dallimore, vol. 1, 383.
409   Ibid., 384.
410   Tyerman, vol. 2, 50.

be coordinated in its efforts and to form an association becoming a safe haven for Calvinistic Methodists.

Tyerman honestly reveals that the first Methodist association was Calvinistic when he stated, "It is a notable fact that the first Calvinistic Methodist Association was held eighteen months before Wesley held his first Methodist Conference in London."[411] This is a remarkable statement because Wesley is given credit for organizing the first Methodist societies. These societies formed the nucleus of the Methodist church after his death.[412]

The Calvinistic Methodist Association reaffirmed the Doctrines of Grace, vindicating Whitefield's position in the matter. Howell Harris led in the formation of the Association but Whitefield assumed the leadership role of the group.[413] The messages he preached were a strong answer to the critic's false-assumptions of his Calvinism. The gospel was being preached and many were awakened, repentant and converted. Changed lives are always the best response to critics attacking their suspicion of someone's ministry.

Whitefield was not even 30 when he assumed the role as leader of the Calvinistic Methodist movement and would become the magnanimous figure as a reconciler, holding the group together, while carrying the torch for revivalism at the same time.[414] He spoke with clarity and truth while seeking to form an association that would survive many attacks. Howell Harris, John Cennick and James Hervey were leaders, but the world looked to Whitefield to enunciate the truths they attested, so it was to no one's surprise that Whitefield was elected lifetime moderator of the movement only a few months later.[415] They trusted him as their spokesman and knew they would not be in the position they were in, had it not been for his steady ministry on both continents.

The movement was bound for expansion with the patronage of Lady Huntingdon and the evangelistic zeal and fearlessness of its leaders. Expansion was taking the form of new chapels built, young ministers rising up in their ranks, and a new movement resulting in England being

---

411   Ibid., 50.
412   Leavell, 71.
413   Tyerman, vol. 2, 50.
414   Dallimore, vol. 2, 157.
415   Ibid., 157-158.

a country heavily influenced by the great revivals still to come. Whitefield was not confined to one place for long. Soon, he accompanied Howell Harris, who had been a leader in the Welsh revival, to Wales, preaching in several places.[416] Scotland and Wales were close to his heart because his wife was from there. General attention was given to the gospel message in a deeper way throughout Wales and the Welsh people heard him gladly from village to village. Harris shared the response of the Welsh people to the gospel, "With us, the work everywhere goes on more and more sweetly. I trust we shall have good order. The exhorters shew a very tractable spirit; each observes his place and we have sweet harmony and love. Great power attends the ministers and exhorters in several places."[417]

The skeptical nature of many in London gave way to an acceptance in Wales, rivaling Whitefield's acceptance in the colonies.[418] Field preaching invigorated Whitefield; field preaching was a tonic, and the open air he preached under was as favorable to him as the Tabernacle and other large edifices.[419]

The crowds grew and began to follow the two revival leaders wherever they went. Whitefield preached at a furious pace in Wales, speaking twice a day for a week or more and the response was encouraging. He also met with and encouraged societies there.[420]

Here, Whitefield experienced a biblical literacy that he had also experienced firsthand in Scotland and in the colonies. People were glad to hear the Word of the Lord and they regarded it as a wonderful experience to hear the Bible preached with great eloquence.[421] The climate was good and vindicating after the formation of the Calvinistic Methodist Association.

Elizabeth Whitefield became pregnant the next summer and Whitefield was soon to be a father; however, an accident caused difficulty for the mother-to-be when their carriage slid off an embankment. Bystanders who saw the carriage go off the road shouted they were dead, but ran to the rescue, pulling Whitefield and his wife

---

416 Tyerman, vol. 2, 53–54.
417 Ibid., 51.
418 Ibid., 54.
419 Ibid., 55.
420 Ibid., 54.
421 Ibid., 55.

out of the wrecked carriage. They were unharmed, but very rattled.[422] Whitefield and his wife avoided injury, but there was concern for Elizabeth because of her pregnancy. A catastrophe was narrowly averted through this trying experience demonstrating God's hand of protection as evident in this accident.

Everything went well as Elizabeth neared the time of delivery, giving birth to a son October 4, 1743. Whitefield, brimming with joy, announced the birth to the Tabernacle as the occasion led to overwhelming excitement. The little boy named John had all the signs of being a healthy baby. Whitefield had longed for an heir and felt his son might succeed him in his ministry, giving him high expectations. The future even gave Elizabeth a sense of anticipation having given birth to a son.[423]

Their joy was short-lived, however, when the baby became gravely ill. Earnest prayer went up from many quarters for his recovery, but it did not happen. The baby's untimely death devastated Elizabeth, and Whitefield experienced great sadness at the loss of his son. They had the unfortunate trial of burying the only child Elizabeth was to give him.[424]

Whitefield did not shrink from the task before him. In his funeral message, he recalled the story of Abraham sacrificing his son Isaac on an altar of sacrifice only to have God stay his hand. This compelling story gave a perfect picture of the substitutionary death of Christ. Abraham had been called to go to Mount Moriah and to give his son back to God. The despondent preacher in his message never doubted God's hand in whatever happened. God had His purposes through this experience, and though he did not know what they were, it does not mean His hand could not be trusted.[425]

The loss of his only child was an immediate shock to Whitefield. More heartache was to come, as Elizabeth had four miscarriages and was never able to carry a child to term.[426] Those hearing Whitefield preach on the story of Abraham and Isaac often testified that they never heard a preacher share it with so much pathos. Through the message, they knew

---

422 Gledstone, 209.
423 Dallimore, vol. 2, 167.
424 Ibid., 167.
425 Gledstone, 211.
426 Dallimore, vol. 2, 472.

of his own heartache and the personal pain, because he had lived it.[427] One of Whitefield's greatest traits was to make the Bible come alive and it was through his own personal grief that he was able to identify with the possible loss of a son in the Scripture of Abraham and Isaac.

Overcoming the great despondency was a major struggle. It was apparent a change of scenery was in order. Whitefield's trip back to the colonies was long overdue. He had administered Bethesda from a distance while it was in the capable hands of James Habersham as superintendent. The anxious evangelist was receiving many invitations to return to the colonies, so he began to schedule meetings.

Gilbert Tennent and others told Whitefield of those anxious to hear him again. They invited him that he might defend the cause of the awakening against critics like Dr. Charles Chauncy, an Old Light pastor of First Church in Boston, where he served for sixty years. Chauncy had taken severe offense to Tennent's preaching against unconverted clergy and the excesses of some of the evangelistic meetings. He published writings against the New Lights and directly, or indirectly, blamed Whitefield for all the commotion.[428]

James Habersham also encouraged Whitefield to go to Bethesda because he had been receiving offerings for its support.[429] The next phase of "the house of mercy" was to make it self-sustaining with its vast farmland and potential for even more children, whom Whitefield wanted to see claimed for the Master. The Spanish were threatening the colony of Georgia itself. The safety of the colony and children in the orphanage were of upmost concern. Fortunately, they were driven back by the British.[430]

Because critics had accused some converts in Whitefield's meetings as extremists, he needed to go back and correct some confusion in various places affected by the awakening where he had formerly preached.[431]

In the two years since Whitefield had ministered in the colonies, he had gone through the fire of theological controversy with Wesley, he had married, lost his only son and he was instrumental in the formation of

---

427   Beaurepaire, 59.
428   Tyerman, vol. 2, 125-126, 128.
429   Dallimore, vol. 2, 211.
430   Fish, 93.
431   Ibid., 96.

the Calvinistic Methodist Association. It was time to return to America, so he looked forward to his third trip to the New World with great joy. The optimistic evangelist believed God would use him on an even grander scale than He had before.

11

Greater Waves

of Revival in the Colonies

(1744-1748)

THE ANTICIPATION OF RETURNING TO AMERICA was tempered by the wait to board a ship sailing there. This time, Whitefield and his wife would go to America for his third visit, even while a state of war existed between England and France.[432] The Whitefields had to wait in Plymouth for a naval convoy as it took six weeks to organize a special attachment that would accompany the ship.[433]

The opposition to Whitefield's ministry was constant and cleverly disguised in one attempt on his life that June. A perceived supporter met with him privately in a local inn after he had spoken in a meeting, his wife being absent. The man spoke of the influence Whitefield had on his life, commending him for his forthright preaching, but at an unexpected moment the scene turned quickly into catastrophe as the imposter used his cane to beat the preacher. He was helpless to defend himself but since the Lord had blessed Whitefield with a loud voice that could carry for great distances, he used that blessing to cry out "Murderer!" even

---

432　Dallimore, *George Whitefield God's Anointed Servant in the Great Revival of the Eighteenth Century*, 138.
433　Ibid., 138.

as the assailant beat him unmercifully. The local innkeeper called the authorities, who arrived in time to save Whitefield's life, but he was badly bruised and beaten. He needed the extra time, while waiting for a ship, to recuperate.[434]

The divine destiny of Whitefield's life was brought to a greater realization than before through this incident. He saw God's hand of protection on his life and knew God had a purpose for him. When he went to the New World, he fully expected to know more concerning that purpose. This would not be the last time his life was threatened; he would face similar experiences in the future. The boldness he exhibited in preaching to thousands on a consistent basis put him in constant danger of attack, either in the meetings themselves or in private places, but Whitefield took the danger in stride.

The Whitefields finally set sail on what was a perilous and arduous voyage. When a ship approached that seemed to be French (who were in a momentary state of war with Britain), Whitefield described their peril with Belden's explanation:

> "All," says Whitefield, "except myself, seemed ready for fire and smoke. My wife, after having dressed herself to prepare for all events, set about making cartridges, whilst I wanted to go into the holes of the ship, hearing that was the chaplain's usual place. I went, but not liking my situation, I crept upon deck, and for the first time in my life, I beat up to arms (summoned by drumbeat the crew to alert), by a warm exhortation." The pursuers turned out to be harmless friends who had also been separated from the convoy![435]

When the ship encountered several storms that threw it off course, those on board grew restless and many, including Whitefield, were afflicted with a fever. He became ill after going into the cabins of the sick, praying for them, and consequently he spent many days in his own cabin without coming out. This exposure caused him to be deadly ill when the ship arrived in Boston Harbor.[436]

The illness struck him sorely, weakening him as he accepted a local minister's flowery greeting, described by Wakeley:

> Whitefield completed his third voyage to America in the autumn of 1744. He had a long, tedious passage and was very sick; but his arrival was hailed

---

434 Philip, 315-316.
435 Belden, 158.
436 Belcher, 256.

with joy, for his name was fragrant throughout New England. The Rev. Moody, an aged minister who had feared the Lord from his youth, gave Whitefield, on his landing in York, New England, where the aged minister was settled, a most cordial and hearty welcome. Said he, "Sir, you are welcome to America; secondly, to New England; thirdly, to all the faithful ministers in New England; fourthly, to all the good people in New England; fifthly, to all the good people of York; and sixthly and lastly, to me, dear sir, less than the least of all." Did ever a welcome transcend this? Mr. Moody then urged Mr. Whitefield to preach. Mr. Whitefield was so delighted with his work, he could not refuse, and he preached to their great joy one of his characteristic sermons, of which he remarks, "God was with me."[437]

Despite the warm welcome, Whitefield's sickness continued to plague him. A description of his illness illustrated the severity of his condition:

> Mrs. Whitefield was with him and several homes were immediately opened to them—among them the princely habitation of one of Whitefield's warmest admirers, Colonel William Pepperell.
>
> Although very unwell, Whitefield began fulfilling the opportunities to preach, hoping as he did so to find the zeal of his spirit to overcome the infirmity of his body. But within a week he collapsed. Two doctors came to attend him and for some days he lay confined to bed, racked with pain, suffering a high fever and seemingly near to death. Much prayer was made for him, the meetings for intercession in some instances being continued both day and night.[438]

Whitefield tried to preach some in Philadelphia, but only got worse. He was confined to bed, and some felt he would not live. At this time a black woman came and had prayer over him. He described the scene in vivid detail:

> Though wonderfully supported within, at my return home I thought I was dying indeed. I was laid on a bed upon the ground near the fire, and I heard some friends say, "He is gone!" But God was pleased to order it otherwise. I gradually recovered and soon a poor negro woman would see me. She came, sat down by the fire and looked earnestly into my face and said, in broken language: "Master, you just go to "heaven's gate." But Jesus Christ said, "Get you down, get you down, you must not come here yet; but go first and call some more poor negroes." I prayed that if I was to live, this might be the event.[439]

---

437 Wakeley, 322-323.
438 Dallimore, vol. 2, 193.
439 Ibid., 194.

Death did not claim the still young 30-year-old. Knowing he would miss the meetings if he canceled them, he got up from his bed and pronounced himself fit to preach. And preach he did, even though he was not totally fit. The illness lingered, and the effects haunted him through the preaching tour he had in the colonies.[440]

Whitefield valiantly sought to preach as normal, believing his health would improve. He did get better and was able to preach in Boston where the whole town, it seemed, came out to hear him. He was a hero to the majority of people, and the opposition kept their distance and their opinions to themselves. He preached in Brattle Street Church in Boston, whose pastor, Dr. Benjamin Colman, was one of his ardent supporters. He assisted in communion at the church and preached to full crowds.[441] Whitefield sought to clear up misunderstandings from the excesses of the awakening, chiefly led by James Davenport. These emotional excess and bizarre demands by Davenport were out of character with the general awakening. In assessing these excesses of the awakening, he said, "But in the mixed state of things, wild fire will necessarily blend itself with the pure fire of God's altar."[442] He assured many he had not meant to cause separation from established churches but was supportive of their ministry.

Whitefield again visited Harvard, where he had, on his first trip, attacked lethargy and questioned some of its instruction. The preacher was reconciling this time, not taking an adversarial position against the faculty or student body and some of his misconceived attacks against them. He accepted a pamphlet entitled, "Testimony," prepared by the faculty, charging him with being an "uncharitable, censorious and slanderous man." The evangelist demonstrated his maturity by asking pardon for "too rash a word I have dropped, or anything I have written or done amiss."[443] This statement shows that Whitefield had grown greatly in his spiritual maturity by this statement.

A spot in Cambridge at Harvard where Whitefield preached was remembered during the American Revolution, as described by Belcher:

---

440 Ibid., vol. 195-196.
441 Ibid., 196.
442 Ibid., 188.
443 Fish, 100-101.

An elm under which Whitefield preached in Cambridge became distinguished; it being under its shade that Washington, thirty-one years after, first drew his sword in the cause of the Revolution, on taking the command of the American army. From this circumstance, it has been called the "Washington elm." The last time the late distinguished Dr. Holyoke, of Salem, Mass., was in Cambridge, then nearly a hundred years old, while passing this tree with a friend, he said that he heard Whitefield's sermon, being at the time a student in college.

The response to Whitefield's preaching was still magnetic. The word spread and he preached to larger crowds than three years before. An expanded account of how people thronged to hear him was described with great excitement by Nathan Cole. The grand event is described in vivid personal language:

> One morning, suddenly there came a messenger that said Mr. Whitefield was to preach at Middletown this morning at 10 o'clock. I was in my field and dropped my tool and ran home, going to my house, bidding my wife to get ready quickly. I ran to my pasture for my horse with all my might fearing I should be too late to hear him, bringing my wife, and going forward as fast as I thought my horse could go. When my horse began to be out of breath, I got down, and put my wife in the saddle, bidding her to ride as fast as she could. I told her not to stop for me except when I bade her to and so I ran until I was almost out of breath and then mounted my horse again...
>
> I saw before me a cloud or fog... As I came nearer the road, I heard a noise, something like a low rumbling thunder and presently found out it was the rumbling of horse's feet.... I could see men and horses slipping along... I found a vacancy between two horses to slip in my horse and my wife said, "Our clothes will be all be spoiled". . . When we got down to the old meeting house there was a great multitude...I looked towards the great river and saw ferry boats running swiftly, forward and backward. When I saw Mr. Whitefield come upon the scaffold, he looked almost angelical, a young slim slender youth before thousands of people and with a bold undaunted countenance, knowing how God was with him everywhere... It solemnized my mind and put me in a trembling fear...for he looked as if he was clothed with authority...and a sweet solemnity sat upon his brow... My old foundation was broken up and I saw my righteousness would not save me.[444]

The social acceptance by people of all stations in the colonies made America Whitefield's favorite place to minister. Indeed, the openness to the gospel message was everywhere.

---

444 Dallimore: *George Whitefield: God's Anointed Servant in the Great Revival of the Eighteenth Century*, 90.

Whitefield renewed his acquaintance with the Tennents and the partnership they had in an itinerant ministry. He preached in the elder Tennent's church several times during his ministry in America. Whitefield had carried on a steady correspondence with Gilbert since they had been together three years before. They began to preach together in several open-air meetings.[445]

People began to follow Whitefield and his party wherever he preached and the response to his preaching in New England was tremendous. The crowds were larger and friends in the press, particularly Benjamin Franklin, reported the current meetings as a great happening. Franklin, though not a believer in Christ, recognized the cohesive value of Whitefield's ministry to the colonies. He was still impressed and enthralled by Whitefield's preaching and the effect it was having on the area. When the news of the orphanage's debt was known, Franklin challenged people to support it, for he knew the good it was doing. He repeatedly told Whitefield the orphanage would do better in New England.[446] Whitefield wanted to help establish a school for blacks, where they could learn reading and writing. He hoped to interest Franklin in jointly sponsoring the school, but that school never materialized, even though he had purchased land.[447]

Franklin was a pioneer of a college in Philadelphia, which eventually became the University of Pennsylvania. As Franklin supported Bethesda, Whitefield supported the college. Further support for the fledgling school was continual throughout the evangelist ministry and his subsequent trips to Philadelphia.[448] A statute of Whitefield preaching was erected and remains today on the present campus in appreciation of all he did as an early sponsor of the school.[449]

In Whitefield's correspondence with Franklin, he commended him for his great discoveries as an inventor and shared how he wished that he would find the great discovery of his life that would reap wonderful rewards: the discovery of the new birth.[450]

445   Belcher, 278.
446   Dallimore, *George Whitefield: God's Anointed Servant in the Great Revival of the Eighteenth Century*, 76-77.
447   Dallimore, vol. 1, 497-498.
448   Dallimore, vol. 2, 370.
449   Johnston, vol 2, 165.
450   Ibid, 244-245.

No substantial record exists of Franklin's conversion, but we do find on his epitaph a strong statement of the resurrection, seemingly reflecting a deep personal faith he may have possessed. If he became a believer, he became one chiefly because of Whitefield's influence.[451] His epitaph read:

The Body of B. Franklin, Printer;

Like the Cover of an Old Book,

Its Contents torn out,

And stript of its Lettering and Gilding,

Lies here, Food for Worms.

But the Work shall not be wholly lost.

For it will, as he believ'd, appear once more,

In a new & more perfect Edition,

(Corrected and amended by the Author.)[452]

Whitefield's influence was more than spiritual during the American Revolution. Ideas were set in place through his preaching that challenged the religious and political systems of the day. The Old Light ministers and churches were more loyal to the King, and the New Lights were more in line with the ideas spawned from the American Revolution. Mahaffey described this difference:

> One could argue that the Anglican Old Lights were closely connected with England and other Old Light denominations were allied with their country of origin (like Dutch Reformed, Scottish Presbyterian, French Huguenots, and German Baptists). But the New Lights were those who had begun in themselves as American. This situation was intensified by the connections between church and state throughout Europe. The Old Lights preferred a strong top-down society led by a king and lords, while the New Lights favored strong, grass-roots, parliamentary self-rule with loyalty to the king as symbolic of their devotion to the British Empire...
>
> The Old Lights could not ignore or ridicule them out of the mainstream. For the Old Light power structure, everything was at stake. Would the equality of New Lights overrun the authoritarian world of the Old Lights? The popularity of revival beliefs and their direct assault on the social order pushed the Old Lights into a corner where they were forced to fight back.[453]

---

451   Ibid., 223.
452   Lambert, 129.
453   Mahaffey, 52-53, 69.

The response to Whitefield's preaching was gratifying it could have tempted him to stay in New England to keep a preaching circuit there. In fact, a benefactor connected to a house where Gilbert Tennent preached in Philadelphia offered to build Whitefield the biggest church in America at the site of the future University of Pennsylvania. He would only have to preach in it for six months out of the year, and the rest of the time, he would be free to pursue an itinerant ministry. He turned down the offer. He would not be held to an agreement where he would preach as a condition for the building.[454] Whitefield, writing from America to a friend in England, said:

> "They came to me lately, assuring me that if I'll consent they will erect in a few weeks' time the outside of the largest place of worship that was ever seen in America." They wished him to become their settled Pastor. Whitefield says, "I thanked them, but at the same time begged leave to refuse their kind offer," and adds, "You know that ceiled houses were never my aim." To many a clergyman the offer would have been a powerful temptation, and would have been accepted with joy.[455]

Whitefield was not confined in one place too long. He preached in Williamsburg, Virginia to a crowd, but the group was not as responsive as those in New England.[456] He was encouraged by some response and other signs of interest in his ministry.

Whitefield started toward Georgia, with a heart toward Bethesda. He had spent a little time in the largest colony of Virginia and agreed to preach there before going south. In Virginia, he became acquainted with the Rev. Samuel Davies, who also had an itinerant ministry. Whitefield was struck by Davies' dramatic style of preaching, and he preached there with Davies to support his ministry.[457]

Whitefield's reputation went ahead of him in Virginia before this current tour. His sermons had a powerful influence on a former bricklayer, Samuel Morris, who had begun to read some of Whitefield's sermons in his home to those gathering there. The sermons had immediate reactions, and many convicted of their need for Christ became Christians. Soon, his home became too small for the crowds who gathered to hear the

---

454   Ninde, 157.
455   Wakeley, 325.
456   Henry, 52.
457   Ibid., 72.

sermon, so Morris built a house that would hold more people. When Whitefield reached Virginia, he discovered that four houses had been built for the express purpose of someone reading his sermons. Although he wasn't there in person, his influence preceded him before he ever arrived in Virginia. The encouragement of Whitefield's sermons through the gatherings of people in churches led to the start of the Presbyterian Church of Virginia.[458]

Several speaking engagements awaited Whitefield in the South, as he headed toward Bethesda. Whitefield began a preaching tour primarily in the Carolinas and when he arrived in North Carolina, his plan was "to hunt for souls and gospelize the wilds for sinners."[459] He spoke in several churches and naturally did not have the great crowds he had in New England because of the sparse population and the differences in the geography of the land. Dallimore shared how "The arrival of Whitefield in Charleston aroused the ire of his old foe, Commissary Garden."[460] Garden had hired a lawyer to prosecute and seek Whitefield's removal from the priesthood, but the matter was still taken lightly by church officials.[461] The evangelist was unwilling to get involved in a long debate with him. He said, "I am willing to wait for a day of judgment."[462] As he moved south, he also spoke in churches supporting his ministry. One of the highlights of his meetings was his encouragement of the brethren through the preaching of the gospel through the Doctrines of Grace. In reflecting on the response his messages had in the southern colonies, he wrote:

> I trust the time for favoring this and the neighboring southern provinces is come. Everywhere, almost, the door is opened for preaching, great numbers flock to hear, and the power of an ascended Saviour attends the word. For it is surprising how the Lord causes prejudices to subside, and makes my former most bitter enemies to be at peace with me... Lately, I have been in seven counties in Maryland, and preached with abundant success.[463]

458   Fish, 102-103.
459   Belcher, 289.
460   Dallimore, vol. 2, 209.
461   Ibid., 209.
462   Ibid., 209.
463   Belcher, 287.

In Charleston, South Carolina, on January 1747, he wrote, "The Lord Jesus is pleased to give me great access to multitudes of souls."[464] After speaking in the Savannah church, he came to the place where God had first given him his vision for ministry in America, at Bethesda. It had been almost six years since he had been there. Although he had been away for a long time, he still remained an ambassador at large for the school. Delays had kept him away, but he knew that James Habersham was a capable leader. When Elizabeth visited the orphanage for the first time, she was captivated by the well-run organization of the school.[465]

The orphan house was doing a good job in offering refuge, training, and instruction for the orphans of the colony, but the need to do more with the land to make the school self-sustaining was urgent. These goals were the next hurdle for Whitefield because of the debts still owed; there was a definite need for more revenue.[466]

Whitefield threw himself into the organizational aspect of the school. His primary job for the next year was to make sure the school attained a measure of security. His plan was to plant and harvest crops of rice and cotton. Slave labor was later used because of the belief that the blacks had a natural inclination to work in humid climates, and there was a shortage of workers for the school.[467] Whitefield became a good friend of blacks, sharing the gospel with them and helping them to understand the need for salvation in Christ and to be free in Him. The greatest way he knew blacks were equal and free was through their response to Christ in salvation.

Farming the land was eventually going to pay off for the school and work to its advantage. The children's instruction time was balanced with the chores as they helped out around the farm. Whitefield found himself in the role of administrator for a year at Bethesda. He met with Habersham and Barber and instructed the children. Many grew to love him; they felt they owed a debt of gratitude to him for rescuing them from their plight. Whitefield had a soft spot in his heart for children because of his own hardships as a boy. Their founder instructing them and being personally available to them was the highlight of the year that

---

464 Ibid., 287.
465 Tyerman, vol. 2, 61.
466 Ibid., 61.
467 Ibid., 169.

he spent with them. After a year's time at the school, the decision was made to go back to England by way of Bermuda. Whitefield did more good raising funds, letting the world know the plight of the school, and the need to support it.[468]

Another reason Whitefield wanted to return to England was because of his health, which had been getting worse. At 33, he was gradually wearing down from the terrific pace he had set for himself. He never fully recovered from the perilous voyage to America, as the hardships of the travels had been a considerable strain. Although still a young man, he had developed a lingering fever and several other ailments that contributed to his ill health. Belden summarizes Whitefield's visit to America with his physical problems, "His brief visit to America had not, however, been in vain, though beset by bodily trials. Once again he had carried the sacred torch of revival through the American churches, kindling thousands of hearts to a purer flame, and he had extended the work of God by at least one whole state, namely Virginia."[469]

One fact was clear: Whitefield needed to rest. He could not continue to drive himself. He went to Bermuda to break up the hardship of the journey and provide himself with some measure of recuperation.

Whitefield left his wife in America, telling her he would rejoin her in England once he was better. The time spent in America represented Elizabeth's longest time to be on a preaching tour with her husband, and her health, too, began to wear down. Elizabeth resigned herself to long periods of separation from her husband, realizing that the pace he kept was too hectic for her. Her return to England marked the beginning of long periods of time when they would be separated.[470]

In Bermuda, Whitefield was at times too exhausted to get out of bed, but gradually, the inactivity was beneficial. Because his fame had preceded him and the word he was in Bermuda was out, he received invitations to speak. He preached a shorter message than usual to a group meeting in a home. The recovering evangelist did get better and was able to preach to several parties.[471] The crowds were not as large as the ones in America, but the smaller crowds probably helped

---

468 Ibid., 181-182.
469 Belden, 163.
470 Ibid., 163.
471 Belcher, 292-293.

him recuperate.[472] With his illness and the small crowds, Whitefield learned, as the apostle Paul, "I have learned in whatever state I am, therewith to be content" (Phil. 4: 11b). He was always at home with those needing to hear the message of the gospel. When he felt strong enough to return to England, he was anxious to continue the ministry to which God had called him.

While on board the Betsy and at sea for a month, he had time to reflect on previous rash statements and impulses early in his ministry. Fish described his remorse for these statements:

> He sailed back to his homeland. He was on the sea for a month before arriving in England. During this time the maturing evangelist looked at his journal published eight years ago being critical of many and the established clergy. He exclaimed, "Alas! Alas! In many things, I have judged and acted wrong. I have been too rash and hasty in giving characters, both of places and person. Being fond of Scripture language I have often used a style too apostolical, and at the same time have been too bitter in my zeal. Wild fire has been mixed with it and... I frequently wrote and spoke in my own spirit, when I thought I was writing and speaking with the assistance of the Spirit of God.
>
> I have likewise too much made inward impressions my rule of acting and too explicitly what had been better kept in longer, or told after my death."[473]

Whitefield continued to reflect on these statements as he returned to England. These misstatements made him admit his shortcomings and brought about a greater awareness of the continual need to trust the Lord to go before him and sustain his ministry regardless of his mistakes. One of his biggest measures of growth was in his being a unifier and encourager to others instead of a divider. As Whitefield continued to mature, he no longer acted impulsively, creating division. His willingness to admit mistakes were seen in this statement:

> No, sir, my mistakes have been too many, and my blunders too frequent, to make me set up for infallibility. I came soon into the world; I have means, I have sometimes been in danger of overstating; but many and frequent as my mistakes have been, or may be, as soon as I am made sensible of them, they shall be publicly acknowledged and retracted.[474]

---

472   Tyerman, vol. 2, 181-182.
473   Fish, 106-107.
474   Tyerman, vol. 2, 221.

These confessions, evidence of his maturing as a leader, endeared him to even more people. He had plans to meet again with the trustees of the colony and raise more money for Bethesda in England. Fellow ministers in the association he had helped form, greeted him and people longed to hear him preach. Many challenges lay ahead, but he knew God would see him through them all.

A Burning and Shining Light

12

APPEAL TO THE ELITE

AS LADY HUNTINGDON'S CHAPLAIN

(1748-1749)

WHITEFIELD'S RETURN TO ENGLAND WAS MET with an interest concerning the work God was doing through him in the colonies. Some who had heard of his illness thought he had died because he had been in America for several years and had received little information on his whereabouts. For instance, The Gentleman's magazine had recently included "The Reverend Mr. George Whitefield" in its "LIST OF DEATHS." Other papers published similar statements.[475]

His wife, Elizabeth, had stayed at Bethesda, assisting the orphanage's administration. She was hardly the matron Whitefield was looking for, but she did teach the girls and assisted in tutoring them. She returned to England in June of 1749.[476]

Andrews marks Whitefield's return to England as a time when he began to enjoy the ardent support of the Countess of Huntingdon. He recalled:

---

475 Dallimore, George Whitefield: God's Anointed Servant in the Great Revival of the Eighteenth Century, 152.
476 Ibid., 151.

Until this event, his opportunities of addressing the upper classes were very few. With the exception of two or three noble families who attended his ministry in Scotland, and he does not yet appear to have obtained any footing among the aristocracy. Lady Huntingdon was, at this time, residing at Chelsea. Left a widow at thirty-nine, she was placed, by the death of her husband, in a position to make a bold stand for the truth. Her piety was well known, and her usefulness admitted generally in the religious world in which she moved.[477]

Lady Huntingdon's conversion to Christ was unusual because she was in the upper echelon of British society. Her conversion made a tremendous difference in her life and her support of the Awakening movement was even more inspiring. Dallimore shared:

> Since her earliest days, Lady Huntingdon had lived an exemplary life, remaining aloof from the coarse pleasures of high society and conducting herself in a highly virtuous and religious manner. In turn, she rested in the assurance that her personal righteousness was sufficient for the saving of her soul. But it was as she lay on a sick-bed and seemed near to death that she especially felt the worthlessness of her self-trust...
>
> Then it was that... from her bed, she lifted up her heart to God for pardon and mercy through the blood of his Son. With streaming eyes she cast herself on her Saviour: "Lord, I believe, help thou mine unbelief!" Immediately the scales fell from her eyes; doubt and distress vanished; joy and peace filled her bosom, and with appropriating faith she cried, "My Lord and my God!"[478]

Lady Huntingdon had communicated with Whitefield regularly and was engaged full time in support of Calvinistic preachers in England. She followed his exploits in the New World with interest and she was heartened to learn of his acceptance throughout the colonies. She longed to have this acceptance in England, not only of Whitefield's preaching, but also the whole of Calvinistic Methodism. Believing that his preaching would expand the movement and that his message was crucial for people to hear, she continued to support him and the Awakening movement. The support Lady Huntingdon gave Whitefield should never be underestimated. In order for her friends to hear Whitefield, she needed a non-threatening place for him to have a proper hearing.[479]

Belden tells of her dilemma and its solution as she made her home a place to reach the upper class of England:

477 Andrews, 215.
478 Dallimore, vol. 2, 262.
479 Stout, 213.

Lady Huntingdon, however, wrestled bravely with her environment and one method she adopted was to fling open her drawing-room for religious services. To these she succeeded in drawing, however unwillingly they may have come, not merely the brilliant and cynical, but also the riotously vicious and notoriously unbelieving elements of her set. Indeed, there could be no more impressive tribute to the sterling character of the Lady of the Revival than the profound respect in which she was held by these elements...[480]

The Lady built tabernacles and sponsored many of "her preachers," as they were called, in addition to supporting Bethesda. The Countess supported the movement generously and defended it valiantly.[481]

The Countess had a new vision: she longed for the royalty and elite of England to hear Whitefield's message, just as the lowest classes of people had and continually wanted to hear him. Finding a place for the nobility to hear Whitefield would be difficult because the majority of the established clergy opposed him.

Knowing the gravity of the situation, Whitefield's demonstrated his dependence on the Lord:

I go with fear and trembling, knowing how difficult it is to speak to the great, so as to win them to Jesus Christ. I sometimes am ready to say, "Lord, I pray thee have me excused, and send by whom thou wilt send. But divine grace is sufficient for me. I can do all things through Christ strengthening me."[482]

Those who attended Whitefield's services were described by him:

Some are here merely to while away an idle hour, attending me just as they would attend Garrick the actor. Others have come, haughty in their assurance of superiority, to scoff should this "commoner" offend some detail of their standards of good breeding, and others smugly assume that as the aristocracy of earth they are also the aristocracy of heaven, and wait to manifest their hostility toward any suggestion that like ordinary mortals they possess a spiritual need. And, the majority feel that religion is all a farce and their attitude is one of examining his Christianity—is it, too, an empty performance or does it contain something real?[483]

Lady Huntingdon knew if the elite heard Whitefield regularly, they would sense the power of his message and be awakened themselves. She

---

480   Belden, 169.
481   Stout, 159.
482   Dallimore, vol. 2, 266.
483   Ibid., 267.

longed for the awakening to spread to the upper classes. Some had come to the Tabernacle in London, but few ventured out in the open to hear the preacher. The new plan was conceived.

Lady Huntingdon enlisted Whitefield as her chaplain and employed him to speak regularly in her house. Tyerman shared, "The Countess made him her domestic chaplain, the only ecclesiastical preferment, except the living at Savannah, he ever had."[484] His first service was conducted in August 1748, although he had been back in England for only a few months.[485]

Whitefield's preaching at Lady Huntingdon's residence resulted in two occurrences: It brought Whitefield to the friendly confines of her house where her royal friends attended in relative safety and comfort. It also erased the stigma of her friends going to the fields to hear him preach.

The opportunity to preach at Lady Huntingdon's home opened a door to preach the gospel and enlist the support of these influential people in England. The support was not only for Whitefield's missionary enterprises, but also for the awakening movement as a whole.[486] Whitefield was hopeful as he assumed the position of her ladyship's chaplain, with cautious trust in the Lord. He believed the venture would be an open door that God had provided, and He would bless his preaching. Belden revealed the responses of the nobility:

> In a few days a most brilliant galaxy of aristocracy gathered about Whitefield in the home of the Countess, and once more we must pay tribute to his amazing adaptability, for he was perfectly at home with his audience. The wife of Lord Chesterfield and his two sisters became consistent, life-long followers of his teaching. Even the Earl was impressed to a degree, declaring, "Sir, I will not tell you what I shall tell others, how I approve of you!" The great Bolingbroke himself would sit in these intense little assemblies "like an archbishop" and rather patronizingly tell Whitefield afterwards that "he had done great justice to the Divine attributes."... Lady Huntingdon, with remarkable determination and foresight, applied her great fortune and her equally great prestige to the task of securing more order and harmony in the new movement by the provision of chapels or preaching centers.[487]

---

484   Tyerman, vol. 2, 193.
485   Ibid., 193.
486   Tyerman, vol. 2, 192-193.
487   Belden, 170.

The responses were varied toward Whitefield. While there was a built-in prejudice toward him through hearsay and the opposition, the opportunity to hear Whitefield gave people a first-hand understanding of his message. These events became a turning point in the acceptance of Methodism by the upper class, as it gained a hearing and made headway into the elite circles of royalty.[488]

Whitefield was a regular fixture at Lady Huntingdon's for many years to come, just as she was at his meetings. The responses featured changed minds and sometimes hearts. In describing a blind man who lost his guide dog, Whitefield likened the man to a sinner in danger of falling into eternal separation from God. As he continued, describing the blind man wandering perilously close to a steep ledge of a mountain ravine, Lord Chesterfield jumped to his feet and cried at the top of his voice, "He's gone!"[489]

It was obvious that Whitefield made quite an impression on Lord Chesterfield. Chesterfield said, "Mr. Whitefield's eloquence is unrivaled, his zeal inexhaustible; and not to admire both would argue a total absence of taste."[490]

Whitefield had surprising reviews from even the opponents of Christianity. Agnostic David Hume noted, "Mr. Whitefield is the most ingenious preacher I ever heard. It is worth going twenty miles to hear him."[491]

Lord Bolingbroke wrote to the Countess of Huntingdon:

> **Mr. Whitefield is the most extraordinary man in our times. He has the most commanding eloquence I ever heard in any person; his abilities are very considerable; his zeal unquenchable; and his piety and excellence genuine-unquestionable. The bishops and inferior orders of clergy are very angry with him, and endeavour to represent him as a hypocrite, an enthusiast; but this is not astonishing, there is so little real goodness or honesty among them.[492]**

While there were positive observations of Whitefield and the messages, there were also negative reactions from the nobility. One

---

488   Ibid., 170.

489   Dallimore, *George Whitefield: God's Anointed Servant in the Great Revival of the Eighteenth Century*, 187.

490   Ibid., 159.

491   Dallimore, *George Whitefield: God's Anointed Servant in the Great Revival of the Eighteenth Century*, 160.

492   Fish, 113.

woman of proper standing heard Whitefield say, "God changes the downcast and gives them a new life." This statement infuriated her. She was especially offended after he related a story of a woman with a questionable past, asking if God would accept "the devil's castaways." The "high placed" woman told Lady Huntingdon she was insulted at the suggestion of one with a questionable reputation having the same standing as she.[493] The woman, as many in British nobility, prided themselves on having a superior standing in many perceived ways. Lady Huntingdon would usually exhort these individuals to hear the man out and not reject him because of one thing he said.

Even the King himself felt Whitefield's influence. He knew of his popularity with the masses and the inroads he was making into the upper classes. When Lady Chesterfield (convicted of the gaudiness of some of her extravagant dresses) appeared in his court with a plain dress, it was out of character for her. King George said, "I know who picked out that dress for you: Mr. Whitefield!"[494] Although said in jest, it did give an assessment of how Whitefield's ministry was affecting even those in the King's court.

Whitefield's ministry was still having wonderful results elsewhere. All around them, the atmosphere was changing minds and hearts toward his message, not only in the nobility. Belden described the reactions to Whitefield's preaching:

> At Sheffield, in 1749, Whitefield by his eloquent preaching completely won over a public that had taken a strong prejudice against the Wesleys, and had actually stoned Charles in 1743. Writing from Sheffield some months after the Awakener's work in the city, Charles Wesley generously admits, "The door has continued open ever since Mr. Whitefield preached here, and quite removed the prejudices of our first opposers. Some of them were convinced by him, some converted and added to the Church."
>
> In the winter of 1749-50, Whitefield enjoyed "golden seasons" in his London Tabernacle. Huge congregations assembled as early as six a.m. morning after morning before the day's business began—whilst the nobility also was treated to a continuous and vigorous bombardment.[495]

Whitefield maintained his influential standing with non-conformist church leaders of his time. Philip Doddridge had heard him speak and

---

493 Ninde, 121.
494 Ibid., 139.
495 Belden, 184.

endorsed his ministry. He spoke in the Tabernacle, and Whitefield spoke in his church at Northampton.[496] Belcher describes Doddridge's support of Whitefield:

> **Dr. Philip Doddridge, as every reader knows, was one of the most pious and accomplished preachers and writers of the Non-conformists of England in his day. Nor was his missionary zeal small in its degree. Though he died as early as 1751, he had said, "I am now content with having something done among the dissenters, in a more public manner, (speaking of Whitefield's ministry and seeing the impact it was having), for propagating the gospel abroad, which lies near my heart."[497]**

Issac Watts was an influential minister of a Non-Conformist church. He is known as the father of English hymnology and his influence in hymn writing is monumental. His hymns, still sung today, reflect an exalted nature of God. Whitefield used his published hymnbooks in his meetings and even for his own personal devotional worship.

When Whitefield died in Newburyport, Massachusetts, Watts' hymnbooks were in his possession on that fateful night.[498] Watts' hymn "Why Do We Mourn Departed Friends," sung at Whitefield's funeral, illustrated his influence on the evangelist's life.[499, 500]

Whitefield visited Watts on his deathbed in Stoke-Newton, where he had labored for many years as the congregation's pastor. When he inquired of Watts' condition he responded, "I am one of Christ's waiting servants." Whitefield helped the older man sit up in bed for him to easily swallow his medicine. Watts apologized for the inconvenience. Whitefield responded: "Certainly I am not too good to wait on one of Christ's waiting servants." Shortly after Whitefield left, Watts died. The two spiritual giants meeting in the parting moments before Watts' death was a lasting memory for the evangelist."[501]

---

496 Tyerman, vol. 2, 256.

497 Belcher, 325.

498 Tyerman, vol. 2, 598.

499 Isaac, Watts, *Why Do We Mourn Departed Friends*, Words: *Hymns and Spiritual Songs 1707*, Music: Dundee, 1615, *The Cyber Hymnal*, Page Design: Richard W. Adams, 1996-2015, (accessed September 30, 2015), http://www.hymntime.com/tch/htm/w/h/y/whydowem.htm.

500 Philip, 536.

501 Dallimore, vol. 2, 253.

Whitefield also relinquished his role as moderator of the Calvinistic Methodist Association because of too many commitments, including his involvement in a ministry on both continents.[502] Howell Harris, however, convened a meeting of the Calvinistic Methodists as the New Year approached. Organization was the watchword, and encouragement through fellowship increased.[503] The group had held together, especially bolstered by Whitefield's presence in England. He shared the blessings of God through his ministry in America, meeting with them and all social strata.

Whitefield shared his vision to preach again to the masses in the meeting of the association with a new resolve to reach all types of people. He would still minister to those who had responded to his message earlier in his ministry. The dynamic preacher left the meeting of like-minded brethren with renewed vigor. He conducted meetings throughout Wales in whirlwind fashion.[504]

In a few months, Elizabeth returned from Georgia. The rigors of sea travel had worn her down. Whitefield had a surprise for his wife: a new home built next to the Tabernacle, which he called "the Tabernacle house." The home served as their "base of operations" for the rest of their lives.[505] His wife stayed close to this new home after her one trip to the colonies.

One reality was abundantly clear in Whitefield's return to England: He was exerting his influence in every echelon of society. The common people had always heard him gladly, and the nobility were becoming acquainted with him. They were impressed with one who "tore passions to pieces," as some had said of him.[506]

Whitefield's influence and his preaching had become a fixture in England. He was no fly-by-night enthusiast, but was leaving his mark on both continents through changed lives in the process.

---

502 Ibid., 256.
503 Fish, 128.
504 Ibid., 128.
505 Ibid, 118.
506 Hardy, 216-217.

13

Expanding the Work

as the Movement Grows

(1749-1751)

WHITEFIELD REVISITED PLACES WHERE THERE had been
responsiveness to the gospel message. In July 1750, he
conducted meetings in Edinburgh and throughout Scotland,
where his support was strong.[507]

It had been eight years since the Cambuslang revival, but the
memories of it were still in its participant's minds and its effects were still
going on. The news that Whitefield would preach drew quite a crowd
and thrust him into the limelight of the religious scene in Scotland.[508]

The Erskine brothers, who had led others to a clear separation from
the established church, must have watched with some displeasure
as Whitefield preached everywhere he had an opportunity. Although
the Associate Presbytery had criticized him, it did not stop him from
speaking wherever he had an invitation; he was no party to partisanship
when the future of souls was at stake.

The response to this fourth visit was remarkable; many Scots were
moved by his preaching, and he found open hearts as well as open Bibles.

---

507   Gillies, 187
508   Ibid., 187

Whitefield used the Scotland's fertile ground to escape the pressures of England and America. His ministry in Scotland was brief, but rapid as described by Philip:

> In this state of mind, he visited many parts of Devonshire and Cornwall. At Gwinnop, he preached to a large audience, although the clergyman had preached a virulent sermon against him in the morning. This worthy had said on Saturday, "Now Whitefield is coming—I must put on my old armour." He did. Whitefield says, "It did but little execution, because not Scripture-proof; consequently, not out of God's armory. I preached to many thousands. The rain dropped gently upon our bodies, and the grace of God seemed to fall like gentle dew, sprinkling rain upon our souls." Thus in Cornwall, "an unthought-of and unexpectedly wide door" was opened. He preached in many churches, and the power of God came down, so that even the ministers were overcome. Such was the flying of doves to their windows there that he ceased for a time to long for the wings of a dove to flee away to America.[509]

Back in England, the coldness was continuing to thaw between Whitefield and John Wesley. First, they began correspondence. Then they began to talk personally. John Wesley had been depressed, with his Brother Charles's counsel for him not to marry Grace Murray. Charles had felt led to steer him away from Murray.[510] He was later to marry another widow as Whitefield did and entered into a very difficult, unhappy marriage.[511]

Wesley was worn down from his preaching schedule. He felt he was dying, and at one point even wrote a will in preparation for the event. Whitefield wrote to encourage Wesley and tell of the value his ministry had been to the world. If it was his time to die, he would be going to a better place, leaving behind a work God had used. The letter revealed a tender side, full of encouragement toward his old friend despite their differences:

> Reverend and very dear Sir,
> If seeing you so very weak when leaving London distressed me, the news and prospect of your approaching dissolution have quite weighed me down.
> I pity myself and the church, but not you. A radiant throne awaits you, and, ere long, you will enter into your Master's joy. Yonder He stands with a massy crown, ready to put it on your head, amidst an admiring throng of saints and angels…

---

509 Philip, 367.
510 Dallimore, vol. 2, 336.
511 Ibid., 344.

...If prayers can detain...even you, reverend and very dear Sir, shall not leave us yet: but if...you must now fall asleep in Jesus, may he kiss your soul away, and give you to die in the embraces of triumphant love. If in the land of the living, I hope to pay my last respects to you next week. If not, reverend and very dear Sir, farewell!

My heart is too big, tears trickle down to fast I fear, are too weak for me to enlarge. Underneath you may there be Christ's everlasting arms! I commend you to His never-failing mercy, and am, reverend and very dear sir, your most affectionate, sympathizing, and afflicted younger brother, in the gospel of our common Lord.[512]

John Wesley's recovery and ministry for another four decades far eclipsed Whitefield in longevity. For several reasons Whitefield offered to help Wesley in his work and preach in some of his chapels, but he was limited in ministry with his old friend because of other commitments and trips to America. He was not able to minister with him until the last decade of Whitefield's life. The sharp theological differences had quelled, as evidenced by another letter to Wesley. Whitefield wrote:

I rejoice to hear, that you and your brother are more moderate with respect to sinless perfection. As for universal redemption, if we omit on each side the talking for or against reprobation, which we may do fairly, and agree, as we already do, in giving a universal offer to all poor sinners that will come and taste the water of life, I think we may manage very well.[513]

The furtherance of the gospel was foremost on Whitefield's mind in his offer to help Wesley. He and Wesley would never be able to reach agreement on the Doctrines of Grace but they could agree that the need of the hour was for the multitudes to hear and respond to the gospel message. The sharp bitterness was gone and was replaced by a willingness to reach others with the gospel. They still maintained separate meeting places but began to pray and encourage each other. The differences were not as defined as they preached Christ in the open fields to the multitudes. Oddly, their powerful and transforming ministries had meeting houses very close to one another. Dallimore shared the similarities and differences in their buildings and worship:

---

512 Ibid, 347.
513 Tyerman, vol. 2, 176.

> It must be recognized that less than a quarter of a mile away and on the same street stood Wesley's meeting-house and headquarters, the Foundery. As long as Whitefield had been in the old wooden Tabernacle the status of the two buildings had been largely equal, but now the Foundery was noticeably put into the shade by this new brick structure.[514]

Whitefield paid close attention to the songs sung at the Tabernacle as Tyerman also illustrated: "In connection with the opening of the new Tabernacle, Whitefield compiled and published a Hymn Book: *Hymns for Social Worship*... designed for the use of the Tabernacle congregation."[515]

Tyerman showed how Wesley bore the influence of the Moravians through the songs sung at the Foundery:

> ...it is somewhat singular that, in the same year, Wesley published his *Hymns and Spiritual Songs*, intended for the use of real Christians of all denominations; and that, in the year following, the Moravians published... *A Collection of Hymns*... designed chiefly for the use of the Brethren's Church. The curious reader may speculate how far Whitefield's little book led to the publication of the other two.[516]

Throughout the Christmas season and into the New Year, Whitefield was ill again, brought on by the pace he labored under. He was not able to maintain his health due to the frequency of his preaching and his extensive travels. Both he and his wife were ill and bedridden together. Some believe one of her several miscarriages necessitated her illness.[517] They both recovered gradually.

The pattern of rest, recovery and preaching again continued through the rest of Whitefield's ministry. After great meetings where the power of God was evident, he would have to rest, recuperate, and seek God's presence and protection, as he went out in His power.[518]

A new Tabernacle was needed because of the constant wearing down of the old wooden one by the elements. Tyerman mentioned the progress of the new Tabernacle:

---

514   Dallimore, vol. 2, 357.
515   Ibid., 357.
516   Tyerman, vol. 2, 295.
517   Fish, 120-121.
518   Ibid., 248-249.

The wooden meeting-house, in Moorfields, stood the storms of a dozen winters. At the best, it was but a huge, ugly shed; and, of course, signs of decay were becoming visible. Still, the uncouth fabric was a sacred one. A more durable edifice, however, was greatly needed; and, in the summer of 1751, while at Lady Huntingdon's residence at Ashby-de-la-Zouch, the project had been discussed, in the presence of her ladyship, Doddridge, Hervey, Hartley, and Stonehouse, all of whom were most cordial in their approval and promise of support. Towards the end of 1752, the subject was renewed at the house of Lady Frances Shirley, in South Audley Street; and, in compliance with the urgent entreaties of her ladyship and of the Countess of Huntingdon, Whitefield began to exert himself in collecting money. He resolved not to begin building till he had £1000 in hand. That amount he soon obtained; the first brick was laid on the 1st of March, 1753; and, within fifteen weeks afterwards, the structure was opened for public worship; the congregations, during that interval, still continuing to assemble in the wooden tabernacle, which was left standing within the shell of the building in course of erection. The new Tabernacle needs no description; for, though a third has within the last few years been built upon its site, there are thousands still living who have often gazed with reverence at the low, unpretentious edifice where Whitefield so often mounted his pulpit throne, and not a few who found salvation within its walls.[519]

Whitefield embarked on his first preaching tour of Ireland, not being one to shrink from a challenge. He had run aground here on return from his first trip to Georgia, but he did not preach to any congregations there.[520] The emerald isle was only a century removed from Oliver Cromwell's crushing the people into submission to English rule by forcing them into the Church of England, reformed under the Puritans. There had been resistance and bloodshed when the armies clashed and Oliver Cromwell was victorious. Emotions were still set against the English and especially their perceived religion as it ran counter to the heavily Catholic influence of Ireland. Whitefield met with moderate success as he gathered believers and preached in the open air in Ireland.[521] He was accustomed and ready for any hostility, having confronted those with such reactions at Moorfields. The hostility would come with greater ferocity on a later trip.[522] Those converted in places he preached

---

519 Tyerman, vol. 2, 290.
520 Ibid., 273.
521 Ibid., 274.
522 These causes were common knowledge for the reason of the hostility between the Irish and English in the time of Whitefield's ministry.

demonstrated that there was a hunger in the country to hear the things of God expounded as in other places.

The work continued to prosper in England under other preachers. Howell Harris, who had spoken in various meetings, was a regular speaker at the Tabernacle in London.[523] Unfortunately, hostility toward field preaching had not quelled; it varied from place to place, but was fueled by local officials' restraint or lack of it. Sometimes the mob turned violent, which caused Harris to narrowly escape death on one occasion in Bala, Wales, at the hands of an angry crowd.[524]

William Seward (an associate of Whitefield) was the first casualty of Calvinistic Methodist preachers. He encountered hostile crowds in South Wales and at Hay-on-Wye on October 15, 1740, in the inception of the Methodist movement. He was heavily stoned by a particularly aggressive mob and a few days later died from his wounds, becoming the first Methodist martyr. He is buried near Hay, in the village churchyard at Cusop in Wales.[525] Whitefield himself was not immune to these attacks and had been the target of many stones, dead cats or whatever the mob found to throw at him. Preaching to crowds opposed to his message and his being there, he became the victim of their hostility.[526]

Howell Harris suffered from the strain of being a field preacher through adversity and the pace he kept in his preaching schedule. Dallimore described his deteriorating condition:

> Moreover, there came now a basic alteration in Harris's life. Physically and nervously exhausted, refused at London and unwanted throughout most of the work in Wales, he gave up the evangelistic labour he had conducted so magnificently for fifteen years and settled down at his home in Trevecka.
>
> By the time, however, Harris was a very sick man. During the next two years he was frequently confined to bed and was in a mentally deranged condition. His diary contains such descriptions of his suffering as "unbearable headache," "excruciating pains in my head," and "feeling that my brain is almost turning."[527]

---

523 Dallimore, vol. 2, 234.

524 Dallimore, *George Whitefield: God's Anointed Servant in the Great Revival of the Eighteenth Century*, 178.

525 Tony Sparrow, William Seward (1702-1740) *Methodist Martyr, A Brief History of Badsey and Aldington*, badsey.net., June 16, 2007, (accessed September 30, 2015). http://www.badsey.net/past/seward.htm.

526 Dallimore, *George Whitefield: God's Anointed Servant in the Great Revival of the Eighteenth Century*, 176.

527 Dallimore, vol. 2, 300.

Field preachers were willing to take the risk of physical violence while traveling through the countryside, in spite of the potential danger. Several times highwaymen robbed Whitefield, once even taking his money that included a collection for the orphanage. Discontented with just the money only, the thief came back for Whitefield's better coat, leaving him with the thief's old shabby coat which happened to have the money in it. The thief's downfall was forgetting to remove the money; his blind greed got the best of him. Whitefield got the money for the orphanage back by the thief's selfish mistake.[528] God's hand of protection was evident on Whitefield. His deliverance from these perils was miraculous in the face of opposition and hostility.

The mere presence of Whitefield in England gave encouragement to the Calvinistic Methodist movement. His preaching in several locations as their guest was a source of great fanfare and excitement. He worked with like-minded preachers to sponsor their ministry when he was in England. He worked with more churches and went beyond the association with a ministry to groups outside this affiliation.[529] Wesley's organizational success would possibly have been realized in the Calvinistic movement if he had confined himself to his native country. He did not pursue this strategy and in the summer of 1751, made another trip to Scotland in the same vicinity of his last trip near Edinburgh.[530]

Whitefield stayed in Scotland for only a short preaching tour. His well-attended meetings met with a fervent reception. The Scots' theological agreement with the evangelist and his preaching the Doctrines of Grace provided great strength for the meetings in Scotland and the reception he received.[531]

Whitefield made immediate plans for a trip to America on his return to England. He longed to visit beloved Bethesda and find out first-hand of its welfare and progress. There were new challenges for the orphanage to face, such as making the farmland productive so it could be a fixture in Georgia for years to come. The trip was a respite for him as Fish described the drive that kept him going:

---

528 Belden, 236.
529 Dallimore, vol. 2, 257.
530 Tyerman, vol. 2, 261-262.
531 Ibid., 262.

While Whitefield himself tended to ignore his body's well-being, friends as diverse as the devotedly secular Ben Franklin and the devout Christian Robert Cruttenden repeatedly expressed concern for the preacher's health. On August 29, 1751, Whitefield left England aboard the Antelope. He was bound for Georgia and was taking several poor children with him. The next day his friend Cruttenden wrote in a letter, "Yesterday I took leave of Mr. Whitefield, who is embarked for America, with little prospect of my ever seeing him again. His constitution is quite worn out with labour." As Whitefield's nineteenth-century biographer Luke Tyerman observed, "It was fortunate that he got away. Without this, he probably would have died. The man was fast becoming a sort of religious suicide. Humanly speaking, his voyage to America saved, or rather prolonged, his life." George Whitefield was only thirty-six years old.[532]

Whitefield longed to be involved in the process of seeing people come to Christ in both continents. This voyage to America led to great anticipation and his full energy.

---

532   Fish 126,

14

Back to Bethesda

and Sponsorship the Work

(1751-1752)

WHITEFIELD BOARDED THE ANTELOPE IN 1752, anxious to get back to Bethesda to see the progression of the work.[533] Several orphans and others he referred to as his family were with him on the trip that was long and arduous.[534] He arrived in the fall, full of hope and excitement for what the Lord was doing, also fully aware the Georgia Assembly had voted in 1751 to import slaves for labor on the farms.[535] Whitefield's consenting to this practice seems strange to those living in the 21st century and it is the one blemish that some have sought to accuse Whitefield of as they chronicle his life. Many of the slaves purchased to work in South Carolina were transported to Georgia and specifically to Bethesda, although slaves were used throughout Georgia.[536] John Pollock, who devoted a whole chapter to this subject in his biography of Whitefield, revealed, "…He carried out a plan which he believed would be good for Bethesda and for Georgia."[537]

---

533 Tyerman, vol. 2, 277.
534 Fish, 125.
535 Dallimore, vol. 2, 368.
536 Dallimore, *George Whitefield: God's Anointed Servant in the Great Revival of the Eighteenth Century*, 147.
537 Pollock, 221.

Although the practice of slavery cannot be justified, several facts led Georgia residents to view slave labor as needful for the orphanage to be self-supporting and productive in the crops it was seeking to produce.

The obvious reason for slave labor was the shortage of workers to tame the massive farmland requiring constant vigilance. Whitefield believed blacks were accustomed to the warm climate of Georgia and had experience in farm labor, so he believed using experienced labor where it was needed was not unwise. The means of attaining this labor through slavery is what was in question. Pollock shares how Whitefield believed, "Bethesda would never expand nor the colony flourish on white labor."[538]

The practice of slavery was accepted as a form of farming the vast raw land of the New World. Africans were enslaved, bought and sold for the task at hand. At the beginning of the slave trade, only the Quakers stood against the practice and managed to prohibit it in Pennsylvania, due in large part to the influence of William Penn. In time, the practice of slavery fell out of favor in the North, due in part to the colonies not needing the labor force.[539] The South was another story in the slavery matter. Plantation owners needed many workers who would be cared for corporately in return for their labor.

The sheer convenience of the slaves working the plantation land in South Carolina led to their transport to Bethesda. It was a short trek to Georgia and their experience in the fields was what was needed to work the 500 acres surrounding Bethesda. Because Whitefield had no time to supervise the buying and selling of slaves, the task was given to the farm manager who did his bidding.[540]

Whitefield described the plight of the orphanage, with the huge amount of farmland to work. The description by Dallimore showed his assessment of the situation:

> **He found "Georgia and Bethesda," he says "in a thriving way." These thriving conditions, however, arose from a deplorable source: They were**

---

538   Ibid., 222.

539   A Common knowledge concerning the founding of the colony of Pennsylvania and the forbiddance of slavery is clear. They offered more freedom than almost any other colony. Rhode Island equally offered this freedom. The economy helped negate the need for slavery being an issue up North regardless of their allowing slave trading in their ports.

540   Cashin, 33.

largely the fruit of slavery. Moreover, it must be recognized that Whitefield had exerted his influence toward having the practice introduced into the Colony (Georgia), and we notice the following letter he had written to the Trustees in December 1748:

"...I need not inform you...how the Colony of Georgia has been declining for these many years...past and at what great disadvantages I have maintained a large family in the wilderness...Proficiency made in the cultivation of my tract of land was made, and their entirely owing to the necessity I lay under of making use of white hands. Had a negroe been allowed, I should now have had a sufficiency to support a great many orphans, without expending above half the sum which hath been laid out.[541]

Bethesda was considerate of the black children, teaching them to read and write in the orphanage as part of the family.[542] Their spiritual lives were also of interest, with every effort made to share the gospel and ground them in the Christian religion. They received equal treatment at Bethesda.[543] Conversion opportunities abounded and were not taken lightly because of Whitefield's motivation to get the gospel to the slaves. Bethesda featured more of a benevolent spirit to the slaves and especially to their children, who considered the orphanage as their home. Whitefield was concerned and believed proper benevolent care was needful for the slaves working hard to make the land productive.[544]

Whitefield disputed Johann Boltzius about slave labor, insisting on the need for it. Boltzius' school for orphans in Ebenezer was the inspiration for Whitefield's school after visiting it. He developed his ministry without slave labor and was against the practice, although the land he owned was of smaller acreage.[545]

Although Whitefield wanted to use slave labor, at the same time he decried their plight:

The Scripture says, "Thou shalt not muzzle the ox that treadeth out the corn." Does God take care of oxen? And will He not take care of the negroes? Undoubtedly He will. "Go to, now, ye rich men, weep and howl for your miseries that shall come upon you." Behold, the provision of the poor negroes which have reaped down your fields, which is by you denied them crieth, and

---

541 Dallimore, vol. 2, 367.

542 Philip, 162.

543 Cashin, 75.

544 William Warren Sweet, *The Story of Religion in America* (New York: Harper and Brothers, 1939), 191.

545 Cashin, 62.

the cries of them which have reaped are entered into the ears of the Lord of Sabbath.[546]

Whitefield used the slaves purchased as a mission field. He went to them often and preached the gospel to them, including them personally in his sermons.[547] He recorded several conversions in his writing: "The everlasting God rewarded all their benefactors. I find there has been a fresh awakening among them. I am informed that twelve negroes, who belong to a planter, lately converted at the orphan-house, and are savingly brought home to Jesus Christ."[548] Whitefield was as joyous with the conversion of slaves as the conversion of any other group of people.

Whitefield was well loved by blacks in many places, by all accounts. He had a favorable hearing with them. His message was well received in the South and in New England.[549, 550] He had meetings in their gatherings on plantations. Many blacks gladly received his message and found joyous fellowship with him.[551] A black woman prayed for him when he was presumed to be dead in New England and he recovered. Another black young woman, Phillis Wheatley, wrote a moving funeral poem in his honor. It captured the love of blacks for his ministry.[552]

Whitefield gave more than token support to the cause of the slaves. He urged the proper care and decent treatment of them wherever he went throughout the colonies. The evangelist refers to the practice of slavery often as "taking unfair advantage of the Africans."[553] He was not sent to lead a crusade against the practice, but actually utilized the practice. He not only moralized concerning the slave's treatment, but had plans with Franklin to start a school in Pennsylvania for black children.[554] He knew their plight and wanted to teach them and give them opportunities they would not have on the plantations. Unfortunately, plans for the school never materialized, partially because of Whitefield's constant travel and preaching on both continents.[555] He had no James Habersham in the

---

546 Belden, 87.
547 Dallimore, vol. 1, 498-500.
548 Belcher, 245.
549 Cashin, 74-75.
550 Philip, 179.
551 Ibid., 176.
552 Mansfield, 233.
553 Ibid., 232.
554 Kidd, George *Whitefield: America's Spiritual Founding Father,* 110.
555 Ibid., 503.

North to supervise the school and help get it on its feet.

Whitefield's decision to use slaves at Bethesda was not a wise decision in light of today's knowledge, but he lived in a primitive time that tolerated the practice. William Wilberforce, who became a leader in Parliament, heard Whitefield preach during his childhood. His motivation to abolish slavery in England led to the campaign that was eventually successful. No armies were needed, and the practice was abolished without firing a shot, unlike America. Wilberforce's reason for abolition came primarily from his Christian faith, aided by his hearing Whitefield's preaching as a child.[556]

Knowledge of various types of slaveholders is necessary to understand the slavery situation. Those at Bethesda were concerned for their welfare and taught them as they did the English children. Whitefield knew the slaves would not be going into a hostile environment. He needed their labor and, in return, offered a true Christian spirit of kindness and acceptance of them as children of God.[557]

When Whitefield got to Bethesda, he found a relatively calm atmosphere this time. The threat of war with Spain had long since dissipated with the battle of "Bloody Marsh" where the Spanish were repelled.[558] The more the school became self-supporting, the more it had a clear separation from Savannah where it had first been temporarily housed. This separation had positive and negative advantages. There were rumors of extreme discipline, especially under Jonathan Barber, the Spiritual Director of the school, who was looked on with suspicion. There was tension with the residents of Savannah and the orphanage.[559] Georgia was probably the roughest colony during its early settlement. The benevolence all around the New and Old World for the orphanage certainly led to resentment from some struggling to survive.

Some of this resentment diminished as the girls who started in the orphanage grew up and were married to local residents, while some of the boys became tradesmen and influential citizens of the town.[560, 561] The orphanage became a fixture in time, especially since it had been

---

556   Ibid., 499-500.
557   Mansfield, 233-234.
558   Cashin, 46-47.
559   Ibid., 41.
560   Ibid., 67.
561   Ibid., 49.

in Georgia from the colony's earliest history.

Charles Tondee was one young man who grew up in Bethesda. After being severely disciplined, he ran away, only to be returned to the orphanage and was put under constant supervision.[562] He continued to live at the orphanage and became a successful citizen tradesman, a leading resident and a Revolutionary war hero.[563] His heroism in the war increased his status in the new state of Georgia, and it all started at Bethesda.[564]

Whitefield quickly surveyed the situation with Georgia's new governor after arriving in Georgia. The leadership of the orphanage, although separated at times, were more closely aligned with Savannah.[565] Both James Habersham and Francis Harris had businesses in Savannah and had become fixtures in the community, seeing no conflict with their duties at Bethesda and in Savannah.[566] Habersham was elected as a representative to the assembly, and represented Bethesda very influentially there.[567] Bethesda was supervised with precision and a balance of work and indoctrination. Cashin describes the daily schedule at Bethesda:

A visitor to Bethesda wrote a letter to his father dated June 1, 1742, describing the daily routine at the orphanage. The wake-up bell sounded at sunrise. The thirty-nine boys and fifteen girls sang a hymn upon rising from bed and prayed before going to the washroom. Next, the bell called all to public worship, consisting of a Scripture reading and the singing of a psalm and a prayer. Only then was breakfast served. After eating, some of the older children went to work and the younger to school. Habersham and Periam instructed the boys, while their wives led the girls. Barber taught Latin to those boys who seemed destined for the ministry. At noon, the children and staff dined together, with a hymn before and after eating. After a half-hour recess, school or work resumed. Time for reading was provided before the bell rang for prayer and supper. And at the end of the day, the schoolmasters and mistresses conducted the children to bed and led them in prayer. When Lord Egmont learned of the routine, he commented acidly, "Not a moment of innocent recreation tho' necessary to the health and strengthening of growing children is allow'd in the whole day." More than ever, he and the trustees believed that Whitefield intended to establish a school or seminary to breed up those of his sect in.[568]

---

562   Temple, 225.
563   Cashin, 120-121.
564   Cashin, 67.
565   Ibid., 67.
566   Ibid., 56.
567   Ibid., 48-49.
568   Ibid., 42-43.

Whitefield was heard gladly in Georgia. His views on issues were important and his opinion in certain matters was often consulted. Because of his influence and his desire for the orphanage to become a college one day, the colony accepted his ideas. Since educational institutions were scarce in the South, he thought the prospect of a school similar to the institutions in New England, with training for the ministry like the Log College, was a glorious prospect. He also believed a school like this would benefit the colony as a whole.[569] Unfortunately, Whitefield's pursuit of his dream would face many future difficulties.

The English Parliament had to approve a charter for the orphanage, giving it official status, because Georgia had become a colony.[570] The great tension Whitefield faced was whether to return to England and personally push for a charter or go to New England where he had received invitations to preach. He chose to go back, seeking the charter for Bethesda.[571] He was a man torn in many directions. Field preaching was his consuming passion and his leadership in the Calvinistic Methodist movement was a pressing concern. The evangelist's best of intentions for returning quickly to Georgia would be stalled and delayed. These concerns allowed him to visit Bethesda briefly and delayed his next trip to America longer than he wished. Whitefield departed as quickly as he arrived, after taking care of the matter. The return trip was a remarkable feat considering the hazard of travel in Whitefield's day on the sea.

Whitefield saw the promise of what Bethesda offered. He continually lauded its cause to the world, and especially to the members of Parliament. The colony now, officially recognized by Parliament, brought him back to his native country sooner than he expected but the charter was obtained.[572] He would never be close to the hands-on supervision of the orphanage because he was absent from it most of his time in America. Bethesda would always be on his heart, however. He remained its greatest ambassador wherever he went.

---

569 Henry, 91.
570 Fish, 126.
571 Ibid., 126.
572 Ibid., 126.

15

Opening Other Tabernacles

and Solidifying the Work in England

(1752-1754)

Whitefield faced new challenges when he returned to England after having been gone for only a few short months. Although he expected to return to America shortly, he had to delay that trip.

Whitefield was concerned about the Calvinistic Methodist movement. He was not there in person to be a strong leader in the movement on a continual basis because of his trips to America, Scotland and other places. The Lady Huntingdon had lent her support to the preachers in the movement as she had to him.[573] Howell Harris, the recognized field preacher in the movement after Whitefield, conducted several meetings with him in Wales, his native country. Each man shared a strong kinship and admiration.[574] Harris showed courage and boldness by going into the fields with the gospel, and he was already out there when Whitefield began his ministry as a field preacher. In Whitefield's absence, Harris had been the leader of the Calvinistic Methodist movement, but now Whitefield was keenly aware of concerns regarding Harris's leadership.[575]

---

573 Dallimore, vol. 2, 309-310.
574 Fish, 128, 129.
575 Dallimore, vol. 2, 298.

When an angry mob attacked Harris in Bala, Wales, his head was bashed with a rock, and by his own admission, he was not the same afterward. According to Dallimore, Harris began to travel with a female prophetess and relied more on impressions and prophetic pronouncements than on Scripture.[576]

Most Calvinists were against strong impressions or casting lots, such as the Moravians and John Wesley used for discerning God's will. Although Whitefield had used impressions he thought to be of the Lord in the beginning of his ministry, he had mostly ceased doing that. Jonathan Edwards had been concerned with his sense of impressions he claimed from the Holy Spirit. Whitefield's impressions supposedly were bathed with prayer and the Scripture. Some of his early impressions had been tempered by age and experience.[577] These impulses were different than Harris who was relying on these sudden impressions for God's leadership.

As Harris became more eccentric, Whitefield was faced with the need to support and lead the movement. He devoted himself to reinforcing the preaching places where he had conducted many successful meetings, but his primary preaching spot was the Tabernacle, where many heard him regularly. Without rebuking Harris openly, Whitefield's presence became a solidifying work in the movement.[578] The people heard him gladly and were grateful that the void in leadership was filled.

The refurbished and enlarged Tabernacle in London gave Whitefield a central preaching point and a permanent place for gathering.[579] Lady Huntingdon was its chief benefactor as well as other chapels.[580] He didn't give up field preaching, but the Tabernacle was the building that highlighted Whitefield's lasting legacy as a structure in England. The large crowds attested to his continuing popularity.[581]

Belden gives a time-frame of the other tabernacles built. He recounted:

> **Next in historical sequence was the commencement by Whitefield of two Tabernacles at Bristol—the first in 1752 at Kingswood, the second in 1753 at**

---

576 Ibid., 298.
577 Marsden, 211-212.
578 Dallimore, vol. 2, 301.
579 Wakley, 189-190.
580 Gledstone, 287-288.
581 Ibid., 271.

Penn Street. The Kingswood cause has a unique fame, for strictly it goes back to the meeting-room of 1741 which sprang directly from that first attempt of Whitefield's at open-air preaching, which took place at Rose Green, only a stone's throw from Hanham Mount, the scene of the second preaching. In the school-room of the present Kingswood Tabernacle, Bristol, there is to be seen a tablet with the inscription: "This building was erected by George Whitefield, B.A., and John Cennick, A.D. 1741. It is Whitefield's first Tabernacle, the oldest existing memorial of his great share in the Eighteenth Century Revival."

This tablet was placed there on Saturday, May 3rd, 1913. Part of this building now used as a Sunday school was Mr. Whitefield's room. Thus, the very first meeting-room he caused to be built, and the one associated with the outstanding feature of his work—the "aeration of religion"—is the only original building still standing and it is still being used for the great original purpose. On July 13th, 1753, the foundation stone was laid of the Penn Street Tabernacle, more familiarly known as the Bristol Tabernacle.[582]

Gledstone described the dedication of the Tabernacle as Whitefield's main preaching chapel:

> With eleven hundred pounds in hand, he, on March 1, 1753, laid the first brick of the new Tabernacle, which was to be eighty feet square, and built round the old place. The ceremony was performed with great solemnity, and Whitefield preached a sermon from the text, "In all places where I record My name, I will come unto thee and bless thee." Three months later the Tabernacle was ready to receive its congregation; and he opened it by preaching in it morning and evening, to four thousand people or more.[583]

Whitefield also raised four hundred pounds from well-wishers to build four almshouses near the chapel—for "godly widows." They received half-a-crown a week from the sacrament money.[584]

The Tabernacle was always crowded when Whitefield spoke there, and it remained a continued evangelical presence through the providence of God into the 19th century.[585]

After the Tabernacle's ministry, Charles Spurgeon's Metropolitan Tabernacle arose as the dominant evangelical force and structure in London. It was as if the legacy was continued, especially with Spurgeon's strong Calvinistic doctrine and his admiration of Whitefield. He attributed Whitefield's influence as his single dominant human example of dedication to Christ and preaching the gospel of Christ. He

---

582   Belden, 196-197.
583   Gledstone, 288.
584   Belden, 288.
585   Ibid., 288.

remarked, "Other men seemed to be only half alive; but Whitefield was all life, fire, wing, force. My own model, if I may have such a thing in due subordination to my Lord, is George Whitefield; but with unequal steps must I follow in his glorious track."[586]

The order of service was generally the same in the Tabernacle. The congregation sang hymns, most of which were by Isaac Watts, and the Scripture was read and explained as a dominant part of the service. People would wait in line to hear Whitefield preach, as they longed to hear his vivid descriptions of biblical characters and his examination of the true importance of a passage in his preaching.[587] They knew God was moving in the Tabernacle, and they sensed His presence when they came.

Other preachers filled the pulpit when Whitefield was away. Howell Harris was a dominant force in the early days of the Tabernacle. James Hervey, Whitefield's old Oxford friend, spoke there, as did John Cennick in the early days before his death. William Grimshaw spoke there before he became a pastor of his own congregation. Cornelius Winter spoke there and became one of Whitefield's closest associates in the later years. The seaman, Torial Joss, was introduced at the Tabernacle in the last decade of Whitefield's life. Joss would preach for him in his absence or when he was too weak to speak. He was one of Whitefield's trusted supporters and friends.[588]

When he was absent, Whitefield often wrote, inquiring about the Tabernacle's services. When he was there, his presence brought a note of authority to the movement, and people flocked to hear him. During the winter months, when outdoor preaching was almost impossible, he and his wife spent the time in London.[589]

Others were indirectly influenced by Whitefield and ministered in other areas. Whitefield influenced John Newton, the famous pastor at Olney. Dallimore revealed the way Newton had exposure to Whitefield in his conversion:

> **This demand came chiefly from spiritual enquirers. Wherever he went people sought him with the question, "What must I do to be saved?"**

---

586 Dallimore, vol. 2, 534.
587 Belden, 288.
588 Fish, 175-176.
589 Ibid., 131, 149.

When the requests were too many he announced certain hours of certain days which he would set aside for meeting with such persons, but in many instances, so urgent was their sense of need, that they tried to come at all hours and he was frequently deprived of sufficient time to eat and sleep. ...We notice in this regard the statement made by John Newton. Newton's conversion may have been assisted, to some extent, by the reading of Whitefield's sermons. It is certain that when, sometime later, he experienced the call of God to the ministry, he felt a deep longing to hear Whitefield preach and to talk with him personally.[590]

The Tabernacle featured services held two or three times a day. Whitefield preached early in the morning, as he had done when he was a young man to the miners in Kingswood.[591] During his ministry, many hungered to hear the gospel. They came to hear him preach even as his messages continued for more than an hour and sometimes longer when he preached inside.[592] The Tabernacle was a sanctuary of the gospel for many years when Whitefield was in his glory and maintained a ministry that continued into the 19th century.[593] Whitefield's health necessitated his speaking once a day. It was difficult for him to accept his inability to preach at the Tabernacle when he was extremely sick and bed-ridden for long periods of time. The services continued on with a worthy associate filling the pulpit, although many desired to hear Whitefield.[594]

Lady Huntington was moved to sponsor the construction of other meeting places when she saw the strength of the Tabernacle's ministry. She saw the potential of the Tabernacle's ministry replicated in other places and regions.

These chapels were regarded as places to hear the gospel and specifically Whitefield, when he was in town. The chapels helped solidify the work by giving the preachers, sponsored through Lady Huntingdon, a visible presence. It was a place to speak and minister, as did Wesley's ministers in similar places preaching on a consistent basis.[595]

---

590   Dallimore, vol. 2, 291.
591   Tyerman, vol. 2, 625.
592   Dallimore, vol. 2, 485.
593   Ibid., 546-547.
594   Fish, 168.
595   Dallimore, vol. 1, 358-359.

The Tottenham Road Chapel was dedicated and opened in 1756. According to Gledstone, "It became 'the mother of many chapels and the birthplace of many souls". [596]

Whitefield had preached here when he was unable to travel since it was close to his London residence. He continued his preaching ministry here into the last decade of his life. The chapel still stands today and contains many Whitefield artifacts seen as a lasting testament to the "Grand Itinerant's" ministry. [597] Whitefield's chair, though originally in the Tottenham Chapel, now resides in the pulpit area of Rodborough Tabernacle, in Gloucestershire.[598] He would sit there while waiting to speak or when he was too weak to stand. He prayed and prepared his heart there before he gave a divine summons. An inscription on the chair reads:

> If love of souls should e'er be wanting here
> Remember me, for I am Whitefield's chair,
> I bore his weight, was witness to his fears,
> His earnest prayers, his interesting tears;
> His holy soul was fired with love divine;
> If thine be such, sit down and call me thine[599]

The inscription is a fitting tribute to Whitefield's passion for souls and preaching the Word of God to people.

Scotland called again for Whitefield with the news he was back in England, prompting many invitations to come preach the gospel. Whitefield did not disappoint when he visited his brethren to the north and was the catalyst of awakening once again. The Scotland tour was a welcome respite from his furious preaching tour of England. Although, he became ill there, he still endeavored to preach at every open door available to him, returning to England to rest and recuperate.[600]

Something in field preaching invigorated Whitefield.[601] It demanded more of him than preaching inside buildings, despite several chapels built

---

596   Gledstone, 301.
597   Wakeley, 333.
598   Digby James, editor of Quinta Press in Shropshire, England informed me the chair had been moved to the Rodborough Tabernacle in Gloucestershire. James' pictures were used in this work and his collection reveals the chair in the Rodborough chapel.
599   Wakeley, 333.
600   Tyermen, vol. 2, 311.
601   Fish, 169.

for him to preach in. The commanding speaker still loved the outdoors and loved to see the crowds amassed, even with the curious coming only to ridicule.[602] All were confronted with the gospel, including drummers, trumpeters, mimics, and those who came only to throw stones. In some incidences, they had a change of heart and were captivated by the message. In other situations, they were miraculously halted from disrupting the meeting and his preaching.[603] Whitefield loved to see the intervention of the Lord and the conviction He brought to people's hearts.

The many meetings in which Whitefield spoke were a tribute to his tenacity and courage to keep going when others would have wilted under pressure or fatigue. At times, he longed to ease up, but the inescapable calling God had placed on his life and the many invitations that came his way drove him and kept him going. The movement was reaching maturity as evidenced by the continued reception Whitefield received when he went throughout England.[604] Chapels built, preachers sent out, and the cause of Christ exalted sustained the awakening movement, while a fraternity of itinerant preachers spawned continued the leadership of the awakening.

Others came forth in both continents to provide leadership and stability to the work God was doing. Whitefield had popularity on both continents and probably had more close friends on both continents than any other man of his time. He longed to return to America again and work with his friends there in an evangelistic effort, but the trip had been delayed for almost a year and a half because of the pressing concerns for the work in England.[605]

The work at Bethesda was better organized and its stature was rising as an integral part of the new colony of Georgia. James Habersham's leadership stability at Bethesda allowed Whitefield to delay his return to

---

602 Philip, 497.

603 Ibid., 281.

604 Whitefield's maturity in relating to more groups of people, growth of the Calvinistic Methodist movement and steady ministry spanning two decades about this time accounted for his continued popularity.

605 This observation is made based on Whitefield's popularity in America, the invitations he received through preachers like Tennent and Davies visiting him in England. The concerns of the leadership of Calvinistic Methodism and other obligations delayed his anticipated trip.

America. His status as roving ambassador for the school had served the orphanage well.[606]

Part of the problem of not being close to Bethesda and its operation was the distance from New England and the great receptivity Whitefield enjoyed there. The invitations constantly came for him to preach there, distracting him from going immediately to Bethesda on his return to America. He was always gathering orphans, but usually, would dispatch them at Charleston and go on his way to fulfill his obligations to preach.[607]

Even when Whitefield was not in America, he was thinking of the work at Bethesda and constantly carried on correspondence with his friends in ministry there. Christmas of 1753 found him entertaining two of his dearest friends from America: Gilbert Tennent and Samuel Davies. They discussed a future trip there and were full of plans for his return visit.[608]

Whitefield's style of preaching was never completely duplicated, although these men shared his passion for evangelism and preaching. He was unique in the gifts and calling God had given him.[609] Henry described Whitefield's style as attractive because of the "intensely confessional character of his preaching."[610] The American preachers, Tennent and Davies, were his strong allies in America. When he preached there, it aided their ministries immensely. Tennent came from a pious family of preachers, with their training grounds at the Log College. Davies' preaching was dynamic and stirring, his preaching style was described as a "dying man preaching to dying men."[611]

Both Tennent and Davies longed for Whitefield's return to America but the return to Bethesda was postponed because of Whitefield's

---

606   Cashin, 66-68.

607   Fish, 136. Whitefield repeated this pattern several times in various trips to America.

608   Philip, 416.

609   This observation is based on John Newton's description of Whitefield's preaching stating in the introduction of this work. Tyerman, vol. 2, 624-625. Newton had many opportunities to experience Whitefield's preaching, being associated with him in the formative years of his ministry when he followed the famous evangelist with great admiration.

610   Henry, 178.

611   C.E. Autrey, *The Great Awakening: A paper at The Awakenings Conference*, (Golden Gate Baptist Theological Seminary, Mill Valley, CA), 1980.

previous preaching obligations in England. The charter for Bethesda was attained in England, permitting him to focus on America again.[612] The orphanage's permanent status secured, the school was not to be without future struggles. However, Bethesda's immediate future was on safe footing.

America awaited Whitefield's return, and when he came back, he would be a wiser, more mature leader. He was almost 40 when he wrote continual admissions in his correspondence that he had been too harsh in his criticism of schools, churches and clergy. He still blamed the spiritual shallowness in England and America on the lack of scriptural teaching in the pulpit. Eventually, he saw that his generalizations of all clergy were not true. Whitefield realized and admitted his pride and arrogance in making allegations that were basically truthful, but not totally correct.[613] England would miss him, but America would welcome him with open arms. The anticipation of Whitefield's return visit to America would soon be experienced through the joy of his preaching in the New World. The population expected him to come preaching again with power.

---

612   Gillies, 208.
613   Haykin, 34.

16

BECOMING A FAVORITE SON

IN NEW ENGLAND

(1754-1755)

WHITEFIELD LEFT ON HIS FIFTH VOYAGE FOR AMERICA, March 7, 1754. He took with him a group of orphans bound for Bethesda.[614] The hard life they would find in America, in the settlement of a new colony would be better than the life they were leaving behind in England.

The voyage to America was by way of Lisbon, Portugal. On Whitefield's first voyage to America, the ship had stopped in Spain, where he became acquainted with the pageantry and gaudiness of Catholicism. He saw this perceived superstition first hand in processions and reenactments of the crucifixion of Jesus and the death of St. Francis of Assisi. The evangelist concluded the pageantry reflected a hollow show, rather than a legitimate expression of internal spiritual commitments. "Vast are the outward preparations," he wrote in one letter. "Altars upon altars are erected. Penitents upon penitents are lashing themselves: but what I want to have erected and adorned is an altar in my heart and the blows and lashes I desire to feel are the crucifixion and mortification of the old man and his deeds. Without this, all is mere parade."[615]

The observant preacher saw in the formalism an outward show of religion. This external religion had plunged England into spiritual

---

614   Fish, 136.
615   Ibid.,137.

decay through rituals, devoid of spiritual life. The awakenings sweeping England and America featured a return to true religious affections, touching the heart and leading to a changed life. The revivals went beyond a performance type of religion that Whitefield found through Catholicism in Portugal.

Whitefield was glad to be on the sea again, headed to Charleston. The voyage took only six weeks and was calm in comparison to other voyages.[616]

When they arrived in Charleston, Whitefield wanted to go to Bethesda, but he had many invitations to preach in New England. His long absence from America led him to go to New England where he had his greatest results.[617] The ministries at Bethesda and New England represented two contrasting styles. He had a burden to help the poor and the unfortunate in the orphanage, yet he also felt led to itinerant preaching in the open fields and to large crowds.

Whitefield went with the orphans from England to Bethesda, but stayed there only a short time to find how the orphanage was doing and see how the supervision of it was going.[618] James Habersham had acted as governor of Georgia until the new governor John Reynolds assumed the position. Habersham's appointment says something of the stature and the trust the colony had in him. He had steadily risen in prominence since he had come to the colony as administrator of the fledgling orphanage.[619] Whitefield had sent a letter of congratulations to John Reynolds, in Georgia declaring: "May the King of kings, enable you to discharge your trust, as becomes a good patriot, subject, and Christian!"[620]

Whitefield was ready to preach to the huge crowds that undoubtedly would flock to hear him. He traveled on the ship, Deborah, from Charleston to New York, where he was reunited with his old friends, the Tennents.[621] He went to New Jersey College to receive a Master of Arts degree after several meetings and preaching opportunities there.[622]

---

616 Ibid.,138.
617 Ibid.,138.
618 Ibid.,138.
619 Tyerman, vol. 2, 335.
620 Ibid., 335.
621 Ibid., 333.
622 Ibid., 334.

This award showed the esteem New England had for him. The academic world had warmed up to him after he had confessed that his early journals had been too harsh and hasty in his judgment of established clergy and teachers. The formerly opposed evangelist would ingratiate himself to Harvard in a generous gesture on a return trip.

Whitefield revisited places of fruitful past meetings and was as popular as he had ever been. The awakening in New England had cooled some, but religious fervor was still everywhere. Jonathan Edwards had been forced to resign from his church because of a communion dispute after 23 years of faithful ministry.[623] The news was probably a shock to Whitefield, who learned that Edwards was continuing to minister faithfully to the Indians in the pioneer town of Stockbridge. He viewed Edwards' action as a tribute to his resilience.[624]

Whitefield returned to Philadelphia, ministering again in one of his favorite places for preaching in America and in the meetinghouse constructed for him in 1740. It had become a school at Franklin's suggestion, and it eventually became the University of Pennsylvania. The building was the first of many housing the fledgling school. The response to Whitefield's preaching was warm, and people flocked from the city and surrounding countryside to hear him preach. Franklin and Whitefield's philanthropy to the school was greatly appreciated by students and residents of Philadelphia.[625]

The fifth visit to America featured continuing dialogue concerning the new birth and Franklin's need for it in his life.[626] Franklin admired Whitefield's Christian influence and benevolent spirit in traveling throughout the colonies. He even suggested that Whitefield go to Ohio with him for the establishment of a new colony and the settlement of many God-fearing pioneers.[627] The prospect excited Whitefield, but his growing concerns from all directions prevented him from seeing Franklin's idea brought to fruition.[628] Franklin by all indications, was still unconverted, but at the same time remained a loyal supporter of

---

623   Marsden, 361.
624   Ibid., 364.
625   Ninde, 157.
626   Dallimore, vol. 2, 446.
627   Ibid., 448.
628   Fish, 139.

Whitefield because of the good he did in the colonies.[629]

Health concerns were again taking their toll on Whitefield, although he was only forty. He was afflicted with cholera, a disease that made him deathly ill, after a week in Philadelphia. As he recovered and regained his strength, he went back to preaching once a day. When he was fully recovered, he set out for Boston.[630]

Whitefield began to see the fruit of his labor in America. The preaching tours were primarily productive in conversions and general awakening in certain areas. Belcher described a chance meeting with a fellow minister who recalled Whitefield's memories of his early ministry in Philadelphia. The story illustrates his abiding influence in America through the years:

> During this first visit of Mr. Whitefield to Philadelphia, another interesting circumstance occurred. Whitefield preached one evening standing on the steps of the court-house, in Market-street, which became, as we have said, his favorite spot during that and subsequent visits. A youth some thirteen years of age stood near him, and held a lantern for his accommodation; but becoming deeply absorbed in the sermon, and strongly agitated, the lantern fell from his hands and was dashed in pieces. Those near the boy, observing the cause of the accident, felt especially interested, and for a few moments, the meeting was discomposed by the occurrence. Some fourteen years afterwards, Mr. Whitefield, on his fifth visit to this country, was visiting St. George, in Delaware. He was one day riding out with the Rev. Dr. John Rodgers, then settled as the minister at St. George's, in the closed carriage in which Whitefield generally rode. Mr. Rodgers asked him whether he recollected the occurrence of the little boy who was so affected with his preaching as to let his lantern fall. Mr. Whitefield replied, "O yes, I remember it well; and have often thought I would give almost anything in my power, to know who that little boy was, and what had become of him." Mr. Rodgers replied with a smile, "I am that little boy." Mr. Whitefield, with tears of joy, started from his seat, took him in his arms, and with strong emotion remarked, that he was the fourteenth person then in the ministry whom he had discovered in the course of that visit to America, in whose conversion he had, under God, been instrumental.[631]

The health problems Whitefield encountered hindered some of his ministry, but he had fully recovered when he came to Boston, where huge crowds attended his meetings. He preached in four church buildings to multiple services of packed houses. At 7 a.m., many came

---

629   Whitefield and Franklin carried on positive correspondence until Whitefield's death. Franklin also spoke of Whitefield's positive influence after he died.

630   Ibid., 158.

631   Belcher, 110-111.

to hear him, crowding the churches with as many as 3,000 people. He had to climb in the building through a window to preach to the crowds thronging one church.[632]

The congregations in Boston loved him, and the excitement of the messages he brought was constant throughout the city. Even ministers who were formerly cold to him warmed up to him. His persistence in coming to America, his softer tone toward the clergy, his experience and his work with the orphanage accounted for this greater receptivity. The meetings were displays of God's power as people were converted and lives were changed.[633] In describing the conversions in Rhode Island and Boston he says, "... souls fly to the gospel, like doves to the windows. Opposition seems to fall daily."[634]

Describing the response of people of New England to his messages, he writes, "In Philadelphia, New Jersey, and New York also, the great Redeemer caused his word to run and be glorified."[635] The freedom to preach and response of the people were great features of these meetings. Whitefield loved preaching in America because of this great receptivity and the Christian influence in the colonies. The influence reborn in the awakening strongly revived interest in the Scripture and the power of the gospel.

Ninde referred to Whitefield's admiration of the Sabbath observance in Boston:

> Nothing in America impressed Whitefield more happily than the way in which the Sabbath was observed, especially in New England. He often referred to it in letters to English friends. Even in a city as large as Boston, the stillness was almost deathlike. Everyone who could do so went to church. There was no strolling, and if a group happened to linger on the street for conversation, they were quickly dispersed by a vigilant constable. Some of the clergy were so strict that they refused to baptize babies born on Sunday.[636]

Whitefield spoke in Rhode Island where he had preached before. He was able to travel by horseback from Boston and back again and thrilled to the results of his preaching. He exclaimed:

---

632   Dallimore, vol. 2, 371.
633   Huge crowds, such as the ones in Boston all over New England indicating Whitefield's continued popularity.
634   Gillies, 212.
635   Ibid., 371.
636   Ninde, 133.

> Surely my coming here was of God. At Rhode Island, I preached five times. People convened immediately, and flocked to hear more eagerly than ever. The same scene opens at Boston. Thousands waited for, and thousands attended on, the word preached. At the Old North (church), at seven in the morning, we generally have three thousand hearers, and many cannot come in.
>
> Convictions fasten and many souls are comforted... I preach at the Old North and the New North (churches). Mr. Pemberton and Dr. Sewall continue to pray for me.[637]

In New Hampshire, he also spoke to big crowds. The spiritual climate in New England allowed for awakening and conversion that followed Whitefield wherever he preached.[638]

Whitefield turned his attention south and made plans to return to Bethesda. He stayed at Bohemian Manor in Maryland, an estate granted by Lord Baltimore.[639] These accommodations were better than the humbler ones he had encountered when he had slept on a bedroll in the wilderness areas and other unusual primitive settings.[640] Whitefield was like the apostle Paul: through his many travels and the varied experiences he had in the places he stayed or the people he encountered (Phil. 4:12). Whitefield's flexibility in many situations accounted for the success of his meetings.

Whitefield used Christmas Day from this august residence to reflect on his ministry and write to Lady Huntingdon. He had a willingness to go to heaven, but also a hunger to do God's will:

> I am now forty years of age, and would gladly spend the day in retirement and deep humiliation before that Jesus, for whom I have done so little, though He has done and suffered so much for me.
>
> About February, I hope to reach Georgia; and at spring, to embark for England. There, dear madam, I expect to see you once more in this land of the dying. If not, ere long, I shall meet you in the land of the living, and thank you, before men and angels, for all favors conferred on me. Tomorrow, God willing, I move again. Before long, my last remove will come; a remove into endless bliss.[641]

---

637 Tyerman, vol. 2, 335.
638 Fish, 141.
639 Ibid., 141.
640 Gledstone, 129-130,
641 Ibid., 141-142.

Whitefield knew God had given him a task, and he was aware of the glory awaiting him that seemed nearer than ever because of his persistent health problems and the furious pace he drove himself.

On his way to Georgia, Whitefield preached in Virginia, a usual stop on his way south where he enjoyed speaking and where he always wished to spend more time. His illness in New England had hindered him from coming earlier. Instead, he preached in only a few places for several days.[642] He recorded the response to his preaching as the same during other times in New England. He exclaimed, "What a wide and effectual door might have been opened here, as well as elsewhere, rich and poor flock to hear "the everlasting gospel."[643] He felt a sense of urgency to reach Georgia, and he departed sooner than he would have wished.

One struggle Whitefield championed in Virginia was the cause of religious freedom. Tyerman reveals how he assisted his friend Samuel Davies in this struggle:

> For nearly eight years Samuel Davies had been laboring here with self-consuming earnestness. His eloquent, faithful and powerful preaching had been bitterly opposed; but it had also been attended with great success. His home in Hanover was about twelve miles from Richmond; and, as early as 1748, he had collected seven congregations, which assembled in seven meetinghouses duly licensed, some of them, however, being forty miles distant from each other, in three years he had obtained three hundred communicants and had baptized forty slaves. He had a long controversy with the Episcopalians, who denied that the English Act of Toleration extended to Virginia; and with great learning and eloquence, he had contended the point of Virginia with the famous Peyton Randolph, the first President of the American Congress. During the first visit to England in 1754, he had obtained, from the English Attorney-General, a declaration that Toleration Act did extend to Virginia, which of course, gave him greater confidence in the legality of his proceedings.[644]

Whitefield stood by Davies in this great cause of religious liberty. The cause became a source of controversy the next two decades in Virginia, especially with the Baptists.[645]

---

642 Ibid., 142.

643 Tyerman, vol. 2, 338.

644 Ibid., 338.

645 This fact is verified by the imprisonment of Baptist preachers attempting to preach in 1769 without a license by the colony. Virginia only recognized Episcopal churches as legitimate and did not recognize the Baptist preachers as valid clergy.

When Whitefield did make it to Georgia, nine months had transpired since he had landed back in America. The persistent time spent in America is a tribute to Whitefield's self-abasement. He would have been more famous and influential had he stayed in England.[646] He decided, however, to pursue the path of pioneer missions instead. The path wore him out physically, but endeared him to the people of the American colonies. Whitefield had no regrets about being gone from his native country for an extended time. The numerous trips to America and the path he trod through the colonies when he arrived, were remarkable.

Whitefield's intentions to spend more time at Bethesda did not materialize, with little known about the few months he spent there. He was concerned that the lack of a strong economy had hindered Georgia as a whole. The debtor's colony had not risen to the level of prosperity as in other colonies.[647] The problem affected Bethesda, where even though the orphan population exceeded one hundred children, it was still not self-supporting. Farming had helped some, and James Habersham and Francis Harris (another worker at Bethesda) had earned income from their own business.[648] It was a sacrifice to work at Bethesda, but the rewards of seeing children become productive members of the new colony were worth it.[649] Harris was also elected the speaker of the first Georgia-elected assembly on January 14, 1751.[650]

When a steady stream of new converts came from the orphanage because of the heavy indoctrination into the Christian faith, Whitefield was even more aware that the children's spiritual lives were worth all the labor and support the orphanage generated.[651] These children grew up to be productive members of the colony also. Cashin reported, "Peter Tondee and Richard Milledge, both alumni of the orphan house, joined with Benjamin Shetfall to organize the Union society that supported laborers in Georgia. April 23rd is still celebrated every year by the society

---

646 John Wesley had more popularity eventually because of his longevity in age and ministry and because of his staying in his native country for his entire ministry. Had Whitefield chose the same path no doubt the popularity of his preaching and associations would have given him many years of successful ministry in England.

647 Cashin, 66.

648 Ibid., 64-65.

649 Ibid., 67.

650 Ibid., 67.

651 Ibid., 67.

as founding day, with the Feast of St. George. The founders of the society intended to lobby for the interests of the artisans of Savannah: carpenters, blacksmiths, tailors, and bricklayers, among whom were many young men formerly of Bethesda."[652]

The staff was trimmed in spite of the moderate success of the school and its continued promise in succeeding years. The cost of the support for the orphanage in the New World was an unknown variable; from its beginning, constant support was always a need.[653] Whitefield's plans for the orphanage brought stability to it, and Bethesda was on its way to becoming a strong institution.

As war was brewing with England and France, Whitefield knew the suspected war would be a long one, making his chances to travel back to the New World almost non-existent. He believed he could help the school more in England by continually raising support for it there.

At the end of March 1755, he embarked from America and his beloved Bethesda.[654] The absence from his life-long work, his passion and responsive crowds in New England would represent the longest time he would ever spend away from the orphanage; the travel restriction because of The Seven Years' War became a reality and forbade him from coming to America in this period of time.

---

652   Ibid., 67.
653   Whitefield never ceased in his fundraising efforts for the school. Ministering in more established places which garnered greater financial support was much more productive economically and in its sponsorship.
654   Fish, 143.

17

SHUT UP IN ENGLAND,

HEALTH PROBLEMS, AND OPPOSITION

(1755-1763)

WHITEFIELD BEGAN HIS LONGEST MINISTRY SPAN for staying in his native country because of the Seven Years' War. The conflict with France and England made sea travel impossible. Several places in America were hot spots of war and unsafe for travel. He was unable to leave the country and minister in America. Confronting hecklers in a sermon was one thing, but armies with weapons were a danger not worth the risk. The civilian travel ban not only affected migration to America, but also brought sea travel to a halt.[655]

Cashin shared Whitefield was restricted from sailing, but kept in contact with Bethesda:

> George Whitefield had been frustrated in his efforts to return to Bethesda from England during the Seven Years' War. He could not obtain passage while enemy ships were on the prowl, but he did not forget Bethesda, however. In September 1756, he had an interview in London with newly appointed Governor Henry Ellis, informing him about the general conditions in Georgia and affairs at Bethesda in particular. He worried about Bethesda, but was relieved by reports that his family there were in no danger. By his preaching alone, he raised enough money in England to pay the obligations he had incurred on Bethesda's behalf.

---

655   Cashin, 82.

"Blessed be God," he wrote, **"that I can send you word, a never failing Providence has put it in my power to pay off all Bethesda's arrears."**[656]

Another reason Whitefield stayed in England was his health. The years of sea travel, preaching several times a day and land travels were taking their toll on him. He had to discontinue the furious pace he had kept because he suffered from fever, intestinal difficulties, respiratory problems and various other ailments. The lack of activity and constant bed rest changed his appearance to a more corpulent person. His pictures in later life did not resemble the appearance he presented as a young man full of enthusiasm and energy.[657]

Even though his wife's health was bad, Whitefield did not spend time solely with her. In the winter, he would be with her, but in the spring and summer months he was off on preaching tours in England, Scotland and Ireland.[658]

Although he was only forty-one, Whitefield felt older because of the wear he had put on his body, yet he refused to cut back. The pace he was trying to continue is revealed in a note from London: "On Thursday evening I came to town, after having preached about a hundred times and traveled about 800 miles. For more than ten days together I preached thrice a day. O, that I could preach 300 times!"[659] He revealed the physical strain he was laboring under:

> For near ten days past, I have preached in pain, occasioned by a sore throat, which I find now, is the beginning of quinsy [an inflammation of the tonsils]. The doctor tells me silence and warmth may cure me: but (if I had my will) heaven is my choice, especially if I can speak no longer for God on earth. However, painful as the medicine of silence is, I have promised to be very obedient, and, therefore, I have not preached this morning.[660]

Toward the end of 1755, Whitefield returned to London. His throat, although not healed, had recovered to the point his voice was restored. He was excited at the prospect of preaching at the new chapel built at Long Acre. Located in London's West End near the theaters, it was accessible to the fashionable members of society where Whitefield had

---

656 Ibid., 82.
657 Gledstone, 300.
658 Fish, 149-150.
659 Ibid., 145.
660 Ibid., 145.

an important ministry. Although he preached only twice a week, they still flocked to hear him, and hundreds of people had to be turned away. There was simply not enough room for the crowds longing to hear the evangelist speak.[661] Whitefield had a more localized ministry in London, in the months of severe weather, and ventured out to the fields again particularly in the warm weather months.[662]

As Whitefield confined his preaching in England, he didn't have to travel long distances. The extended trips had weakened him in the past because of various hardships. He was able also to visit historic places in his native country during his preaching tours. He preached at Kidderminster where Richard Baxter served.[663] He visited and preached in Bedford where John Bunyan ministered. Wakeley shared of his time at Bedford:

> Whitefield was a great admirer of John Bunyan, in Bedford, the immortal dreamer, the author of the "Pilgrim's Progress" and wrote a preface to his works.
>
> Whitefield had the high honor of preaching in the pulpit of John Bunyan, in Bedford, in 1758. He had been ill for several days, but, occupying the pulpit where that unyielding champion of the cross had stood, we wonder not that his spirits were revived, and that he received a fresh anointing for his mighty work. We are not surprised that he wrote, "O how sweet communion did Bunyan enjoy in Bedford jail! I really believe a minister will learn more by one month's confinement than by a year's study."[664]

William Grimshaw, a faithful pastor from Haworth began to travel and preach with the evangelist.[665] Their ministry together began during Whitefield's confinement in England. There were many unusual events in his sermons, but one was extremely shocking. Belden shares the immediate account of this experience:

> As he proceeded to preach, a wild shriek of terror arose from the midst of the crowd. Grimshaw plunged into the crowd to see what had happened and presently cried "Brother Whitefield, you stand amongst the dead and the dying, an immortal soul has been called into eternity; the destroying angel is passing over the congregation. Cry aloud and spare not." One of the audience had fallen dead! Once again, Whitefield began and read his solemn text once

---

661   Ibid., 145.
662   Ibid., 150.
663   Andrews, 183.
664   Wakeley, 285.
665   Dallimore, vol. 2, 286.

more. Immediately, from a spot close by Lady Huntingdon and Lady Margaret Ingham who were in the crowd, a second dreadful shriek arose. Imagine the awe that swept over those thousands as they learned that another soul had been called to its account. Yet, Whitefield calmly continued and finished his sermon in a strain of tremendous eloquence.[666]

It is hard to imagine this scene. The shock of seeing someone die in the congregation certainly must have brought sudden conviction on those at the meeting. Definitely, it was an unforgettable experience in itself, bringing urgency to their need for Christ's salvation.

Whitefield began to preach regularly in a new chapel at the Long Acre district of London.[667] The dramatic preacher (known for his public criticisms of the theater) knew that many in the audiences had come from the nearby theater performances, adjacent to his Long Acre Chapel. He incorporated these criticisms of the theater into his Long Acre sermons. The evangelist did not hold back in his criticisms. He described the actors and their performances as the "devil's children grinning at you."[668]

Some members of the actors' guild took steps to disrupt the services. Soon, every sermon he preached was interrupted by people outside the building ringing bells, banging drums and singing rowdy songs. When Whitefield continued to preach and people continued to listen to him, the hecklers began throwing stones at both Whitefield and those supporting him. It was a very chaotic scene. "Drummers, soldiers, and many of the baser sort had been hired by subscription. A copper furnace, bells, drums, clappers, marrow bones and cleavers and such like instruments of reformation have been provided for and made use of them, from the moment I have begun preaching to the end of my sermon," he wrote.[669]

Stout observed how Whitefield was very competent to handle hecklers and those deliberately trying to disturb his preaching: "When Whitefield was most successful, the mob was most determined to silence him. Instead, he would patiently wait the rioters out; sometimes singing, sometimes praying, until they grew bored or tired, and then he would pick up where he left off."[670] The disturbances at the Long

---

666   Belden, 186.
667   Gledstone, 296.
668   Stout, 239.
669   Ibid., 362.
670   Ibid., 177.

Acre chapel were different than any he had previously experienced. These disturbances were a real concern given the continued opposition. The instances caused Whitefield to write the King for protection. He described the scene he encountered:

> By these horrid noises, many women have been almost frightened to death, and mobbers encouraged thereby coming and rioting at the chapel door during the time of divine service, and then insult and abusing me and the congregation after it hath been over.
>
> Such a scene, at such a juncture, and under such a government, as has been transacted in your lordship's parish, in the house or yard of Mr. Cope, who, I hear, is your lordship's overseer, ever since last Twelfth-day, I believe is not to be met with in English history.
>
> Not content with this, the chapel windows, while I have been preaching, have repeatedly been broken by large stones of almost a pound weight, which, though leveled at me, missed me, but sadly wounded some of my hearers. If your lordship will only ride to Mr. Cope's house, you will see the scaffold, and the costly preparations for such a noise upon it, as must make the ears of all who shall hear it to tingle.[671]

Early in April 1756, Whitefield received three anonymous letters threatening that his preaching in Long Acre stop or he would have a "certain, sudden and unavoidable death." He knew his enemies were plotting to kill him.[672]

To compound the conflict and continue opposition to his preaching, Whitefield had begun to speak more vocally against the danger of the Roman Catholic influence and the differences he felt were evident in the Church of England. He expressed support for the Anglican Church, but cautioned against Catholicism. Undoubtedly, this criticism was brought on by the war against Anglican England and Catholic France. Expressing his support as a loyal, though dissenting, churchman, he addressed a church official regarding this difference and support of the church:

> I shall continue to adhere to her doctrines, and pray for the much wished-for restoration of her discipline, even to my dying day. Fond of displaying her truly Protestant and orthodox principles, especially when Church and State are in danger from a cruel and Popish enemy, I am glad, my lord, of an opportunity of preaching, though it be in a meeting-house; and I think it discovers a good and moderate spirit in the Dissenters, who will quietly

---

671 Dallimore, vol. 2, 384.
672 Fish, 146-147.

attend the Church service, as many have done and continue to do at Long Acre Chapel, while many, who I suppose style themselves her faithful sons, by very improper instruments of reformation, have endeavoured to disturb and molest us.[673]

Many have preferred to believe Whitefield's opposition to Catholicism was direct and purposeful. Fish described the hostility against Whitefield for defending his native country:

> Some Roman Catholics reacted to a pamphlet Whitefield wrote about the ongoing war between England and France. When war broke out between France and England in 1755, the Church of England had been Protestant for generations. The official French church was Roman Catholic. In supporting Britain's war against France, Whitefield charged Catholic priests with inciting Native American tribes to kill English subjects in America, mentioning "shocking accounts of horrid butcheries and cruel murders committed." He charged Roman Catholic countries with martyring thousands of innocent Protestants.[674]

Lambert suggests Whitefield's publication stirred up fear of the war abroad in America coming to England when he disclosed:

> On the eve of the Seven Years War, he struck a patriotic theme in a pamphlet that went through six editions in a single year. The work warned against a possible invasion of England by the Catholic French and denounced French and Indian attacks on British North America. Viewing the war as a struggle between good and evil, Whitefield called on Protestants of all denominations to shield themselves with the safest moral armor; true Protestant principles.[675]

Caution and warnings arose due to Whitefield's accusations, but nothing further materialized. The pamphlet fueled more opposition toward Whitefield, hurting him later when he preached in Catholic Ireland. The English Catholics' anger over the pamphlet was noticeable and led to opposition in Ireland.[676]

Whitefield decided to build another chapel in London at Tottenham Court Road. He chose the site because it was close to Long Acre, so people attending services there would be able to reach it easily. At the same time, it was far enough away from the theater district to discourage the rioters from disrupting his sermons.[677]

---

673   Gledstone, 298.
674   Fish, 147.
675   Lambert, 203.
676   Fish, 147-148.
677   Wakeley, 266.

In November of 1756, Whitefield held the first meetings in the new facility. He loved the building and even offered it as a burial place for the Wesley brothers, whose headquarters, an old cannon factory, was not suitable for burial. Relationships had thawed with the Wesleys and Whitefield. Unfortunately, Whitefield's early death and the Wesleys' longevity disrupted these plans. Although these arrangements were never finalized, he had generously made the offer to them.[678]

The futility of ministering at Long Acre made the Tottenham Chapel more manageable in comparison. Although intervention by the King to protect the congregation from the violence of the hecklers undoubtedly discouraged the would-be assassins, Whitefield saw it would be unwise for him to try to carry on permanently at Long Acre.[679]

The initial size of Tottenham Chapel eclipsed the size of the current building. Dallimore reveals how it was added to the initial building and became quite an impressive facility a short while after its initial construction: "...an addition was built, thus giving the total edifice a breadth of seventy feet, a length of 127 feet and a height to the top of the dome of 114 feet. In this completed form it was the largest non-conformist church building in Britain and probably in the world."[680] The building, though damaged and replaced, still houses a church that meets there and contains artifacts of Whitefield's ministry.[681] Whitefield spoke of the chapel as "the most promising work the Redeemer ever vouchsafed to employ me in."[682] Shortly after it was opened he gave this report: A neighboring doctor hath baptized the place, calling it "Whitefield's Soul-Trap."[683]

The doctor came to Christ through his exposure in "Whitefield's Soul-Trap" since it was instrumental in his salvation experience. He later testified that he found salvation there, through hearing the famous evangelist. He described the evangelistic setting of the new chapel and his response to that testimony:

---

678   Fish, 149.

679   Dallimore, vol. 2, 386.

680   Ibid., 386.

681   Dallimore, *George Whitefield: God's Anointed Servant in the Great Revival of the Eighteenth Century*, 187.

682   Ibid., 387.

683   Ibid., 387.

"A thought came into my mind last Sunday morning to go and hear you at the new tabernacle, and to see what sort of a place it was. In one part of your discourse, my heart trembled, and the terrors of the Lord came upon me. I then concluded that I must prepare for hell, and that there was no hope of salvation for me"...Whitefield says, in speaking of this letter, "I have answered my new friend, and pray the Friend of sinners to make the chapel a "soul-trap" indeed to many wandering creatures." [684]

Wakeley illustrated the effect of Tottenham Chapel, thus earning the name it was called:

It so proved, for multitudes were there converted and brought to "walk in the light," and when God writeth up the people it will be said that this and that man was born-again there. There Garrick heard him with profound admiration; there Shuter heard him, and was almost persuaded to be a Christian. Some of the nobility became his stated hearers, and took seats in the new chapel. [685]

Whitefield often preached there when in London, and every time there was fruit through conversions. He called it his "Bethel." [686] The name itself reveals a distinction from the Tabernacle and its history of birthing other new chapels, as Tyerman describes: "From this venerable sanctuary, sprang separate congregations in Shepherd's Market, Kentish Town, Paddington, Tonbridge Chapel in the Euston Road, Robert Street, Crown Street and Craven Chapel." [687]

After Whitefield's passing, a ministry continued at the chapel under John Fletcher. Wakeley shares Whitefield's influence on Fletcher and his continuance of a strong biblical preaching at the chapel:

Mr. Whitefield and Rev. John Fletcher were intimately acquainted, and were excellent friends. In 1766 Whitefield invited Fletcher to come to London and preach in his chapel. Fletcher accepted the invitation, to the great delight of Whitefield, who wrote thus: "Dear Mr. Fletcher has become a scandalous Tottenham Court preacher...Were we more scandalous more good would be done... Still a shout of a king is heard in the Methodist camp." No wonder Whitefield rejoiced, for Mr. Fletcher was one of the purest and truest ministers that ever adorned the Church. Fletcher testifies not only to Whitefield's great oratorical powers, his "divine pathos," but also to his fidelity. [688]

---

684 Wakeley, 266.
685 Ibid., 266.
686 Ibid., 266.
687 Tyerman, vol. 2, 374.
688 Wakeley, 284.

Fletcher long remembered Whitefield's choice phrases:

> "How often," he says, "has that great man of God, the truly Rev. Mr. Whitefield, said to his immense audiences, "You are warned. I am clean of your blood. I shall rise up as a swift witness against you, or you against me, in the terrible day of the Lord! Oh, remember to clear me then!" And is not this just as if he had said, "We shall all be justified or condemned in the judgment by what we are now doing, I by my preaching, and you by your hearing? And will any say such expressions are only flights of oratory? If they do they will touch the apple of God's eye."[689]

Whitefield continued to spend the winter in London with his wife. Not only did he speak fifteen times a week at Tottenham Chapel and the Tabernacle, but he also oversaw the building of twelve alehouses where many poor widows lived rent-free.[690] The evangelist tried to maintain contact with friends in both America and the Georgia orphanage, but because of the war of England against France, it took longer for the ships carrying his letters to cross the Atlantic.

In 1757, Whitefield did not start his preaching tours until late April. After traveling for sixteen days, he arrived in Edinburgh, where he stayed for a month. This was his ninth visit to Scotland, and, as he had done before, he held open-air meetings each morning and evening.[691]

Reconciliation with Ralph Erskine quelled any organized opposition against his ministry in Scotland.[692] A deeper friendship was established with John Gillies, (his earliest biographer).[693] Gillies shared how, "… the whole multitude stood fixed, and hung upon his lips. Crowds grew steadily "larger than ever."[694]

From Edinburgh, the evangelist traveled to Glasgow where he raised money for relief work with the poor in the city. Afterwards, Whitefield decided to go to Ireland.[695]

"He arrived in Dublin in mid-June and continued preaching there for several weeks. Most of his preaching took place in arrangement with the

689   Ibid., 284.
690   Fish, 149.
691   Ibid., 150.
692   Stout, 208.
693   Ibid., 208.
694   Ibid., 208.
695   Fish, 150.

Wesleyan societies, scattered throughout the area."[696] The co-operation was evident in Ireland with Whitefield and the Wesleys.

Fish described the scene in Whitefield's Ireland ministry erupting in a violent incident, almost costing him his life:

> Whitefield was already well-known for his anti-Catholic statements. One afternoon an enraged mob, finding Whitefield alone in the field, began stoning him. Whitefield kept walking, but was soon covered with blood. He was hit on the head by several stones...
>
> When he reached town he found a Methodist minister's house and managed to stagger into the door. Temporarily, Whitefield found safety. But the mob surrounded the house, and the minister's wife was terrified that the people would destroy her home. Still, she didn't want to send Whitefield on his way to certain death. Just at that moment another Methodist preacher with two friends pulled up in front of the house in a coach. Whitefield leaped from the doorway to the vehicle and was carried away to safety, but for the rest of his life he carried a large scar near one of his temples.[697]

Gledstone noted the contrast with Scotland and Ireland in their response to Whitefield's preaching. The responses were drastically different, illustrating the divergent responses to gospel preaching Whitefield encountered wherever he went:

> In May 1757, Whitefield was the most highly honoured man in Edinburgh, the next month he was mobbed and stoned in Dublin. Several Scotch towns had previously made him a freeman, and this year he received the marked respect of the ministers of the General Assembly and of the Lord High Commissioner.[698]

In Ireland, it was a different story. The opposition to his preaching turned violent and he encountered the opposite response in the attack on his life when he escaped from the angry mob in the coach:

> ...he found a brief shelter in a minister's house, and some friends bringing him a coach, he rode "in gospel triumph" through the oaths, curses, and imprecations of whole streets of Papists. This assault, of which he bore the scar the rest of his life, was entirely owing to his having exhorted all ranks to be faithful to the Lord Jesus Christ and to King George, not to having spoken against Popery.[699]

In reflecting on the incident, Whitefield was resilient, yet he realized the attack had led to a near death experience where he barely avoided

---

696 Ibid., 150.
697 Ibid., 151.
698 Gledstone, 309.
699 Ibid., 309.

fatal consequences. Whitefield did not preach in Ireland to stir up trouble. He shared his honest intentions of going there and ministering:

> When I came to Ireland, my intention was to preach the gospel to all and if it should ever please the Lord of all lords to send me thither again, I purpose to pursue the same plan. For I am a debtor to all of every denomination and have no design, if I know anything of this desperately wicked and deceitful heart, but to promote the common salvation of mankind. The love of Christ constrains me to this.[700]

In a letter written to a friend soon after this event, he revealed what the experience did to him physically: "I received many blows and wounds; one was particularly large, and near my temple; I thought of Stephen, and was in hopes, like him, to go off in this bloody triumph to the immediate presence of my Master."[701]

Fish disclosed, "In spite of the attack, Whitefield continued to preach in Ireland for another three weeks. He never returned to the country again. In August he left for London, where he spent the rest of the year."[702] His stint and reception in Ireland were limited compared to Scotland and the America colonies.

Whitefield began to fully realize his physical limitations, but somehow, he continued. In a letter to Professor Francke of Halle University in Germany, he wrote, "In the winter I am confined to this metropolis; but to my great mortification, through continual vomiting, want of rest and of appetite, I have been reduced for some time to the short allowance of preaching only once a day except Sundays when I generally preach thrice."[703]

"These concessions were only the beginning for Whitefield, learning to deal with physical weakness. As soon as spring arrived, he left London, determined to preach through England and Wales."[704] He tried to return to his old pace to no avail. ... "in Wales, he was so weak that he couldn't even sit up in bed when people came to visit him."[705]

Navigating the roads also became a burden to him that further added

---

700 Belcher, 336.
701 Ibid., 337.
702 Fish., 152.
703 Ibid., 152.
704 Ibid., 152.
705 Ibid., 152.

to his physical difficulties. He tried various helps to aid him. He had "changed from riding horseback to a two-wheeled chaise." He said, "The Welsh roads played havoc with the chaise." Whitefield's obstacles became more challenging because of his physical difficulties.[706] He revealed his physical limitations while traveling:

> I am just now setting forward towards London, but fear I cannot reach it before Sunday. My chaise wanted repairing here. O how good hath Jesus been to a worthless worm! Once a day preaching, I can bear well; more hurts me. What shall I do with the Chapel and Tabernacle? Lord Jesus, be thou my guide and helper! He will! He will! Send word to the Tabernacle that you have heard from me. We have had sweet seasons.[707]

Because travel became more treacherous for Whitefield due to his physical infirmities, he purchased a four-wheeled vehicle that made travel more comfortable. "He was frequently called back to London to preach in the Tabernacle or Chapel" because no one was available to preach or "some administrative crisis had erupted."[708]

Circumstances restricted Whitefield and his boundless ministry in a way he had never encountered before. He was still carrying the burden of his health and the barrier of not being able to travel to Georgia and the colonies to continue the ministry. The evangelist rejoiced because of the advancement of the gospel in England even with continued opposition, as Tyerman described:

> Whitefield began the year 1757 with mingled feelings. He rejoiced because of the prosperity of the work of God; he was distressed by political and Church contentions and he was full of care respecting his distant Orphan House. Hence the following selections from his letters:
>
> LONDON, January 12, 1757.
>
> "A wide door seems to be opening at Tottenham Court Chapel. The word flies like lightning in it. O that it may prove a Bethel—a house of God—a gate of heaven! I believe it will. As the awakening continues, I have some hopes that we are not to be given up. Alas! Alas! We are testing and contesting, while the nation is bleeding to death. We are condemning this and that; but sin, the great mischief-maker, lies unmolested, or rather encouraged by every party.[709]

---

706 Ibid., 152.
707 Tyerman, vol. 2, 454.
708 Fish, 152-153.
709 Tyerman, vol. 2, 389.

When Whitefield began to experience personal losses, grief was added to the personal load he was carrying. He learned of the death of his friend Jonathan Edwards, who had been serving as the new president of Princeton University for only a short time.[710]

Whitefield had always admired Edwards, although he spoke in his pulpit only a few times. Edwards had strongly influenced him in having an evangelistic ministry along with a heavily Calvinistic theology. The twin combination is thought to be difficult by various theologians. Edwards and Whitefield were able to hold these views and office with a great deal of success.[711]

A letter to an ailing friend, James Hervey, December 19, 1758, revealed Whitefield's remorse over his inability to follow the path of Edwards and apparently Hervey's also. He offered this comfort to Hervey in light of his pending demise:

> And is our dear friend about to take his last flight? I dare not wish you return to this vale of tears. But our prayers are continually ascending to the Father of our spirits that you may die in the embraces of a never-failing Jesus, and in all the fullness of an exalted faith. Oh when will my time come! I groan in this tabernacle, being burdened, and long to be clothed with my house from heaven.[712]

On Christmas Day James Hervey died, adding to Whitefield's discouragement because of the death of many of his closest friends. The thought of never seeing them again in this life caused him great remorse, but Whitefield sought to carry on in his weakened condition.[713] Dealing with physical infirmities created a trying time for him.

The Seven Years' War continued and featured the crowning of a new King in 1760, George III, who pursued the war to its successful conclusion.[714] The King's aggressive policies in stepping up involvement in the colonies by a stronger presence and taxation were later regretted by Whitefield and caused anxiety, as mentioned in his letters to his friend Benjamin Franklin.[715]

---

710 Fish, 153.

711 Calvinism's view of particular election has used been by its opponents to say it restricts reaching all people because of its emphasis on a certain number of people only being elected for salvation.

712 Fish, 153.

713 Ibid., 153.

714 Ibid., 153.

715 Dallimore, vol. 2, 452.

The year also featured the lampooning of Whitefield in the play, *The Minor*, written by Samuel Foote. Dr. Squintum (a hypocritical preacher in the play), ridiculed him, making fun of the squint he had in his eye, a result of his bout with the measles as a child.[716] It seemed Whitefield's preaching against the theater at Long Acre had come back to haunt him. Although many leaders of English society called the play blasphemy, it drew large crowds and was a financial success for Foote.[717]

Henry explained that the intent of the play was to ridicule Whitefield, making his work seem hypocritical at best, and not taken seriously at worst. He stated, "In *The Minor*, which appeared at the height of Foote's popularity, the Methodists were made the butt of his wit."[718]

The drama was first acted in July 1760. A month later, Whitefield wrote to a friend: "Satan is angry. I am now mimicked and burlesqued upon the public stage."[719] The piece scandalized the Methodists, particularly Lady Huntingdon. She waited on both the Duke of Devonshire (then Lord Chamberlain) and David Garrick. She made an unsuccessful effort to have the license canceled and the production of the play suppressed.[720]

The play served only to remind Whitefield and those impacted by him of his monumental ministry. There was still a wide divergence of opinions toward Whitefield's ministry even with his aging, and his settling down to certain chapels and permanent preaching stations. Whitefield's ministry had the effect of a lightning bolt, and individuals were still divided because of his ministry and the message he preached. Cashin declares the mixed reaction to him:

> By this time, Whitefield had achieved celebrity status, and fame brought both praise and ridicule. The poet William Cowper wrote in admiration, "He followed Paul; his zeal and kindred flame, His apostolic charity the same…" Fashionable society tended to ridicule rather than praise him. Alexander Pope called Whitefield "a braying ass." On the other hand, the great actor David Garrick once said, "I would give a hundred guineas if I could only say 'O!' like Mr. Whitefield."[721]

---

716 Fish., 154.
717 Ibid., 154.
718 Henry, 159.
719 Ibid., 159.
720 Ibid., 159.
721 Cashin, 83.

In November of 1761, Whitefield caught a severe cold, further weakening his health. He was a bedridden invalid, unable to preach at all. His physical condition was a hard blow for Whitefield emotionally. He did recover completely by following the doctor's instructions. Although he had recovered, when he started preaching in the spring, he had a relapse.[722]

In 1762, Whitefield was weaker than he had been the year before. Many believed he was near death. He halted his preaching tour and went to Rotterdam, Holland to recuperate; there his health did improve significantly.[723] Cutting back his preaching schedule and then halting it totally was one of the most difficult decisions in his life. It was a needful act though, if he was to have any hope of future ministry.

Whitefield realized steps had to be taken to relieve the burden he was laboring under. He recovered to a level of normal function as the Seven Years War ended. He designated the management of the Tabernacle and chapel to three friends who had assisted him in ministry: Robert Keen, Charles Hardy, and Mr. Beckman. "O that the Lord may incline your hearts to accept this trust!" he told them. "It will take off this ponderous load that oppresses me so much."[724]

Whitefield now saw his improved health, the end of the war, and the delegation of the management of the Tabernacle and Chapel.[725] These events gave him an opportunity to return to America after eight long years of being in England. He wished to see his old friends with whom he had little communication with during the war. He had plans for Bethesda's future and wanted to preach to the receptive crowds he always found in America. He felt he was once again able to the task.

---

722   Fish., 154-155.

723   Ibid., 155.

724   Ibid., 155.

725   All these events allowed Whitefield the freedom to return to America. They represented what his ministry would be in the final decade of his life. It was more of a maintenance ministry instead of a pioneering one the way his ministry had been in early years.

18

ACCEPTANCE IN AMERICA

AND FUTURE PLANS FOR BETHESDA

(1763-1764)

Whitefield preached again in Scotland in first few months of 1763. He tried returning to England after a grueling ministry, but his body did not cooperate. He was too weak to board the Jenny in April 1763. He delayed his trip back to his native country to try to regain his strength. The evangelist finally returned and did recover somewhat to continue his ministry, although severely hampered by his decline in health.[726]

Whitefield was determined to attempt a voyage on the Fanny, destined for Virginia on June 4, 1763, because the Seven Years' War had ended and his extended rest in England. He wanted to return to America and minister there but had been prevented from going for eight years.[727]

A voyage across the Atlantic was possibly the worst action for his health. He described his physical struggles and his slow recovery that accompanied his preaching tour in Scotland:

> For some weeks, I was enabled to preach once a day when in Scotland, and, I trust, not without Divine efficacy. But, being taken ill of my old disorder at

---

726 Fish, 156-157.
727 Ibid., 157.

Edinburgh, I had to remain silent for near six weeks, and sometimes I thought my intended voyage would be retarded, at least, for one year longer. Having however, obtained a little strength, I embarked, for the eleventh time, in the ship Fanny, and I have not been laid by an hour through sickness, since I came on board…Often, have I thought of my dear London friends, when I guessed they were assembled together; and as often prayed, when I knew that they were retired to rest, that He, who keepeth Israel, would watch over them, and make their very dreams devout.[728]

The ship arrived in Virginia on August 24. Whitefield wished to visit Bethesda, but the summer heat prevented him from going immediately. Instead, he turned northward and headed for Philadelphia, longing to see his lifelong friend Benjamin Franklin, but found he was inspecting the post offices throughout the colonies on an 1800-mile trip. He reacquainted himself through his preaching with many of the residents in New England, while waiting to meet with Franklin. Because it had been eight years since they had seen Whitefield, they were shocked at his corpulent and visibly weakened appearance.[729]

When Franklin did return from his trip, he was happy to see his favorite evangelist. During his time with Franklin, Whitefield probably shared his plans to develop Bethesda into a college. Franklin received these plans with great enthusiasm, since he felt an institution of higher learning was needful in the South and particularly in Georgia, the poorest of the colonies. After Whitefield's death, Franklin was appointed a trustee of Bethesda, maintaining an interest in the school although it never became a college.[730] Whitefield's health forced him to delay his trip to Georgia. He had to wait until he was stronger because the doctor would not allow him to travel.[731] When Whitefield was able to return to Bethesda, Franklin agreed to lend his support to the cause of Bethesda becoming a college and speak in favor of Whitefield's dream becoming a reality.[732]

Whitefield had broached the idea of a college for several years in England and America. The college was thought to be a work in progress so he continued to explore the level of interest throughout the colonies

---

728 Tyerman, vol. 2, 465.
729 Fish, 157.
730 Gledstone, 343.
731 Ibid., 158.
732 Stout, 259.

and his homeland. Whitefield's vision had obvious implications; he wanted it to be a place for training ministers, a place that would rise to the caliber of the other schools in New England and Virginia that had been established longer and had served those areas well.[733] He shared his vision for the school with the Governor, the Council, and the Assembly in Georgia, and found positive responses.[734]

Whitefield slowly recovered and was able to preach in many familiar places. The people were glad to hear him, but were preoccupied with other matters as well. The perceived encroachment of England into the colonies was getting worse. The British had fought for seven years and seemed destined to control the colonies in a way they previously had not maintained.[735]

Whitefield moved northward, preaching at New Jersey College, and then he moved on to New York, preaching there for seven weeks.[736] He also raised money in New York for the Benjamin Wheelock School for Indians in Lebanon, Pennsylvania. A local newspaper reported how he had preached charity sermons and took up offerings for the poor and Wheelock's school. The offering for Wheelock was double the amount of the other offerings.[737]

Whitefield's help for Wheelock's school was a sign of his keen interest in the gospel going to Native Americans. He was intensely interested in the school and visited it in 1764. He had always supported these types of enterprises to open up new avenues for sharing the gospel. He had been at the forefront of expanding its message with field preaching and considered it a seed-bed for the training of future missionaries to the Native Americans.[738] The support for the school continued through the benevolent evangelist's sponsorship back in England during the succeeding years. In 1767, Rev. Nathaniel Whitaker and Occum, an Indian preacher from Wheelock's school, visited England. Whitefield arranged for their meetings with influential people while they were in England at the same time and introduced them to people of wealth.

733 Cashin, 85.
734 Tyerman, vol. 2, 483-484.
735 These were the understood purposes of the British government from parliamentary history and leaving British troops to man forts in the colonies.
736 Tyerman, vol. 2, 469-470.
737 Dallimore, vol. 2, 427.
738 Hardy, 270.

The evangelist raised large sums for the college and of him it was said, "Whitefield took it (the school), by the hand, and commended it to the kind charity of his English friends."[739] From the New York area, the preacher longed to be in Boston, where he had enjoyed an enormous response eight years before.

As Whitefield made his way toward Boston, his recurring health problems continued to plague him. He wanted to go to Canada, where he had never been, but his health prevented him from going northward. He remained for several days in Portsmouth, New Hampshire where he was unable to get out of bed. A stalemate confronted the evangelist in his ministry at this point. He had to rest and recuperate to have any semblance of a ministry in Boston. Whitefield did get better and his time spent in Boston was basically without complications.[740]

Four years before, a fire damaged Boston and it left inhabitants homeless, disrupting normalcy. After learning of the devastation, Whitefield immediately began to sponsor a fund to help those victims of the catastrophe.

His first order of business was to give the total of the Boston charitable fund to the mayor. This act of generosity increased his stature enormously with the residents of the oldest and most influential city in the colonies.[741]

Whitefield contacted friends about helping Harvard replace their library that had been lost in the fire, in addition to the fund he delivered for the citizens of Boston. Although they were already in the process of replacing the library, Whitefield's donation was a significant gesture.[742] The action was a far cry from his first time at the school in the early 1740s when he was a young preacher. Hardy elaborates about the donation and Whitefield's newfound acceptance at Harvard and Yale:

> He nearly always preached in Cambridge whenever he was in Boston and always with marked acceptability. When the Harvard Library was destroyed by fire, Whitefield at once appealed to his English friends, and the response was so generous that the officers of the college voiced their appreciation in a very hearty vote of thanks.

---

739 Ibid., 270.
740 Fish, 162.
741 Dallimore, vol. 2, 428.
742 Ibid., 429.

Whitefield's relation to Yale College was rather more intimate than with Harvard but he lacked definite opportunity to contribute to its welfare. On one occasion after preaching there, "The President came to me as I was going off in the chaise, and informed me that the students were so deeply impressed by the sermon that they had gone into the chapel and earnestly requested me to give them one more quarter of an hour's exhortation."

Whitefield was more than happy to patch up old differences at Harvard. Remembering the school's opposition to itinerant preaching, seeming lack of devotion, and burden for evangelism of the students, it was a complete turnaround. The maturity of the evangelist, the wide acceptance of his ministry and his generosity went a long way extinguishing any differences that had existed between the school and Whitefield.

The President of Harvard expressed the new receptivity of the school and the city. His endorsement was a sign Whitefield had matured and was a trusted leader to many, even in the colleges where he had once had a shaky relationship. By 1764, the controversy of the Great Awakening had diminished, with the school and town exhibiting friendliness toward the evangelist.[743]

Another encouraging feature of Whitefield's ministry on this trip to America was the reception of ministers who previously had opposed him. They were no longer hostile to him and many preachers were referred to as "New Lights."[744]

The popularity of Whitefield's ministry in Boston resulted in the residents of the town refusing to let him depart after his scheduled time there. A huge crowd literally followed him out of the city and forced him to turn back.[745] New challenges for this controversial city were to come with the British oppression and their resistance. The residents clung to the preacher as a bridge to England from America, instead of erecting a wall of separation they had previously begun to build. He did stay eight more weeks and immensely enjoyed his time within the city.[746]

Whitefield's popularity was enormous in America. Philip reveals his stature as equal to George Washington:

---

743   Ibid., 271.
744   Mahaffey, 52-53.
745   Fish, 162.
746   Ibid., 162.

> **It is worthy of American Christians, that whilst they would feel at a loss between two of their patriarchs—one of whom had shaken hands with George Washington, and the other with George Whitefield—with which to shake hands first,—they would venerate most a veteran who had known both. Again I tell them, that I have not dared to do Whitefield full justice, in reference to their father-land, because I was afraid of doing injustice to their fathers, who acted with him, and followed after him.[747]**

Whitefield made his way back to Philadelphia, but eventually turned south. As he turned south, he had fellowship with "New Light" preachers all the way through Virginia and into South Carolina.[748] Whitefield shared the openness of many in America with John Wesley and impressed him with the importance of the work. Because of Whitefield's excitement, Wesley sent more missionaries to America in the following years.[749]

In December, Whitefield finally made it to Bethesda. He was happy to celebrate the Christmas season at the orphanage with the children and staff.[750] The decade's absence represented the longest time span he had been away from the orphanage. He found it in good financial shape primarily because of a legacy it received in Scotland from a wealthy donor.[751]

He shared his plans for a college with the leaders of the school and asked the governor for 2,000 acres of land for the future college. Whitefield's dream for a college was as alive as it had ever been, as he shared it with the growing population. He felt he could get support from the colony for the college since it would represent educational advancement for Georgia.[752] Habersham's influence as president of the governor's council was providential also in gaining support for a college.[753] Unfortunately, the decision on the orphanage to become a college would have to wait for several years.

---

747 Philip, 472.

748 Since the Church of England, clergy had ostracized him from several churches in his denomination. Out of necessity, Whitefield reached out to what many would have considered evangelical churches today.

749 Fish, 181.

750 Gledstone, 322.

751 Dallimore, vol. 2, 471.

752 Tyerman, vol. 2, 479-481.

753 Ibid., 480.

Governor Wright received Whitefield's request for land and transmitted his request of a college to Parliament with positive support for the school. Parliament delayed the decision because they questioned the affiliation of the president with the Church of England.[754]

Cashin related the problem of the college president's affiliation requirement with the Church of England; Whitefield believed the president should come from any denomination. The division was a sticking point:

> The facts of the college negotiations, to the extent that Whitefield knew them, were straightforward. He gave a copy of the petition to Granville Sharp, the clerk of the King's council, who delivered it to the Archbishop of Canterbury, Thomas Secker. Whitefield gave a second copy to Lord Dartmouth and Dartmouth referred it to the same archbishop, Thomas Secker. That dignitary wrote Whitefield to inquire, "Would the president of the college be a member of the Church of England? What endowment could be provided?" Whitefield answered candidly. He could not require the head of the college to be a minister or even a member of the Church of England. He said that the College of New York (Columbia) had been retarded in its progress by a similar provision. He preferred to build his college on a "broad bottom." The College of Philadelphia and the College of New Jersey had no such qualifications, yet they prospered nonetheless...Whitefield said he had no intention of becoming the chief administrator: "Alas! My shoulders are too weak for the support of such academic burden." In fact, he would not even nominate the first president himself. Rather, he would ask Lord Dartmouth to name the first head of the college.[755]

The granting of land was a blessing and Whitefield was more successful in securing this acquisition. There was land aplenty and the worthy purpose of having an educational place in Georgia was well received. Cashin explained the agreements leading to the proposed use of the land:

> As for the endowment, Whitefield could guarantee an income of £500 a year. Besides that, Bethesda owned nearly 2,000 acres in the immediate vicinity, plus two thousand acres on the Altamaha. The Reverend Bartholomew Zouberbuhler willed another 1,000 acres on the condition that slaves there be taught religion. In 1767, Bethesda owned thirty slaves. Negro children belonging to the college would be instructed by one of the students in lieu

---

754 Ibid., 481.
755 Cashin, 88.

of tuition. Whitefield intended to instruct Indian children also. The whole [effort] would be a free gift to the colony of Georgia.[756]

The orphanage was still supervised through the excellent administrative skills of James Habersham, although he was playing more of a limited role in its operation and more of a role in the government of the colony.[757] Because of the danger of winter crossings, Whitefield was determined to stay several months at Bethesda and review its operation, resting from his busy schedule since arriving in America.[758]

When the orphanage underwent a successful audit of its books, Whitefield was satisfied that all debts had been paid and Bethesda had some cash available because of crops and lumber harvested from the preceding year.[759] The orphanage's firm establishment was refreshing.

Smallpox had recently taken the lives of six slaves and four orphans, but Whitefield was pleased that in twenty-four years of existence only four other children had died. The small number of deaths was a remarkable record, because childhood diseases were rampant in the colonies with no effective treatment. These diseases normally would spread more quickly in an institutional environment like the orphanage, so it was evident that the administration of the school maintained a healthy environment for the children.[760]

Whitefield enjoyed the relative quiet of the orphanage and focused on managing its needs instead of simultaneously carrying the responsibilities of itinerant preaching, running two churches in London and raising funds for various charitable causes. The books were audited and everything found in order.[761] He continued correspondence with friends, including Franklin, about his plans for a school at Bethesda.

Whitefield stayed at Bethesda through the spring and into the early summer. He hated to leave beloved Bethesda, but after almost a year in America, he felt it was time to return to England. He set sail on June 9 and arrived there July 7. After being on the sea for this long period of time, he was worn out, so he stayed in Falmouth for several days. He

---

756 Ibid., 89.
757 Ibid., 65-66.
758 Fish, 165.
759 Ibid., 165.
760 Ibid., 165-166.
761 Tyerman. vol. 2, 483-484.

wrote to Robert Keen, "I am very low in body and yet undetermined what to do. I must have a little rest, or I shall be able to do nothing at all."[762] This revealing statement in itself describes the physical and emotional dilemma plaguing Whitefield the last decade of his life.

---

762   Ibid., 166-167.

19

CHAPELS, SCHOOLS, & WORKERS

WHO CARRY ON THE LEGACY

(1764-1768)

THE SEVERITY OF WHITEFIELD'S TRIP TO AMERICA was realized as he returned to London. The possibility of making the journey again seemed remote. He did have hopes of a college at Bethesda and preaching connections to consider, so he attempted to improve his health, trusting the Lord to protect him and touch his ravaged body.

The smoky air in London irritated his respiratory problem, giving some truth to the belief that field preaching was a tonic for him physically, emotionally, and spiritually.[763] He continued to rest throughout the summer, the period he usually would be out preaching.

Whitefield did try to direct the efforts of the Tabernacle although he was no longer managing it. His securing speakers for both locations gave rise to others who assisted in ministry there. One of the first preachers to heed the call was Cornelius Winter, who eventually became a traveling companion. After returning from America, Whitefield came to the realization that he would no longer be able to travel by himself; he needed to have assistance to help him get medical attention if needed. Winter was to become a confidant and fellow traveler in his remaining

---

763   Fish, 169.

journeys.[764] Another traveling companion who helped was Richard Smith, accompanying him on his last trip to America.[765]

Winter, who fit the itinerant evangelist mold, got his start speaking at the Tabernacle. His destiny had been set through hearing Whitefield preach during the period in the rebuilding of the Tabernacle. Tyerman shared the influence Whitefield had on Winter:

> Cornelius Winter, then a boy in the thirteenth year of his age, was induced to hear Whitefield preach. Cornelius was an orphan, whose father had been a shoemaker, and his mother a laundress...He then became the inmate of a workhouse.... When his "schooling closed," he "had merely learned to write, without being set to put three figures together, or to learn one line in any of the tables."... However, he writes, "At last, I got to hear Mr. Whitefield, and was particularly struck with the largeness of the congregation, the solemnity that sat upon it, the melody of the singing, Mr. Whitefield's striking appearance, and his earnestness in preaching. From this time, I embraced all opportunities to hear him."[766]

Winter had a close association in his later years with Whitefield as his traveling companion, as well as Smith. Winter and Smith knew of the peculiarities, if not trademarks, of Whitefield's daily routine while traveling with him. He was always a neat person with perfect deportment in appearance and manners. He left his office and room the way he had found it. Everything had a place and he positioned objects in their place that had been misplaced, to the point of putting his gloves in a neat position on the table when he left the room. Whitefield went to bed at an early hour. When he had friends staying late, he would show them to the door no later than 10 p.m., reminding them it was time for all good men to go to their homes and get the rest they needed to employ in God's work in a wholehearted way.[767] Another personal preference in Whitefield's life was dining on cow's heel. He dined on this quite often; it was one of his favorite dishes though it would seem strange to some.[768]

A very revealing picture of Whitefield's preparation, study, and drama in preaching was recorded by Winter. His routine was seen in a way

---

764   Dallimore, vol. 2, 480.
765   Belden, 218.
766   Tyerman, vol. 2, 346.
767   Dallimore, vol. 2, 485.
768   Ibid., 485.

seldom captured and only by one like Winter who lived in his home, catching personal glimpses of him. This sketch gives a glimpse of the man communicating God's truth eloquently to the masses:

> The time Mr. Whitefield set apart for preparations for the pulpit, during my connection with him, was distinguished from the time he appropriated to other business. If he wanted to write a pamphlet, he was closeted; nor would he allow access to him, except on an emergency, while he was engaged in the work. But I never knew him engaged in the composition of a sermon, until he was on board ship, when he employed himself partly in the composition of sermons, and partly in reading the history of England. He was never more in retirement on a Saturday than on another day; nor sequestered at any particular time for a period longer than he used for his ordinary devotions. I never met with anything like the skeleton of a sermon among his papers, with which I was permitted to be familiar, and I believe he knew nothing of such a kind of exercise as the planning of a sermon.

He usually claimed retirement for an hour or two, before he entered the pulpit. Then, on the Sabbath morning especially, he was accustomed to have Clarke's Bible, Matthew Henry's Commentary, and Cruden's Concordance within his reach...

> His rest was much interrupted, and he often said at the close of an address, "I got this sermon when most of you were fast asleep." He made very minute observations; and in one way or another, the occurrences of the week, or of the day, furnished him with matter for the pulpit. ...I have known him, at the close of a sermon, to avail himself of the formality of the judge putting on the black cap to pronounce sentence. With his eyes full of tears, and his heart almost too big to admit of speech, he would say, after a momentary pause, "I am now going to put on my condemning cap. Sinner, I must do it. I must pronounce sentence upon thee." And then, in a strain of tremendous eloquence, he would recite our Lord's words, "Depart, ye cursed." It was only by hearing him, and by beholding his attitude and his tears, that the effect could be conceived.
>
> My intimate knowledge of him enables me to acquit him of the charge of affectation. He always appeared to enter the pulpit with a countenance that indicated he had something of importance to divulge, and was anxious for the effect of the communication. His gravity on his descent was the same...
>
> He was averse to much singing after preaching, supposing it diverted attention from the subject of his sermon. Nothing awkward, nothing careless appeared about him in the pulpit. Whether he frowned or smiled, whether he looked grave or placid, it was nature acting in him. Professed orators might object to his hands being lifted up too high, and it is to be lamented that in that attitude, rather than in any other, he is represented in print...

> I hardly knew him to go through a sermon without weeping, and I believe they were tears of sincerity. His voice was often interrupted by his affection; and I have heard him say in the pulpit: "You blame me for weeping, but I cannot help it, when you will not weep for yourselves, though your souls are on the verge of destruction, and, for aught I know, you are hearing your last sermon!"
>
> When he treated upon the suffering of our Saviour, it was with great pathos. As though Gethsemane was in sight, he would cry, stretching out his hand, "Look yonder! What is that I see? It is my agonizing Lord!"...[769]

The concern for the lost drove Whitefield in his evangelistic ministry and cannot be separated from his preparation and delivery of sermons. Belden shared the earnestness and energy of Whitefield in his zeal for souls:

> Nothing is more impressive in Whitefield than his consuming zeal for the saving of men. He was as ready to spend himself for the individual and for the few as for the vast congregation. His individual work must have been simply colossal, costing him, as it did so often, whole days of patient endurance, and leaving him scarcely any time even for food. As lesser ministers know, there is no work that can be so mentally and nervously exhausting as this. His Calvinism did not suffice to hinder his deep and passionate humanitarianism. He would, if he could, place the offer of salvation at the feet of all human beings on the face of the earth, whatever their ultimate fate might be.[770]

Those close to Whitefield the last decade of his life were able experience his devotion to his calling and godly habits till his life's end. Their insights are valuable in understanding the reason God used him so mightily. These traveling companions also offered a relative measure of safety, and Whitefield had assurance of their physical help whenever he needed it. Richard Smith's assistance was essential on his last preaching tour in America.[771]

As Whitefield continued to recover, he renewed his friendship with the Wesleys. When he dined with them, his appearance surprised them, because he looked like a man well beyond his years. Charles was especially surprised that his old friend looked so much older than fifty years of age.[772]

---

769 Tyerman, vol. 2, 510-511.
770 Belden, 234-235.
771 Tyerman, vol. 2, 598.
772 Dallimore, vol. 2, 353.

Whitefield clarified one final doctrinal point to allow him to utilize some of John Wesley's preachers. He learned Wesley did not believe in sinless perfection, the belief that one reaches a point of holiness as a Christian where he or she will never sin again. John Wesley denied the doctrine although one of his early assistants, George Bell and other members of the societies believed they were as "holy as the angels" and "incapable of sinning again."[773] Wesley encouraged the belief that a believer could reach a sanctification demonstrating spiritual maturity but did not hold to the extreme position of sinless perfection. Whitefield concentrated on the furtherance of the gospel instead of Wesley's disagreement on Arminianism and Calvinism. His actions proved his willingness to use Wesley's preachers who were plentiful because of the growth of the Wesleyan movement.

Tyerman gave Charles Wesley's impression of the meeting with Whitefield and his associates and his description of the importance of these leaders:

> "1767, August 18. Tuesday, I met in conference with our assistants and a select number of preachers. To these were added, on Thursday and Friday, Mr. Whitefield, Howell Harris, and many stewards and local preachers. Love and harmony reigned from the beginning to the end." ...A trio, like Wesley, Whitefield, and Howell Harris, were a sight worth seeing, three great reformers, because three great revivers of pure and undefiled religion. "Mr. Whitefield not only attended the conference, but also invited the preachers to the Tabernacle, ordered them to be placed round the front of his galleries, and preached a good sermon, to encourage them in their holy calling. When he had done, he took them to his house, by ten or twenty at a time, and entertained them in the most genteel, the most hospitable, and the most friendly manner."[774]

Whitefield's agreement with Wesley was realized by these actions that went beyond lip service.

Lady Huntingdon remained a strong ally of Whitefield and Calvinistic preachers, while favoring an alliance between Wesley and Whitefield in supporting each other's preachers.[775] She gave her support to other preachers and the orphanage, in Georgia. She hated to see Whitefield suffer through deteriorating health. A painting of

---

773   Fish, 170.
774   Tyerman, vol. 2, 531.
775   Dallimore, vol. 2, 463.

Lady Huntingdon, a tribute to her sponsorship of the orphanage, remained for many years in the main house at the orphanage.[776]

Whitefield started chapels that were practically supported in their construction by Lady Huntingdon. She also built her own chapels for the preachers she sponsored at Brighton, Norwich, Tunbridge Wells, and Bath, her home.[777]

A high point of Whitefield's ministry was when he was asked to preach the dedication sermon at the Countess' chapel at Bath, and being physically able to speak at this momentous occasion. God had used Lady Huntingdon as an instrument in the sponsorship of those leading the awakening. The final chapel dedicated in her hometown was a tribute to the power the gospel had through her preachers and their sponsorship by her. God got the glory, but He, in his sovereignty, had used this strange combination of nobility and profound preachers to awaken many to the gospel of Christ. They marveled that despite Whitefield's illness, he was able to deliver such an eloquent sermon.[778] Perseverance was woven into his character and would be until he died. He never let anything stop him from preaching the gospel; he would use any strength he had in him for that purpose.

New leaders arose to assist Whitefield in the work. These men, who had come to Christ in various ways, were destined to be his successors through their ministries. Each was unique in his style and background, but they all were committed to preaching the gospel and continuing the flame lit by Whitefield.

Torial Joss was a young man that God used to become Whitefield's successor at Tottenham Chapel. Whitefield supported him as a wonderful preacher. Dallimore described the evolution of Torial Joss becoming one of his trusted assistants:

> Joss' youth had been spent in much suffering—first as a sailor, then at the hands of the press-gang, and finally as a French prisoner of war. His first knowledge of the Gospel came by overhearing some persons talk about their conversion, which was followed up by his reading Bunyan. Thus he came to know the Lord and amidst terrible persecutions that followed he proved unflinching in his stand for righteousness.

---

776 Cashin, 107.
777 Gledstone, 323.
778 Tyerman, vol. 2, 490.

> For a time he was associated with one of Wesley's Societies in a sea-port village and did some preaching. Later he became captain of his own ship and because of his bold Christian witness the sailors termed it: "The pulpit."
>
> As the years passed Joss became strong in the Lord. He gained knowledge of the Scriptures and was known as a powerful and courageous Christian.[779]

Joss joined a Wesley society and began preaching in his free time, encouraged by Wesley to continue preaching. He was promoted to first mate of the ship and continued preaching every time the ship came to port. Joss later became captain and held regular worship services for the crew. Word of the Captain/Preacher reached Whitefield when he was headed for London.[780]

Dallimore describes the response to Joss's preaching:

> When Joss was thirty-four Whitefield had him preach at the Tabernacle. It was immediately evident that the hand of the Lord was upon him and Whitefield urged him to quit the sea and devote himself to Christian work. Determined, however, to take such a step only at the unmistakable call of God,...
>
> In London his congregations were crowds, and his sermons full of converting power. Four or five months every year he spent in itinerating regularly visiting Bristol, Gloucestershire and South Wales.[781]

He left the comforts of these congregations to pursue the ministry of a traveling evangelist the same way his predecessor Whitefield had done. He thus continued this tradition of being confined to one place and preaching from place to place, indoors and outdoors.

Whitefield took the initiative, giving Joss the opportunity to speak at the Tabernacle and entrusting the ministry at Tottenham to him. Hardy described his encouragement to Joss and his ministry:

> On his arrival, Joss was astounded to find himself announced by Whitefield to preach at the Tabernacle. Torial Joss made such an impression that Whitefield begged him to leave the sea and take to preaching altogether. Thus, in 1766, Torial Joss became one of Whitefield's assistants, and great crowds waited upon a ministry full of converting power and ripe with chequered and tragic experience. Four or five months each year, like Whitefield himself, Joss would be on itinerating work. In Wales, the people followed him in multitudes. He became known later as the "Archdeacon of Tottenham" because of his powerful ministry at Tottenham Court Chapel. There he died and was buried there in 1797.[782]

---

779 Dallimore, vol. 2, 467.
780 Fish, 175-176.
781 Dallimore, vol. 2, 467.
782 Hardy, 195.

Another similar conversion and call to ministry came from Captain Jonathan Scott, who commanded a regiment in the Seven Years' War. He contemplated his soul in the heat of battle. Hunting with some friends after the war, he found refuge in a storm at a farmer's cottage. The farmer witnessed to him of Christ's salvation and invited him to a nearby village church, where he was converted. He immediately started sharing the gospel with his soldiers. Many Christians encouraged him to start preaching. Whitefield invited him to the Tabernacle to preach. People were so moved by his message that he resigned his army commission to become one of his preachers and assisted in the work of the Tabernacle and Chapel.[783]

Rowland Hill was another preacher deeply influenced by Whitefield, who emulated him in many ways as Dallimore described:

> **Rowland Hill patterned his ministry after that of Whitefield. He preached in the open air, itinerated extensively, and after filling certain Church of England appointments he built a large nondenominational meeting house in London, the Surrey Chapel. The word "eccentric" has often been applied to him but it is misleading. He was a highly zealous and powerful preacher, he ministered constantly to great crowds, and Lady Huntingdon said he was the nearest to Whitefield of any preacher she ever heard.[784]**

Hill aided Whitefield in his work through the various ministry opportunities that Whitefield was enthusiastically relinquishing to him and others.

The long term solution to continuing the work of the awakening was finding and training more ministers God had called. A school for training ministers started at the ruins of an old castle Lady Huntingdon renovated in Trevecka, Wales. Her idea was to have young men God had called stay at the school for three years during their education process.

Each student received free education, room and board, and a suit of clothes each year. Graduates would be able to seek ordination either from the Church of England or from the Methodists.[785]

Whitefield did not continue the pace he had set in his early ministry. He relied on younger men trained at Trevecka to carry on the ministry

---

783   Fish, 176.
784   Dallimore, vol. 2, 469.
785   Ibid., 473.

he and others had begun.[786] Belcher described Whitefield's perseverance and plan to continue the itinerate ministry:

> Rest and quietness! With Whitefield, such things were impossible as long as he could move or speak. His fire must burn till its whole material was expended; his heart overflowed, and he must labor till his body sank under exhaustion. No persecution could appall him, no sickness could long keep him from his beloved engagements. He would preach till he died, being fully assured that his "labor was not in vain in the Lord."[787]

Although Whitefield continued to serve as long as the Lord gave him breath, he did realize the need to train younger men to succeed him and other leaders. These men were a part of the next generation who would inherit the last generation's glorious legacy. They were going to step in and hopefully continue the leadership in the awakening movement. Belden shared of their need for training:

> Many of the men engaged under his direction, and preaching in what was already called "Lady Huntingdon's connection," needed, as they well knew, a better education than they possessed. Hence her ladyship obtained a lease of an old structure, supposed to have been part of an ancient castle erected in the reign of Henry the Second. The date over the entrance, now almost effaced, is 1176. It was called Trevecka House, and was situated in the parish of Talgarth, in South Wales, and was for some time the residence of Howell Harris. This building was opened as a college for religious and literary instruction, and the chapel dedicated to the preaching of the everlasting gospel, Aug. 24, 1768. Mr. Whitefield preached from Exod. 20:24: "In all places where I record my name, I will come unto thee and bless thee;" and on the following Sabbath he addressed a congregation... "Other foundation can no man lay than that is laid, which is Jesus Christ." When speaking of the dedication of the college, Mr. Whitefield says, "What we have seen and felt at the college is unspeakable."[788]

Whitefield had high hopes for the school at Trevecka. He realized the pressing need for more ministers in the work. He had returned in the summer of 1768 from his fifteenth and final trip to Scotland where he was as popular as ever. He threw his support behind the school, realizing

---

786 The utilization of the younger ministers in the Tabernacle and Tottenham chapel were evidence of Whitefield's confidence in them and recognition of the limitations he had in the last few years of his life.

787 Belcher, 412.

788 Ibid., 413.

it was long overdue.[789] As every movement ages, it faces new challenges essential for its survival. One new challenge was a disturbing trend that had developed under the new wave of Methodist preachers. Many of the younger workers in Methodism chose to work in one parish and not be involved in itinerant ministry. Although their commitment to stay with one congregation was acceptable, Whitefield hated to see field-preaching become a thing of the past.[790]

Whitefield felt he must continue his ministry until God called him home. He believed others would replace his ministry and God would prepare future evangelist in schools like Trevecka.[791] The prematurely aging preacher longed to see the awakening movement continue in the hands of able ministers called of God, trained and fully able to preach the gospel of Christ. To this end, he labored in the last years of his life.

---

789 Dallimore, vol. 2, 370-371.
790 Fish, 174.
791 Dallimore, vol. 2, 473.

20

DEATH OF WHITEFIELD'S WIFE

AND FINAL GOODBYE TO ENGLAND

(1768-1769)

THE YEARS OF 1768 AND 1769 WERE ONES OF SAYING goodbye for Whitefield. He said goodbye to Elizabeth, his wife of twenty-seven years, and he bid farewell to his native country and his work there, never to return.

Whitefield knew the day was coming when his wife would pass away because she had experienced poor health for years. In the last decade of his ministry, she had not traveled with him at all. He would come home to her in the winter months, but she had seldom gone with him on his travels and had no longer gone to America.[792]

At times they were apart for a year or more. They had even separated on occasion; once when Whitefield had gone alone to Bermuda, Elizabeth stayed behind in Bethesda. She was always a dutiful wife when she accompanied him to the Tabernacle and chapels; she always stayed in the background.[793]

It is not known whether Elizabeth had understood the type of union she was entering when she married a global traveler. She must have lived

---

792   Fish, 149.
793   Dallimore, vol. 2, 223.

a lonely life separated from Whitefield for many months and even years at a time. Elizabeth had left a simple life in a Welsh village to marry one of the greatest preachers in history. Her new life was not easy and was far from what she was accustomed to. Whitefield's work to which God had called him undoubtedly made it difficult for him to love a wife while his primary concern was for the lost, but he possibly sought to love her with the love he exhibited for them. [794]

Elizabeth attended to Whitefield more during their travels together and whenever she went with him personally. They affirmed their love for one another in a quiet respect. It was not manifested as openly as it was treasured in their hearts. Whitefield must have sorely regretted leaving her for long periods.[795] Elizabeth understood her calling in their marriage and had endured these periods and poor health. Now her suffering was over.

We must not forget the heartache both Elizabeth and her husband had experienced in losing their only child John at four months. Whitefield had predetermined that John would be a preacher if God had willed it, a determination that God evidently had not willed.[796] Other attempts to have children had failed certainly resulting in much discouragement.[797]

Whitefield reduced his ministry opportunities in an effort be with Elizabeth more and to improve his own health. However, their being together more never became a reality. After he returned from his final trip to Scotland, Elizabeth took sick with a fever and never recovered. She died on August 9, 1768.[798] Whitefield mourned her passing and possibly wished he had been there more for her. He preached at Elizabeth's funeral a few days later. It was a sad time of mourning her passing, but also a glad time of knowing she was released from all the physical suffering she had experienced the last few years of her life. Belcher discloses Whitefield's sermon and remarks at his wife's funeral:

---

794 Ibid., 290.

795 Belcher, 136.

796 Dallimore, *George Whitefield God's Anointed Servant in the Great Revival of the Eighteenth Century*, 114.

797 Stout, 171.

798 Dallimore, vol. 2, 471.

> On the death of his wife somewhat suddenly, August 9, 1768, Mr. Whitefield himself preached her funeral sermon, from Romans 8:28: "And we know that all things work together for good to them that love God, to them that are the called according to his purpose." In describing her character, he particularly mentioned her fortitude and courage, and suddenly exclaimed, "Do you remember my preaching in those fields by the stump of the old tree? The multitude was great, and many were disposed to be riotous. At first, I addressed them with firmness; but when a gang of desperate bandits drew near, with the most ferocious looks, and horrid imprecations and menaces, my courage began to fail. My wife was then standing behind me, as I stood on the table. I think I hear her now. She pulled my gown"—himself suiting the action to the word, by placing his hand behind him and touching his robe—" and looking up, said, 'George, play the man for your God.' My confidence returned. I again spoke to the multitude with boldness and affection; they became still; and many were deeply affected."[799]

This story illustrates Elizabeth's fearlessness. Her preparation of gun cartridges on Whitefield's third voyage to America feeling an enemy ship was following them also demonstrated this fearlessness.[800] God had chosen to call Elizabeth home before him, and he acknowledged the providence of God. The "all things" were part of God's eternal plan, and, as she served God on earth, she would now be with Him in eternity. The interment was conducted in the burial vault at the Tottenham Court Road Chapel.[801] Whitefield's work was not done but he would no longer leave a wife behind on his trips. She would be in heaven and was in God's comforting and consoling care while he continued on.

The verdict is still out on the Whitefields' marriage. Cornelius Winter came to live in their household in January of 1767 and was with them for a year and a half. He remarked, "He was not happy in his wife, but I fear some who had not all the religion they professed, contributed to his infelicity. He did not intentionally make his wife unhappy. He always preserved great decency and decorum in his conduct towards her. Her death set his mind much at liberty."[802]

One last trip remained for Whitefield to America. His health seemed improved because his reduced travel forced him to cut back minimally

---

799   Belcher, 136.
800   Gledstone, 231.
801   Dallimore, vol. 2, 471.
802   Ibid., 471.

on preaching and ministry the last four years. These cutbacks had helped him somewhat. Whitefield had preached his way out of a job at the Tabernacle and Tottenham Chapel, although he was as popular as ever when he spoke. He knew others would have to carry on the work in the places where he had often preached.

Two big concerns were constantly in Whitefield's mind as he communicated with his friends in America. His first concern was the political situation involving America and his native country because he had been a bridge between both worlds. The Boston Massacre (as it was called), in the spring of 1770, would make a bad situation worse leading to open hostility against England by America. The quartering of soldiers and the Stamp Act came next and the Tea Act was yet to come. Whitefield's friend, Franklin, shared his concerns in 1768. He warned:

> I am under continued apprehensions that we may have bad news from America. The sending soldiers to Boston always appeared to me a dangerous step; they could do no good, they might occasion mischief I cannot but fear the consequences of bringing them together. When I consider the warm resentment of a people who consider themselves injured and oppressed, and the common insolence of the soldiery, who are taught to consider that people as in rebellion, I cannot but fear the consequences of bringing them together. It seems like setting up a smith's forge in a magazine of gunpowder.
>
> I see that our affairs are not well managed by our rulers here below; I wish I could believe with you, that they are well attended by those of above.[803]

Whitefield was well aware he would be going into a political hot bed on his last trip to America.

His second concern was still Bethesda. He wanted to see Bethesda become a college sponsored by the trustees and the Church of England. This initial offer had ended in rejection. Whitefield's proposed plans to allow someone other than a minister of the Church of England to be the president were rebuffed. He was encouraged that a charter was granted by the governing council of Parliament. However, Thomas Secker, the Archbishop of Canterbury did not approve the charter because of Whitefield's refusal to guarantee that the college's president would be a Church of England man and the charter was rejected.[804] This rejection led to another plan to start an academy that would develop into a

---

803 Dallimore, vol. 2, 452.
804 Cashin, 91-92.

college. Whitefield did not think he had the time to pursue this goal. He would take his plan for a college to the colony itself and the political leaders in Georgia.[805] He would share his vision with top officials and explore their interests in a college. Unfortunately, he was unable to meet with the Assembly and the Revolutionary War disrupted continued discussion on this subject.[806]

Edwin Cashin mused about what the college might have been to Georgia:

> Bethesda boys and indeed all Georgians might wonder: "What if a charter had been granted?" Bethesda College would today rank with other eighteenth-century colleges, like Columbia, Princeton, and Pennsylvania. Whitefield came so close to getting the charter. He could have accepted the condition that the head be a member of the Church of England; after all, he assumed that such would be the case. However, he promised his donors a "broad bottom," and we cannot fault him for being a man of his word. Instead, Whitefield would seek to persuade the officials of Georgia to sponsor a school.[807]

Land was no problem for the school. It was easier to attain property than it was to establish a college. More land had been obtained for the school in an anticipation of a college beginning there.[808]

Whitefield diligently made plans to go to America, along with plans for a farewell sermon at the Tabernacle. This parting was with a greater degree of uncertainty because he did not know if he would see his native country again.

In one of his final messages in his native country, Whitefield spoke on the figure of the vine and the branches in John 15. The aging evangelist used the symbol to illustrate the ministry he had shared with his native country for the last thirty-three years. God had done great things and he was trusting that the work God had used him in would bear fruit in the form of new ministers. His dream was a new generation continuing the legacy he was leaving behind.[809]

The final service featured a bittersweet parting from the Tabernacle. Friends and supporters were glad Whitefield was able to make his seventh trip to America but, because of his poor health, some knew it

---

805 Ibid., 92-93, 97.
806 Dallimore, vol. 2, 476.
807 Cashin, 92.
808 Fish, 182-183.
809 Belden, 216- 217.

would probably be the last time they would see him personally. They sensed, as with the Apostle Paul, "…they would see his face no more" (Acts 20:30). As they bid him farewell, those in the congregation knew they were saying good-bye to a legend.[810] Even if he did return safely, the chances of his making other trips were very remote because of his condition.

Whitefield and Richard Smith left aboard the Friendship on September 4, 1769. He intended to stay longer in America since he no longer had a wife waiting for his return.

Whitefield received a copy of his farewell sermon, as dictated, that he read as they embarked from the port of Deal. His sermons in written form never really captured the man and his total message. He was disappointed with the sermon in written form, feeling it was not an accurate rendition of what he had said. He had spoken on the Scripture concerning the Good Shepherd from John10:27-28. "My sheep hear my voice, and I know them, and they follow me: and I give unto them eternal life; and they shall never perish, neither shall any man pluck them out of my hand."[811]

Whitefield's disappointment was short-lived because of the prospect of preaching once again in America. He was to see his beloved Bethesda again and he would try to convince the local government there to sponsor a college. He was to speak in old places to new faces. The steadfast preacher still thrilled at the call to do what he loved best: preach the gospel of Christ to those he knew would respond when they heard it. The trip to America was an adventure he did not pass up, even in his weakened physical condition. The journey was what God had called him to until the day he died.

---

810   Ibid., 219.
811   Belcher, 418-419.

21

The Fateful Last
Tour of the Colonies
(1769-1770)

WHITEFIELD'S RETURN TO AMERICA SEEMED foolish to many, given the hardships of travel and his deteriorating physical condition. There were few hindrances, however, in going to the colonies since his wife had passed away. He had relinquished the management of the chapels and Tabernacle to others. There was nothing stopping him from going on his seventh trip to America. Philip shared why Whitefield felt he was able to make the trip to America:

> Many things conspired to enable Whitefield to embark again for America, without suspecting that he was not likely to return. Both his health and spirits were unusually good. He had often raised his old war cry, "Field preaching, field preaching forever!" He followed it up with the shout, "Ebenezer, Hallelujah, Pentecost!" He would be preaching in the spots of his former triumphs. His chapels in London also were well provided with acceptable supplies, and his affairs at Georgia all prosperous. Indeed, he appears to have had nothing to vex him but the heavy expense incurred for coach-hire, in making his last excursions. It had "mounted very high," he says; "and means must be found to save the last great expense."... "I am brave as to my bodily health, and have not been in better spirits for years," is his own account of himself, when he went on board the Friendship; and of his prospects, he said, "I am persuaded this voyage will be for the Redeemer's glory, and the welfare of precious and immortal souls." It was—but not in the way he anticipated. Cornelius Winter's account of his general tone of mind and body agrees, on the

whole, with Whitefield's own account of himself. He had occasional seasons of "remarkable lowness and languor."[812]

Whitefield's voyage on the Friendship began September 4th. Strong storm winds sent the ship back to port and on September 19th they tried again to set sail. The ship encountered another storm and turned back. The ship finally sailed onward to America. He preached to the passengers and crew, working also on sermons aboard the ship.[813] Whitefield wrote letters communicating with many of his friends. One of the letters he wrote was to John Wesley. It was a letter of reflection on what God had done the last three decades in both men's lives. He declared:

> What hath God wrought for us, in us and by us! I sailed out of these Downs almost thirty-three years ago. O the height, the depth, the length, the breadth of Thy love, O God! Surely it passeth knowledge...One would hope that these are earnests of good things to come, and that our Lord will not remove His candlestick from among us. Duty is ours. Future things belong to Him, who always did and always will order all things.[814]

Whitefield had been urging Wesley to send missionaries to America for years. On the day Whitefield left for America during his last voyage, two young men sent by Wesley were leaving on another ship to come to America. These preachers contributed to the Methodist movement forming societies when they reached America.[815]

Whitefield's ship arrived safely in Charleston on November 30, 1769 after an extended time at sea. Although the voyage was initially rough, things did settle down and the sea was calm as the ship pulled into South Carolina.[816]

When he arrived in America, Whitefield was determined to go south to Bethesda, having recovered with improved health. He wanted to tackle the issue of Bethesda becoming a college head-on by taking his plea to the colony itself. Whitefield preached for ten days to crowds in Charleston, heading toward Bethesda on December 10 to meet with Mr. Ambrose Wright, the manager.[817] He arrived during the Christmas season, in time for a special program the children presented. All the hard

---

812 Philip, 497.
813 Fish, 180-181.
814 Tyerman, vol. 2, 570.
815 Fish, 181.
816 Ibid., 181.
817 Ibid., 181-182.

work in the orphanage's establishment and maintenance had paid off through the providence of God.[818] Writing to Charles Wesley, who was responsible for giving him the idea of the orphanage he exclaimed, "All admire the goodness, strength and beauty of the late improvements. In a few months the intended plan, I hope, will be completed and a solid, lasting foundation laid for the support and education of many as yet unborn."[819]

The orphanage was in excellent financial shape. The substantial legacy left by a supporter in Scotland had paid off all debts, giving freedom for the orphanage to continue without financial disparity.[820] Whitefield turned his attention toward the charter from the colony. He invited the governor and his council to the orphanage. During a meal, the evangelist preached and later conducted a tour of the grounds.[821] He had consulted Benjamin Franklin concerning the continued support in the colonies for the orphanage and Bethesda's pursuit of a college.[822] The interest in a college was positive. Bethesda owned 5,000 acres deeded to the orphanage free and clear.[823] Land was not the problem for establishing a college in Georgia.

The chief sticking point in Bethesda becoming a college was the continuing conflict with the Archbishop of Canterbury concerning the presidential affiliation. Whitefield did not want to restrict the office to a member of the Church of England. Dallimore explained the conflict: But the chief authority in the matter remained with the Archbishop and during 1767 he and Whitefield exchanged letters seven or eight times. Dr. Secker insisted that in order to ensure the Anglican character of the College, "...the head of the College be a member of the Church of England...and that public prayers should not be extempore ones, but the liturgy of the Church, or some part thereof...." Whitefield, however, was not willing to accept this requirement. Bethesda's possession of the land and international good will would constitute an important part of the endowment of the College. The money for the original construction and the many years of maintenance of the Orphan House had come, not solely from members of the Church of England but, chiefly from persons who were Dissenters.[824]

---

818   Cashin, 93-94.
819   Tyerman, vol. 2, 574.
820   Dallimore, vol. 2, 471.
821   Tyerman, vol. 2, 575-578.
822   Dallimore, vol. 2, 451.
823   Ibid., 559.
824   Ibid, 456.

The obvious reason for the failure in a succession of the orphanage to college was Whitefield's death. No one else was willing to keep battling for the orphanage's transitioning into a college. Certain events curtailed future plans for the school:

> Unfortunately, the plans for a college never materialized at Bethesda. Other events postponed consideration and eventually halted the plans. The greatest obstacle was Whitefield's death. Although Lady Huntingdon supported Bethesda, she could not give it the care Whitefield had given it. The large house was struck by lightning in 1773 and burned down. The Revolutionary War also delayed any future plans...[825]

In 1791, the State of Georgia assumed the care and maintenance of the orphanage. It still exists today and is the oldest orphanage in America still active today. Whitefield's dream may not have materialized as he wished, but the continuance of Bethesda is a tribute to the vision and hard work he devoted to it.

Whitefield's assessment of the orphanage was wonderful, even without the unfulfilled dream of a college. He loved Bethesda and was warmly received there because of his role in its founding and his sacrifice to labor for its continuance. Whitefield's final assessment was positive and encouraging as Cashin related:

> Whitefield was pleased with the good work of his new superintendent Ambrose Wright. Wright had made much needed repairs on the big house, also stocking it with provisions and putting all its accounts in good order. Everything seemed to be going well. Whitefield wrote, "What a blessed winter have I had! Peace and love, and harmony, and plenty, reign here!" The next logical step was the presentation to the king's council of his request for a college charter. He loved Bethesda better than any other place, but he never stayed there long. Again, as in the past, it was for Bethesda that he traveled back to England. "Now farewell, my beloved Bethesda," he wrote, "surely the most delightful place in all the southern parts of America."[826]

Whitefield's parting was not secret, but with great fanfare. A parting message profoundly affected Olaudah Equiano, a former slave. He would later team up with William Wilberforce to lead to the abolishment

---

825   Cashin, 110-112.
826   Ibid., 86.

of slavery in England.[827] Cashin described Equiano's response to Whitefield's final sermon in this account:

> The Itinerant preached a farewell sermon in Savannah. As usual, the church was crowded, the attendees spilled out into the yard, and individuals climbed on ladders to see through the windows. One interested observer happened to be the famous Olaudah Equiano, a Nigerian-born slave who later wrote a narrative of his own life. Equiano had rarely seen a church so crowded, and one of the locals informed him that George Whitefield was speaking inside. The incident remained fresh in Equiano's memory when he penned his life story many years later: "I had often heard of this gentleman, and had wished to see and hear him; but I never before had an opportunity. I now, therefore, resolved to gratify myself with the sight and pressed in amidst the multitude. When I got into the church I saw this pious man exhorting the people with the greatest fervor and earnestness, and sweating as much as ever I did while in slavery on Montserrat beach." Equiano had never before witnessed clergymen exerting themselves so forcefully.[828]

Whitefield turned north to places where he had ministered before. He set sail on a coastal vessel on April 24 and arrived in Philadelphia on May 6, 1770.[829] He planned to preach throughout the summer in New England and return to Georgia for the winter, but again his health began to fail. His short trip on the ship had worn him out. He did speak twice on Sunday in Philadelphia and three or four times during the week.

The crowds flocked to hear him, realizing this could be the last time they would get to do so. They had thought him incapable of returning to America, as his condition kept deteriorating.[830] They had a rendezvous with destiny and wanted to hear the gallant warrior for Christ one more time.[831]

Whitefield traveled 150 miles to the Philadelphia vicinity in June. People came to hear him one more time as he preached throughout the countryside and moved toward his fate. "There were so many new as well as old doors open," he remarked.[832] He headed north to New York from there.

---

827   Ibid., 86, Cashin does not describe Equiano's future work when he labored with Wilberforce as a leader in the successful abolishment of slavery in England.

828   Ibid., 86.

829   Tyerman, vol. 2, 588.

830   Fish, 183.

831   Tyerman, vol. 2, 589.

832   Fish, 184.

The traveling evangelist spoke July 29th at a horse stealer's execution. "Thousands had come to hear Whitefield speak and the local sheriff allowed the thief to listen to the sermon before he was executed."[833] Whitefield conversed with the prisoner about his soul, but the results concerning the prospect of his conversion before his execution are unknown. He preached at his coffin pressing the need to be right with God before slipping into eternity.[834] The urgency of the moment impressed his hearers with the uncertainty of life.

As Whitefield moved northward it was good to see the surviving Tennents one more time. Gilbert had died in 1764 and William had passed away several decades ago from this time.[835] He recalled many fond memories of the Tennents as he visited with them one more time. An episode from the past through an exchange with William Tennent Sr. before he died in 1745 may have come to mind to keep him preaching. As Whitefield dined with William Tennent and his family, a group of ministers were conversing about the joy of going to heaven. Whitefield talked of the joy of soon dying and going to heaven. He asked the elder Tennent if he did not rejoice his end was soon. Tennent replied, "No sir, it is no pleasure to me at all; and if you knew your duty, it would be none to you. I have nothing to do with death. My business is to live as long as I can." Refusing to let up, Whitefield asked if he would choose to die if he could. "Sir," answered Tennent, "I have no choice about it. I am God's servant, and have engaged to do His business as long as He pleases to continue me therein."[836] Reflection on these words by the evangelist, may have been a factor in causing Whitefield to drive himself and continue the pace of his preaching even more not only then but on his final tour.

Whitefield had lost none of his style, making him colorful to hear and see. A shipbuilder contrasted him to many other preachers in his day, after hearing him for the first time. He shared how during other preachers' sermons he built a whole ship in his mind as it wandered from the sermon. So captivated was he by Whitefield's sermon, that he said, "With Mr. Whitefield, I could not lay a single plank in my mind

---

while he preached." This response was typical of the total absorption and involvement in Whitefield's message. The preacher never lost the gift God gave him.[837]

On July 31, Whitefield sailed from New York to Newport, Rhode Island, where he arrived August 3. With the exception of six days, Whitefield preached daily until he died. The days he did not preach, he suffered from a variety of ailments, causing him to travel throughout northern New England in a weakened condition.[838]

Whitefield encountered growing resentment toward the British while he was in Massachusetts, at the site of the Boston Massacre. The confrontation with the British soldiers had taken place in March. The trial for the soldiers was set for October. In spite of resentment toward the British, the colonists were still very open to the message the English evangelist preached, and did not associate him with the oppression of the British government and its soldiers.[839] Whitefield actually sided with America. He wrote, "Poor New England is much to be pitied; Boston people most of all: How falsely misrepresented."[840]

It was this constant understanding of the American cause that endeared Whitefield to the colonies. His extensive travels served as a constant reminder of his labor and giving his life for the establishment and support of Bethesda. Whitefield disassociated himself from the British problems because of the countless lives changed through his messages. Lambert explained:

> Colonists viewed Whitefield as a symbol of American patriotism not only for his outspoken support but for his selfless service to suffering people. They recognized him as one who extended himself for the community rather than personal benefit, citing the thousands of pounds he had raised and given to charities. In 1770, how one spent his or her money was a measure of patriotism.[841]

Whitefield had many friends and interests in America. His good friend, Benjamin Franklin, had communicated with him and supported

---

837 Ibid., 185.
838 Tyerman, vol. 2, 592-593.
839 Fish, 186.
840 Ibid., 186.
841 Lambert, 224.

him for years, regardless of his unbelief in a personal religion.[842] The institution the evangelist had given his life to supporting and prospering was in America. Bethesda was his vision of how the gospel of Christ was used as a wonderful example of reaching out to not only the spiritual, but also to physical needs of those destitute. Whitefield loved America and America loved him. The response to his sermons and the openness to him wherever he went were strong indications of the affection that existed for him. America was his adopted home as well as England his natural one, and he would as soon meet the Lord there, as in his native country.

Note his compassion and tender devotion to the cause of America when he says, "I can't in conscience leave the town without acquainting you with a secret. My heart bleeds for America. O poor New England! There is a deep laid plot against both your civil and religious liberties, and they will be lost. Your golden days are at an end. You have nothing but trouble before you."[843]

Stephen Mansfield believes Whitefield aided in the cause of revolt against his mother country. Future remembrances of him in the war would follow, illustrating the fond memories soldiers had for his support of the colonies' liberty. Benedict Arnold's army, on their way to Canada to fight the British, stopped at the burial place in a church at Newburyport, Massachusetts to worship and visit Whitefield's crypt during their trek to Canada before engaging with the British in battle.[844]

Mansfield describes this affinity and labels him as the "forgotten founding father":

> So now the forerunner of the revival that made them one became the forerunner of the war that set them free. It is why men marched into battle chanting: "No King but King Jesus! No King but King Jesus." It is why they pledged to God their lives, their fortunes, and their sacred honor. It is also why George Whitefield must be remembered as a founding father of the American cause."[845]

Mahaffey detailed how, as the American colonies grew nearer to their revolution; Whitefield began to use rhetoric that was more political. He

---

842 Dallimore, vol. 2, 444-445, 447.
843 Mansfield, 256.
844 Ibid., 27-31.
845 Ibid., 256.

described the response of this language in an earlier tour of the colonies when he had been in better health:

> ...Whitefield's increasing use of republican language and how he blended it with theology was seen in his celebrated sermon "Britain's Mercies and Britain's Duties." In his desire to preserve religious freedoms, Whitefield began to include the idea of "liberty" in his messages. The Revolution was still thirty-one years away, so the audiences hearing his messages were the parents of those who actually fought in the Revolution, making Whitefield's direct influence one step removed. But his teachings held incredible power as parents taught their children the difference between right and wrong, good and evil.[846]

The ideas Whitefield espoused in his messages were easily translatable to the ideas rising to the surface that promoted liberty in the colonies. The equality of redeemed sinners at the foot of the cross easily applied to the ideas of equality facing an oppressive provincial government giving its citizens no representation. Thomas Kidd, in his work *The Great Awakening*, echoes these sentiments: "Since the 1960s, a generation of historians have conclusively demonstrated that these republican ideals fueled the Revolution. Evangelicals championed republicanism as eagerly as their more liberal or skeptical Patriot friends."[847]

As Whitefield preached in New Hampshire, he had plans to return to Georgia and see Bethesda, but his health prevented him from doing that immediately. The evangelist had immediate plans to preach at Newburyport, Massachusetts, where his old friend Jonathan Parsons served as the pastor of the Presbyterian Church. Whitefield had preached in the church many times, and Parsons was one of his most ardent supporters in New England.[848, 849] He would first go by way of Portsmouth and Exeter, New Hampshire, where he would preach in the open air one more time.[850] Fall was upon him, the winter was approaching, his destiny lay before him. He was unafraid, but confident in the Lord's ability to prevail.

---

846   Mahaffey, 103.

847   Thomas S. Kidd, *The Great Awakening: The Roots of Evangelical Christianity in Colonial America* (Yale University Press: New Haven, CT: 2007), 289-290.

848   Stout, 279.

849   Tyerman, vol. 2, 597.

850   Ibid., 596.

22

FINAL DAYS OF LIFE

AND GLORY

(1770)

THE LAST DAYS OF WHITEFIELD'S LIFE WERE dramatic ones. He died as he lived, full of God's power and desperately looking to Him for strength and help. The way his life ended is probably the way Whitefield would have wanted it to end. A burning candle is a fitting way of describing his last days of ministry and preaching. When the candle of his life burned down, he accomplished the task the Lord had for him on earth.

Whitefield set out from Portsmouth, New Hampshire, toward Newburyport, Massachusetts, and eventually Boston on Saturday morning, September 29, 1770.[851] When he stopped at the village of Exeter, some fifteen miles from Portsmouth, people begged him to give a sermon. The evangelist's continuous preaching was a fitting tribute to his ministry until the very end, because even then people were still longing for him to preach.[852] They wanted to hear his golden voice, experience those animated gestures one more time and hear a message from God. A friend observed, "Sir you are more fit to go to bed than

---

851 Tyerman, vol. 2, 596.
852 Ibid., 596.

to preach." "True," replied Whitefield, and then clasping his hands and looking up to heaven, he added: "Lord Jesus, I am weary in Thy work, but not of it. If I have not finished my course, let me go and speak for Thee once more in the fields, seal Thy truth, come home and die!"[853]

Whitefield did not heed his friend's advice, determining to preach anyway, which he did standing on a large barrel to address the crowd. A person hearing his last sermon to the large crowd described the experience:

> Mr. Whitefield rose, and stood erect, and his appearance alone was a powerful sermon. He remained several minutes unable to speak: and then said, "I will wait for the gracious assistance of God; for He will, I am certain, assist me once more to speak in His name." He then delivered, perhaps one of his best sermons. "I go," he cried, "I go to a rest prepared....My body fails, my spirit expands! But I die to be with Him."[854]

The sermon is said to have lasted two hours or more as a testament to Whitefield's willingness to give his very all to preaching in the last few hours of his life. Whitefield used as his text, II Corinthians 13:5, "Examine yourself, whether ye be in the faith." The old glow and passion to preach the unsearchable riches of Christ was still there. He spoke with power and authority, not diminished but only intensified, as he got more into the message. Tyerman said, "Whitefield's sermon was two hours in length—characteristic of the man, but, in his present health, quite enough to kill him."[855]

Stout related how the people saw him and the final remarks he made in this, his last sermon:

> He rose up sluggishly and wearily, as if worn down and exhausted by his stupendous labors. His face seemed bloated, his voice was hoarse, his enunciation heavy. Sentence after sentence was thrown off in rough, disjointed portions, without much regard to point or beauty. [But then] his mind kindled, and his lion-like voice roared to the extremities of his audience. He was speaking of the inefficiency of works to merit salvation, and suddenly cried out in a tone of thunder, "Works! Works! A man cannot get to heaven by works! I would as soon think of climbing to the moon on a rope of sand."[856]

---

853   Belden, 222.
854   Dallimore, vol. 2, 503-504.
855   Tyerman, vol. 2, 597.
856   Stout, 279.

There was a note of finality to the scene when the spent preacher finished his message. The Reverend Jonathan Parsons met with Whitefield after the message, and the two had dinner together before starting to Parson's church in Newburyport. Traveling by boat, Whitefield needed help getting off the boat because he was too ill to get off by himself.[857]

When Whitefield was ready to retire for the night, he said, "I am tired, and must go to bed," but a crowd had gathered outside the house. People who had gathered below begged him to preach as he headed up the stairs to his room. The weakening evangelist did not turn down this opportunity, but stood by the landing and exhorted his hearers. He stopped speaking immediately when the candle he carried flickered, burned itself out and died away.[858]

Whitefield's life, like the candle, burned brightly until the very end. When it was extinguished, it left those seeing it to marvel at how great the light brightly burned till the very end. There is no record exactly what words Whitefield spoke, but it was probably only a few remarks, while the candle burned down.[859] Then he went inside completely spent and worn out.

Richard Smith describes the scene in his room after he joined Whitefield when he retired for the night. "I found him reading the Bible with Dr. Watts' Psalms lying open before him,"[860] Smith reported. Whitefield prayed and conversed with Smith for a short time before going to sleep. At two in the morning, Whitefield woke and asked Smith for something to drink. Smith noticed Whitefield to be panting for breath. When Smith asked how he felt Whitefield told him that his asthma was returning.[861] When Smith said that he wished Whitefield would not preach so often, the preacher told him, "I'd rather burn out than rust out."[862] Burn out he did indeed, in a figurative sense, with his life ebbing away because of his intense ministry. Whitefield began to pray for his friends and areas of ministry where he had responsibility.[863]

Whitefield asked Smith to completely open the window although

---

857 Tyerman, vol. 2, 597.
858 Dallimore, vol. 2, 598.
859 Tyerman, vol. 2, 598-599.
860 Ibid., 598.
861 Ibid., 598.
862 Ibid., 598.
863 Ibid., 598.

it was already half-way open. He cried, "I cannot breathe, but I hope I shall be better by-and-by. A good pulpit sweat today may give me relief. I shall do better after preaching."[864]

The weakened evangelist went back to sleep, but the sleep didn't last long, for he woke up again, complaining of more difficulty breathing. He asked Smith to warm some gruel for him. Parsons heard the sound of the fire being made and came in to see what was going on.[865]

Parsons went quickly to Whitefield and asked what was happening? He responded, "I am almost suffocated. I can scarce breathe. My asthma quite chokes me."[866] He went to the open window, seeking relief in his breathing but it gave him none.[867]

By 5 a.m., Richard Smith rushed to Dr. Sawyer's home for emergency care. When they returned, Whitefield was coughing up phlegm. Sawyer felt Whitefield's pulse and said, "He is a dead man," but Parsons refused to believe the pronouncement. "You must do something doctor," he said. "I cannot," the doctor said. "He is near his last breath."[868]

The doctor's pronouncement was correct, for at 6 a.m. Whitefield breathed his last breath.[869] The spiritual giant went home to be with God, leaving only his weakened and totally spent body behind. George Whitefield was now "...absent from the body and...present with the Lord" (II Cor. 5:8). His work was done, but what a rich legacy he left behind.

At six o'clock on Sunday morning, September 30, 1770, Belden said, "He, who had awakened so vast a multitude of souls from the death of sin to the life that is life indeed, was himself awakened from this mortal dream to the life that is without end."[870] Basil Miller recalled, "As the dawn of that beautiful Sunday morning of September 30, 1770, gilded the hills with its golden glory, the beauty of an eternal morning broke upon his soul, for Whitefield had gone home."[871] Quietly and gently, God took him home. His ministry was finished.

---

864   Ibid., 599.
865   Ibid., 599.
866   Ibid., 599.
867   Fish, 188.
868   Belcher, 440.
869   Tyerman, vol. 2, 599.
870   Belden, 224.
871   Basil Miller, *Ten Famous Evangelists* (Grand Rapids, MI: Zondervan, 1949), 13.

When the news traveled to Boston that Whitefield was dead, representatives from there traveled to Newburyport requesting his body for burial in their city.[872] Others recalled in conversations with him, his request for burial at the Newburyport Presbyterian church. Even Bethesda later wanted the body to be shipped there. Due to the proximity of the place of his death, and remembering his request, the church in Newburyport became his burial place.[873] The man who spent most of his life in the pulpit was buried– under the pulpit.

The cenotaph later placed in the Newburyport church commemorating his ministry and his influence on the world through his preaching reads:

> This Cenotaph is erected, with affectionate veneration, to the memory of the Rev. George Whitefield born at Gloucester, England, December 16, 1714; educated at Oxford University; ordained 1736. In a ministry of thirty-four years, he crossed the Atlantic thirteen times, and preached more than eighteen thousand sermons. As a soldier of the cross, humble, devout, ardent, he put on the whole Armor of God: preferring the honor of Christ to his own interest, repose, reputation, and life.
>
> A Christian orator, his deep piety, disinterested zeal, and vivid imagination, gave unexampled energy to his look, utterance, and action. Bold, fervent, pungent, and popular in his eloquence, no other uninspired man ever preached to so large assemblies, or enforced the simple truths of the gospel by motives so persuasive and awful, and with an influence so powerful, on the hearts of his hearers. He died of asthma, September 30, 1770, suddenly exchanging his life of unparalleled labors for his eternal rest.[874]

The funeral arrangements for the great preacher were carried out with clockwork execution. Jonathan Parsons fulfilled Whitefield's request to be buried in Newburyport. He instructed men to construct a vault under the pulpit they had ready for burial at his funeral on October 2.[875]

Six ministers, including the first bishop of the Church of England in Massachusetts served as pallbearers in the mile-long procession to the church where he was buried under the pulpit in the basement.[876]

The funeral service itself included prayers, singing and a sermon.

---

872   Fish, 189.
873   Ibid., 189-190.
874   Belcher, 444.
875   Belcher, 442-443.
876   Fish, 189.

The congregation sang Watts' hymn, "Why Do We Mourn Departed Friends."[877] Ministers continued for two hours, conversing about his great usefulness and prayed that God would scatter his gifts and drop his mantle among them.[878]

Fond remembrances of Whitefield's influence were given in the funeral service after the corpse was placed at the foot of the pulpit, close to the vault. The Rev. Daniel Rogers gave an affecting prayer, and openly confessed, under God, that he owed his conversion to the labors of this dear man of God, whose remains now lay before them. He cried out, "O my father, my father!"— Stopping and weeping, as though his heart would break, and the people wept all through the place. He finally recovered, and finished his prayer, sitting down, and continuing to weep.[879]

Jonathan Parsons gave a short message remembering Whitefield. He commented on his zeal despite hardships and his preaching style that captivated the crowds who came to hear him. He said, "In his repeated visits to America, when his services had almost exhausted his animal spirits, and his friends were ready to cry, "Spare thyself," his hope of serving Christ, and winning souls to him, animated and engaged him to run almost any risk."[880]

Remembering Whitefield's classic preaching style, Parsons commented:

> His popularity exceeded all that ever I knew; and though his asthma was sometimes an obstruction to him, his delivery and entertaining method were so inviting to the last, that it would command the attention of vast multitudes of his hearers...He had something so peculiar in his manner, expressive of sincerity in all he delivered, that it constrained the most abandoned to think he believed what he said was not only true, but of the last importance to souls;...
>
> The last sermon that he preached, though under the disadvantage of a stage in the open air, was delivered with such clearness, pathos, and eloquence, as to please and surprise the surrounding thousands.[881]

The solemnity of the occasion was gripping. The Great Awakener

---

877   Watts: *Cyber hymnal*: http://www.hymntime.com/tch/htm/w/h/y/whydowem. htm. Why do we mourn departed Friends? (September 30, 2015).

878   Philip, 536.

879   Ibid., 536.

880   Johnston, vol. 2, 461.

881   Ibid., 461.

who had preached to thousands was dead. Now was the time to remember his legacy. Philip detailed the major emphasis of the funeral message preached by Jedediah Jewet:

> Jedediah Jewet, of Rowley, Massachusetts, preached a funeral discourse. His affectionate address to his brethren was to lay to heart the death of that useful man of God, begging that he and they might be upon their watchtower, and endeavor to follow his blessed example. Jewet spoke of Whitefield's "peculiar and eminent gifts for the gospel ministry, and his fervor, diligence, and success in the work of it." "What a friend," cried Jewet, "he has been to us, and our interests, religious and civil; to New England, and to all the British colonies on the continent."[882]

The corpse was placed in the vault, and all concluded with a short prayer, and dismission of the people, who went weeping through the streets to their respective homes. Crowds continued to arrive at Newburyport begging to be allowed to see the corpse.[883] Whitefield was finally buried a gallant champion for God till the end.

The place where Whitefield was laid to rest is even remembered in American poetry by John Greenleaf Whittier when he recounted:

> Under the church of Federal Street,
> Under the tread of its Sabbath feet,
> Walled about by its basement stones,
> Lie the marvellous preacher's bones.
>
> No saintly honors to them are shown,
> No sign nor miracle have they known;
> But he who passes the ancient church
> Stops in the shade of its belfry-porch,
>
> And ponders the wonderful life of him
> Who lies at rest in that charnel dim.
> Long shall the traveler strain his eye
> From the railroad car, as it plunges by,
>
> And the vanishing town behind him search
> For the slender spire of the Whitefield Church;
> And feel for one moment the ghosts of trade,
> And fashion, and folly, and pleasure laid,

---

882   Ibid., 537.
883   Tyerman, vol. 2, 600- 601.

By the thought of that life of pure intent,
That voice of warning yet eloquent,
Of one on the errands of angels sent.
And if where he labored the flood of sin

Like a tide from the harbor-bar sets in,
And over a life of time and sense
The church-spires lift their vain defense,
As if to scatter the bolts of God

With the points of Calvin's thunder-rod,—
Still, as the gem of its civic crown,
Precious beyond the world's renown,
His memory hallows the ancient town!

—From Whittier's "The Preacher."[884]

Whitefield's death affected many in several ways. One of the moving tributes was given by a young man, Benjamin Randall, who heard Whitefield preach in Portsmouth, New Hampshire, though he wasn't converted then. When he heard the news of his death he exclaimed, "Whitefield is in heaven but I am on the road to hell! He was a man of God and yet I reviled him. He taught me the way to heaven, but I regarded it not. O that I could hear his voice again."[885] The death of Whitefield moved Randall to be converted to Christ, and he became a Baptist minister. He later founded the Free-Will Baptist denomination.[886]

The Free-will Baptists and Randall's predecessors championed the cause consistently opposing slavery. Belden added, "…today they number some one hundred thousand strong in membership. Thus did God own the Awakener's message and seal his power in the very hour and article of death."[887]

A struggle for the remains of Whitefield ensued after his death. The news of his death reached Georgia, and the pews of the governor and council in the Savannah church were draped in black, as were the pulpit, chandelier and organ. The leaders in the council approved money to bring Whitefield's remains back to Georgia to be buried at Bethesda,

---

884 Dallimore, *George Whitefield: God's Anointed Servant in the Great Revival of the Eighteenth Century*, 201.
885 Tyerman, vol. 2, 601.
886 Ibid., 601.
887 Belden, 224.

but the people in Newburyport strongly objected. They insisted his remains stay in the church where they are till this day. The request was finally given up. Some forty-five years later, when Georgia formed a new county, it was named Whitefield County in memory of the man who was an early leader in the colony.[888]

American slaves greatly mourned Whitefield's passing. He had spoken in their defense and had insisted on sharing the gospel with them, caring for their souls as he would the highest member of the British aristocracy. He took steps to see their living conditions improved in his contacts with them. Phillis Wheatley, a seventeen-year-old Boston slave, had converted to Christianity and taught herself to write poetry with the instruction of her mistress. One of the poems she wrote was an elegy for George Whitefield.[889] It was widely distributed, because not only did it describe his magnetic appeal to all classes, but it also identified him in the colonists' struggle with the British government and included a tribute to the Countess of Huntingdon.[890] These emphases made the poem popular in America and Great Britain.

The last few lines are a moving tribute to Whitefield's influence. They read:

> "Take him, ye wretched, for your only good,
> Take him ye starving sinner, for your food;
> Ye thirsty, come to his life-giving stream,
> Ye preachers, take him for your joyful theme;
>
> Take him ye dear Americans, he said,
> Be your complaints on his kind bosom laid:
> Take him, ye Africans, he longs for you,
> Impartial Saviour is his title due:
>
> Wash'd in the fountain of redeeming blood,
> You shall be sons, and kings, and priest to God."
> Great Countess, we Americans revere
> Thy name, and mingle in thy grief sincere;
> Their more than father will no more return.

---

888 Fish, 190.
889 Ibid., 191.
890 Gillies, 302.

> But, though arrested by the hand of death,
> Whitefield no more exerts his lab'ring breath,
> Yet let us view him in th' eternal skies,
> Let every heart to this bright vision rise,
> While the tomb safe retains its sacred trust,
> Till life divine reanimates his dust.[891]

Whitefield was dead, but his memory would live on. His influence was realized in the years after his death and is still felt today by those who carefully study his life.

On November 5, the jolting news reached London of Whitefield's death. The thought of the Grand Itinerant gone was a shock to many. Many articles appeared in newspapers and magazines recounting the facts of his life and discussing the impact of his preaching.[892] Friends and fellow ministers wrote eulogies to Whitefield. Whitefield had instructed Robert Keen to contact John Wesley to preach his funeral sermon at the Tabernacle in London. There was unity in the gospel with Wesley at Whitefield's passing. When asked earlier who he wanted to give his funeral sermon, Whitefield said without hesitation, "John Wesley, he's the man." Wesley gave a flowing account of the effect of Whitefield's ministry.[893]

Charles Wesley composed an elegy that recalled with great fondness the day they first met and the blessing his friendship with Whitefield had on him. He tells of the influence his ministry had on the world. Portions of the poem recount Whitefield's eventful life:

> Can I the memorable day forget,
> When first we by divine appointment met?
> Where undisturbed the thoughtful student roves,
> In search of truth, through academic groves,
> A modest, pensive youth, who mused alone,
> Industrious the frequented path to shun,
> An Israelite without disguise or art
> I saw, I loved, and clasped him to my heart,
> A stranger as my bosom-friend caressed,
> And unawares received an angel-guest...

---

891 Ninde, 210-211.
892 Fish, 193.
893 Ibid., 193.

Soon as he thus lifts up his trumpet-voice,
Attentive thousands tremble, or rejoice:
Who faithfully the welcome truth receive,
Rejoice, and closer to their Saviour cleave:
Poor Christless sinners, wounded by the word
(Lively and sharper than a two-edg'd sword,
Spirit and soul Almighty to divide)
Drop, like autumnal leaves, on every side,
Lamenting after him they crucified!...

What multitudes repent, and then believe,
When God doth utterance to the preacher give!
Whether he speaks the words of sober sense,
Or pours a flood of artless eloquence,...
Opposers struck by the powerful word admire
In speechless awe, the hammer and the fire,
While Whitefield melts the stubborn rocks, or breaks,
In consolation, or in thunder speaks,
From strength to strength, our young apostle, goes,
Pours like a torrent, and the land o'erflows,
Resistless wins his way with rapid zeal,
Turns the world upside down, and shakes the gates of hell!...
How blest the messenger whom Jesus owns,
How swift with the commissioned word he runs!
The sacred fire shut up within his breast
Breaks out again, the weary cannot rest,
To pluck poor souls as brands out of the flame,
To scatter the good seed on every side,
To spread the knowledge of the crucified,
From a small spark a mighty fire to raise,
And fill the continent with Jesus' praise...

Lover of all mankind, his life he gave,
Christ to exalt, and precious souls to save:
Nor age, nor sickness could abate his zeal,
To feed the flock, and serve the Master's will.
Though spent with pain, and toils that never ceased,
He laboured on, nor asked to be released;
In deaths immortal, till his work was done,
And wished, for Christ his latest breath to spend,...
That life and labour might together end.

**He speaks—and dies! Transported to resign
His spotless soul into the hands divine!
He sinks into his loving Lord's embrace,
And sees his dear Redeemer face to face![894]**

Old differences were laid aside. In heaven, there would be no differences, only sweet communion with the Lord. The Wesleys labored on for two more decades, establishing Methodism in England and America as a fixed institution.

The mourning was great at Whitefield's death, and he was long remembered. His testimony and character are tremendous examples and he is revered unto this day as one of the greatest preachers in Christian history.

---

894 John Edwards, *Charles Wesley's Reflections on George Whitefield*, August 20, 2008, "Elegy on the Life of George Whitefield" 1771, (accessed September 29, 2015). http://www.christian-faith.com/forjesus/charles-wesleys-thoughts-of-george-whitefield.

23

LASTING CONTRIBUTIONS

OF GEORGE WHITEFIELD

THE INFLUENCE OF WHITEFIELD'S MINISTRY on the history of Christianity up to our present day has been enormous. Some of the practices he pioneered are usually taken for granted in succeeding centuries. Hopefully, you have experienced what God did through his committed life in the time span he ministered on both continents. Many have looked to him as a model, while others view his life with admiration. It is imperative to identify these influences through seeing how God used Whitefield and how they have helped shape us in modern day Christianity. The evaluation of his influence will help gain a better understanding of the impact of his ministry.

WHITEFIELD WAS ONE OF THE LEADING
FORERUNNERS OF EVANGELICAL CHRISTIANITY

The origin of evangelical Christianity is traced back to the influence of the awakening movements. The movements dealt with personal religion and were in stark contrast to the staid and ritualistic worship and ministry of the established churches of England. Although the Puritan and Separatist movements brought some life to the Church of England, their struggle was more for religious liberty. These movements were not as aggressive in going out to the masses with the gospel the way early Methodists were.[895]

George Whitefield stands at the forefront of what God was doing to get the gospel out to the masses, creating a fellowship of believers known by their experience of the new birth. The new birth was the primary theme of the majority of Whitefield's preaching. His last open-air message was on the need to examine one's self and come to an assurance of personal salvation in Christ.[896] Everywhere Whitefield went, he found a warm fellowship through his trademark of preaching the new birth.

A new group of preachers had formed a denominational affiliation, primarily known as New Lights. They gave "new light" on the need for personal salvation through Christ's atoning work. They felt a calling to lead the lost out of darkness into the light of the gospel.[897] People hearing Whitefield and any New Light preacher understood the gospel and so vivid was he in his presentation, that no one missed this grand theme. The New Lights were not a contrived fellowship, but one bound together by the Spirit of God. Cashin refers to a kinship among evangelicals we have with Whitefield, as key in their support of the Bethesda orphanage:

> George Whitefield, the "Grand Itinerant," changed the religious character of Colonial America more than any of his contemporaries. Many of today's Christians, especially those who think of themselves as "born again," are his theological heirs. Only a few Americans realize that the religious history of this country would have been remarkably different had it not been for the institution Whitefield loved dearly enough to call his "Beloved Bethesda.[898]

We experience a current unity of believers today in joint outreach efforts. The fellowship believers have with each other is akin to what they will have in heaven, because the primary thrust of their fellowship is in the gospel of Christ. This fellowship does not force conformity by some grand scheme, resulting in the minimization of the major doctrines of Christianity. It is instead, a fellowship of believers who share a common belief in the gospel and its power to transform lives that are bound together with this emphasis.

---

895   These were historical movements within primarily English Christianity and America that were at play during the time period culminating into the period of the awakening movement and paving the way for the New Light movement.

896   Tyerman, vol. 2, 596.

897   Mahaffey, 35-36.

898   Cashin, Preface I.

Kidd was definite in his conclusion of Whitefield's leadership in evangelical Christianity when he stated:

> Once evangelist George Whitefield arrived in America in 1739, the religion of the new birth became a permanent fixture of American religious life. The Old Lights could protest, but for better or worse, evangelicalism was here to stay. The most interesting question in the first generation of American evangelicalism, then, was what kind of movement it would become. How socially radical would it be? Would it tolerate the dramatic mystical experiences of laypeople? Would it reaffirm traditional boundaries set by race, class, gender, education and age? The struggle over these questions played out chiefly between moderate and radical evangelicals, not between Old Lights and New Lights.[899]

Peter Hoffer revealed, "Born-Again Christians are a force in American cultural and political life. They are the inheritors of the revivalism that George Whitefield brought to America in 1739."[900]

Whitefield believed there were no barriers for preaching the gospel that God could not overcome. He knew no boundaries when it came to fellowship with like-minded brethren. The New Lights shed light in dark places during the awakening movements. The primary leader in this effort that spawned the awakening was Whitefield.

WHITEFIELD WAS AN EXAMPLE
OF POWERFUL PREACHING

Whitefield was known by many characteristics of his ministry. He was a dynamic preacher to the world and believers, a student of the Bible who made Calvinistic doctrines come alive. He was a model of devotion in his personal and public persona who preached with power and the conviction of the Holy Spirit. Authoritative truth followed him wherever he went in his preaching schedule.

Hoffer describes Whitefield's preaching revealing, "Whitefield's sermons were superb examples of the "plain style" pioneered by the Puritans. For them, the guide through the long process was the Word and the guide through the Word was the sermon. The sermon came "flaming from the hand of the minister."[901]

---

899 Kidd, *The Great Awakening*, xv.
900 Hoffer, 121.
901 Ibid, 55.

Spurgeon's earlier comment said of Whitefield that he was, "all life fire, wing and force."[902] This statement revealed the admiration he had for Whitefield's pattern of ministry. Spurgeon, often called the "Prince of Preachers," followed his practical Calvinism, glorying in his example and pattern for ministry. He appreciated Whitefield's strong doctrinal emphasis and appeal to mass crowds which were also a part of Spurgeon's ministry.[903]

The examples of ministry Spurgeon emulated included Whitefield's preaching pattern and extended to his benevolent causes, such as Bethesda, and his receiving offerings for oppressed Christians. These causes were similar to Spurgeon's ministry to people in need.[904]

The influence on young children was indelible and inspired them as they grew up to great acts of Christian activism as with this famous British statesman:

> The year was 1769. Whitefield was preaching the last sermon he would ever preach in England. The boy listened intently, and as he did, he felt something eternal stamped upon his soul. In time, the imprint dimmed as the boy became a man and threw himself into the ways of the world. Later, as he traveled in Italy, he happened to pick up a hotel copy of Philip Doddridge's *The Rise and Progress of Religion.* As he read it, his heart melted. All that Whitefield had preached those many years before came roaring back and the young man gave his life to God. His name was William Wilberforce and one day he would almost single-handedly drive slavery out of the British Empire.[905]

WHITEFIELD FOSTERED
FORCEFUL DOCTRINAL PREACHING

The trend of the preaching in Whitefield's day was to give moral platitudes that resembled lessons on doing good deeds as the primary way to be a Christian instead of what the Bible said. Wherever Whitefield spoke, he "thundered out the Word of God." He actually said, "I love those that thunder out the Word. The Christian world is in a deep sleep. Nothing but a loud voice can awaken them out of it."[906] His preaching attracted many for the simple reason that he would express doctrinal truth in an understandable way. He did not shrink

---

902   Dallimore, vol. 2, 534.
903   Mansfield, 258.
904   Ibid., 258.
905   Ibid., 259.
906   Wakeley, 371.

from doctrinal truth and denounced those withholding it from people. Whitefield did not seek to stir up doctrinal controversy, but he did respond when attacked. He chided those who omitted the new birth and did not put an emphasis on the major doctrines of the faith.

Tyerman illustrated Whitefield's love for doctrinal truth:

> The man's faith filled and fired him with enthusiasm. On themes such as the ruin of man, the love of God, the death of Christ, the salvation of souls, the felicities of heaven, and the torments of hell, it was impossible for Whitefield to be calm. If Whitefield had preached on little subjects, he might have been as cool as many of his fellows, and might have courted favour by yielding to the fastidious tastes of respectable congregations, desiring the sentimental, the picturesque, and the imaginative, but turning with disgust from the solemn, the alarming, the awakening. Whitefield was not a coward.[907]

Whitefield was not ashamed of being known as a Calvinist. He was thrilled to employ these doctrines for evangelistic purposes. He saw God's sovereign plan in predestination, the limited atonement and eternal salvation. The evangelist sought to ground the orphans at Bethesda in the doctrine of original sin. He saw the necessity of sinners understanding their lostness in order to understand God's gracious choice in bringing the gospel to their heart.[908]

Many have found a beacon of light in Whitefield's example. The passion of his preaching was in stark contrast to the philosophical musings of the day. Whitefield took the truths of God's Word to a level of understanding so that many children gathering around him in his open-air meetings could comprehend them. They brought notes to him from the crowds of the hearers who had been awakened and converted.[909] The excitement of sharing scriptural truth with his hearers who waited in anticipation to hear them was linked to Whitefield's themes in his preaching.

Whitefield's use of theological ideas in his sermons linked listeners to his own personal experiences. His audiences did not simply hear about his conversion experience in Oxford; they lived through it with him.

---

907 Tyerman, vol. 2, 629.
908 These were recurrent doctrinal themes in Whitefield's preaching.
909 Ninde, 79.

WHITEFIELD WAS ESPECIALLY NOTED
FOR HIS DRAMATIC PREACHING

Whitefield's preaching was dramatic and the envy of many actors of his day. His preaching captivated audiences and moved them to action.[910] Whitefield always played the part of one telling a narrative and was especially fond of describing biblical characters and places so vividly that listeners were transported to those places.[911] Ninde reveals, "As people watched by the extraordinary play of the passions of the soul in his eyes in every feature ...Certain it is that no preacher of his age if, indeed of any age, equaled his histrionic power. He knew the untold value of a good delivery in holding people's attention."[912]

Whitefield deserved the credit for using the dramatic element as a new motivation in his preaching. Before Whitefield, preaching consisted of a teaching sounding more like a lecture on moral relativism. After Whitefield, preachers began to direct their messages more to the heart and not exclusively to the intellectual and learned.[913] Many of the established clergy of Whitefield's day shunned and disdained his approach to preaching while the ordinary people welcomed it. Haykin shared, "Unlike many of his Anglican contemporaries who addressed only the mind and whose preaching lacked zeal, Whitefield spoke to the whole man with passion and without mincing any words."[914]

Whitefield revolutionized preaching in the English-speaking world. Seventy years later Joseph Campbell, a pastor at the London Tabernacle stated, "The bulk of the best gospel preachers of Whitefield's day presented their instruction in a form so scholastic as to require extraordinary intelligence to follow them. But after the star of Whitefield set in, the metaphysical form of instruction gradually disappeared from the British pulpit."[915]

Whitefield had the ability to mesmerize his audiences. Because the majority of preachers had adopted the styles of a bad academic lecturers, Whitefield's messages were different that listeners were moved to strong emotions. Basil Miller recalls Whitefield's preaching to the masses:

---

910   Mansfield, 123-124.
911   Ibid., 198.
912   Ninde, 162.
913   Mansfield, 124.
914   Ibid., 39.
915   Fish, 199.

His voice could move listeners to laughter, melt men to tears and his power of portrayal was so vivid that audiences could not restrain their feelings... "I have left the people full of fire," he said. "Thousands have flocked to hear the gospel. Awakenings I have heard of in every place. My eyes gush with tears of joy at the very thought of it." He was hardly ever known to preach a sermon without tears filling his eyes.[916]

He seldom spoke without winning souls to his Redeemer. John Wesley says in his journal that it was Whitefield's prayer life that enabled him to win so many souls. John Newton, gifted song writer of his era, said Whitefield's vital prayer life was a potent factor in his spiritual victories. When he spoke he was eloquent, not with an earthly or human eloquence, but an eloquence given him by God. When he preached, men saw not him but God, whose cause he pleaded, and whose message he delivered.[917]

Typical preachers of Whitefield's age used a complex vocabulary only a few in the audience followed, but he chose simple and direct words that a child could follow.[918] Haykin noted the impact Whitefield had on children in lasting ways after hearing his messages: "Whitefield spoke as one who sought to awaken and grip the heart."[919] The passion in his sermons was long remembered by an elderly man who heard him as a child:

Unlike many of his Anglican contemporaries who addressed only the mind and whose preaching lacked zeal, Whitefield spoke to the whole man with passion and without mincing any words. In 1844, John Knight, an elderly man of eighty-one, recalled the time that he had heard Whitefield preach on the evangelist's final visit to Gloucestershire in 1769. According to Knight, he was "about 6 years of age" at the time. "My father held me up in his arms," he wrote, "and though so young I well remember to see the tears run down the cheek of the servant of God while preaching the love of the Master to dying sinners."[920]

People traveled for miles to hear Whitefield preach. They knew any message he gave would be filled with animation and descriptive imagery. He got down where the people were as they visualized the scenes and events of the Bible. Dramatic preaching made an impression on the world in which Whitefield lived. This impression came through his efforts to give the gospel to people and a greater

---

916 Miller, 12.
917 Ibid., 12–13.
918 Mansfield, 124.
919 Haykin, 39.
920 Ibid., 39-40.

understanding of it in their own context.

Philip recounted how another child was moved by Whitefield's calm dealing with those trying to disturb his preaching:

> I asked him whether he remembered Whitefield's person. The old man brightened at the question, and said, "Ay, sure: he was a jolly, brave man; and what a look he had when he put out his right hand thus, to rebuke a disturber, as tried to stop him under the pear-tree. The man had been very threatening and noisy: but he could not stand the look. Off he rode and Whitefield said, 'There he goes: empty barrels make the most din.'"[921]

The more vivid Whitefield's illustrations were, the homier was the language he used. This language had a great effect on people through the style of delivery they experienced.[922] Truth came to life with Whitefield's preaching. Visualizing truth in vivid descriptions is very valuable in today's culture.

WHITEFIELD PIONEERED
MODERN CRUSADE EVANGELISM

Some believe that without Whitefield there would have been no Billy Graham. The explanation is that God in His providence used Whitefield as the forerunner of mass evangelism resulting in the crusade ministries of Moody, Sunday, and Graham. Billy Graham was actually converted in a crusade meeting led by Mordecai Ham.[923] This open air ministry of an itinerant preacher was popularized by George Whitefield. Others had used the method before Whitefield began his ministry: Howell Harris, Theodorus Frelinghuysen and the Tennents in America were leaders, but Whitefield took field preaching to a new level. Both Billy Sunday and Billy Graham followed in Whitefield's footsteps when they made use of tents, athletic stadiums, and other large venues for their meetings.[924]

These 20th century leaders have been criticized for the converts in their meetings who did not continue in the faith. Whitefield received the same criticism concerning his ministry. An interesting account of one

---

921 Philip, 561.

922 Donald, E. Demaray, *Pulpit Giants: What Made Them Great* (Moody Press: Chicago, 1973), 162–163.

923 John Pollock, *Billy Graham: The Authorized Biography* (McGraw-Hill: New York, 1966), 5-7.

924 Robert Ferm, *Cooperative Evangelism* (Zondervan: Grand Rapids, MI, 1958), 49.

convert to Christ in one of his meetings and her life-long walk with the Lord reveals the continued influence he had on her. Her testimony was told to J. B. Wakeley, author of a collection of anecdotes on Whitefield:

> We had the pleasure nearly forty years ago of becoming acquainted with an old lady, at that time nearly ninety years of age, residing in a village near Sharon, Connecticut, who had been converted under Whitefield's preaching when he was in Sharon, and who still retained the primitive fire which he had then kindled. She had always venerated the name of Whitefield, and she described to us with great fervour his person and his eloquence, saying that his followers were in those days called New Lights. Having prayed one morning at her house in a large kitchen, we were much surprised on closing to hear her commence praying, and such a prayer we never before nor afterward heard. She prayed as if she were used to wrestling with the Angel of the Covenant.
>
> She was at one end of the room when she began, with a kitchen chair before her, which she lifted up and put down at every petition; and on saying Amen she was at the other end of the kitchen. She was the only convert of Whitefield's we ever saw, and she had more life and fire in her than some whole churches.[925]

There would be no John Wesley as we know him had it not been for Whitefield's ministry of field preaching. Whitefield brought him to Bristol after Wesley's conversion and impressed on him the need to engage in ministry there to the miners. Wesley was reluctant at first, but the thrill of seeing the response to Whitefield's sermons by many made him throw care to the wind. Wesley literally took on Whitefield's makeshift congregation at Bristol, made up of the Kingswood Collier's miners. The move, bringing Wesley to pastor the Bristol congregation, catapulted him into notoriety, while Whitefield went to Georgia and stepped out of the limelight.[926]

John Wesley's concern for the poor and unfortunate (long a trademark of Arminian Methodism), was nurtured during his time in Bristol when Whitefield turned over the Kingswood ministry to him. Whitefield's encouragement to Wesley was incalculable.[927]

Whitefield was deeply hurt when Wesley turned against him and incited people to oppose his beliefs after he went to the New World. He was puzzled and deeply pained by the attacks Wesley launched on Whitefield's Calvinistic theology after he had encouraged Wesley. It is

---

925   Wakeley, 382-386.
926   Dallimore, vol. 1, 274-275.
927   Ibid., 276-277.

to the honor of both men, this doctrinal rift was remedied when they worked together in ministry before Whitefield's death. Both men agreed the furtherance of the gospel had to be pre-eminent over other issues.[928]

Whitefield did not create the scheme of field preaching, but took it up when established churches rejected his ministry. Field preaching worked because of the lack of buildings large enough to seat the crowds who came to hear him. He primarily went wherever the people were, and the people came to hear him wherever he was. As God thrust Whitefield into field preaching, he "looked upon the world as his parish" long before Wesley used this as a theme.[929] A pattern was established for what we know today as crusade evangelism. The Tabernacle and chapels became mainstays of Whitefield's ministry later in his life, but the last sermon he preached was to a mass of people in the open air.[930]

Whitefield was the first evangelist to use the popular media. He used newspapers, religious magazines, pamphlets, posters and ordinary correspondence to draw huge crowds to his meetings. Whether Whitefield's publicity was positive or negative, he found a way to turn notoriety to his advantage and to the advantage of the gospel. As a young preacher, Whitefield profited from Benjamin Franklin's printing of his sermons and Franklin following his ministry in America. Weeks before he arrived in a town, Whitefield and his supporters would send letters to pastors and other people in the area, informing them of the upcoming meetings. These supporters, in turn, would contact friends, neighbors and local newspapers; the methods created a ripple effect. Some would even hold meetings and read letters Whitefield had sent.[931]

It is easier to get the non-Christian to go to a special meeting if it is in larger venue. The special nature of the event brings people out as it did in Whitefield's day. Surely, Whitefield would be amazed and happy at the fulfillment of this ministry he began more than two and a half centuries ago.

---

928   Ibid., 467.
929   This was a major theme of Wesley's ministry found in his writings. Whitefield actualized this more than Wesley by his extensive world travel. Wesley sent missionaries but personally chose to stay in England and lead the movement from there.
930   McConnell, 180.
931   Fish, 197–198.

WHITEFIELD PROMOTED THE MASS
APPEAL OF PREACHING AND THE GOSPEL

Hand in hand with crusade evangelism is the appeal of preaching the gospel to the masses. Gospel preaching would have long ceased to exist if it were only a fad as seen predominantly in Whitefield's ministry. However, gospel preaching is still prevalent today. This preaching may possibly be in other forms, but is still vibrant in the mass appeal of God's plan of salvation. The directness and simplicity of one taking the Bible and revealing God's plan of salvation is time-tested and effective. Whitefield illustrated the value of gospel preaching in a dynamic way.

Many who have prejudice against evangelism and don't preach the gospel can easily dismiss Whitefield's appeal to the people in his preaching. Criticism of the methods of evangelism has not changed. Shallow converts, excessive emotionalism, seasonal decisions are just some of these criticisms and are still viewed as typical of mass evangelism. The criticism is as constant as it was in Whitefield's day and there have been abuses.[932] The furtherance of the message is the important emphasis still alive today in the Christian movement. It is evidence to the great exclamation by the Apostle Paul, "I am not ashamed of the gospel of Christ for it is the power of God unto salvation to everyone that believeth" (Rom. 1:16). This statement was proven by Whitefield's ministry and is still being evidenced today as the gospel is preached with power.

There is an approach today to emphasize contemporary worship as the means of reaching an unchurched, postmodern culture. John MacArthur stated, "The easiest thing many of these churches can do without, is preaching."[933] Preaching has almost become an inconvenience to some churches and definitely has been downgraded to some type of a rap session in some quarters. Christian history helps students understand that no great movement of God has occurred without masses converted through the preaching of the gospel. Some say there are more ways to communicate the gospel than through sermons. It is important to note preaching is the method God chose to use to "...save those who would

---

932   Mansfield, 144.

933   John MacArthur Shepherd's Conference: Grace Community Church Panorama City, CA, 2007 Pastor's Conference, Question and Answer Session.

believe" (I Cor. 1:21). Any church service, no matter how modern, will never have a ministry God will bless without preaching as the main event in the service.

The word Whitefield would preach at certain places brought people out who would assemble with great anticipation. Whitefield did not only preach; but he used Isaac Watts's hymns, he read the Scripture and he made impromptu comments, but these were not substitutes for the preaching event. If preaching is not the main event in the worship service, how does one explain Whitefield's ministry?[934] We pay homage to the fact that Whitefield powerfully preached the direct message of the gospel to people. His preaching was the source of the mass movement featuring hearing and responding to his message.

WHITEFIELD LED IN THE GREAT AWAKENING
SPREADING TO UNREACHED AREAS

The primary intent of Whitefield's ministry was to bring awakening to regions, masses and countries wherever he used the method of preaching the gospel. He became a world traveler because the goal of spiritual awaakening was always at the forefront of everything Whitefield did. His purpose to reach the lost is seen in his journal entries, correspondence and in the focus of his ministry.

Whitefield could have been very successful staying in one place, but it was to his credit that he roamed the countryside, preaching wherever people would hear him instead of preaching only in church buildings.

Hoffer shared the reasons for Whitefield's popularity in the preaching: "The size of his audiences, his ability to be heard, the way in which he used publicity to gain a mass following—all of these were a phenomenon in themselves that kept the awakening alive. And when they seemed to pall, Whitefield himself stirred the ashes of enthusiasm to rekindle the revival."[935]

Whitefield was a Christian leader who demonstrated a life of religious commitment and intensity that would reform a society instead of tear it apart. The people living in Great Britain, in the middle of the eighteenth century were part of a culture that had only recently escaped

---

934 These religious practices used in Whitefield's meetings were secondary to the preaching event.

935 Hoffer, 92.

from more than 200 years of religious warfare. A peaceful atmosphere was established and many viewed religious enthusiasm with suspicion, if not outright fear. Yet, their fears were short-lived.[936]

Awakening did come to both continents and, although Whitefield was not the only person God used in the movement, he greatly contributed in many ways as God worked through him. The First Great Awakening took many avenues, but the preaching of George Whitefield was a key element of what God accomplished in this great movement. The awakening movement needed his leadership and fellowships began on both continents because of the awakening that Whitefield led. People were brought together, moral ills were corrected, and a Christian influence was extended through Whitefield's ministry. The abolition of slavery, the elevation of the working class, and even a segment of the industrial revolution were results of the awakening's influence. John Wesley's continued ministry after Whitefield's death is credited with averting the violence and bloodshed in England associated with the French Revolution in France. The awakening was of value to every aspect of society.[937]

The goal and motivation for church ministry need examining, as one asks why we do ministry and what the purpose of our church is? Awakening in any generation is the floodtide sweeping everything in its path into the sovereign plan of God for the world. We are not involved in church just to get individual needs met and let the world perish without Christ. We have a noticeable outward focus if we are to have a gospel preaching and reaching ministry. Spiritual awakening must be our heart cry as it was with George Whitefield. Activities, prayer efforts, focus, and our money should be given to the ultimate end of awakening happening in every generation before the return of Christ.

Whitefield believed God was sovereign and that He would awaken individuals and churches. He believed that we need to trust God to send awakening, while putting ourselves in a position for God to send it to us.[938] The purpose of worship, evangelistic efforts, teaching

---

936 Fish, 202.

937 The historical result that came from the effect of the awakenings that took place in Britain and America was very apparent.

938 A marked difference in the First and Second Great Awakenings was the beliefs concerning the sovereignty of God and the free will of man.

and prayer is to allow God to do what He desires when we become available to Him. When the church is revived, spiritual awakening is a supernatural consequence. This supernatural move of God is a need in every generation as it was in Whitefield's day. May God grant awakening to come in our lifetime, in God's time, in God's way, the same way it happened in the life and ministry of George Whitefield.

24

What We Must Experience

Through Studying Whitefield's Life

I WILL CLOSE THIS WORK WITH ANSWERS to the question "so what" about Whitefield's life. Some characters in the history of Christianity stand alone through time and eternity. We do not have to search for reasons to study their lives, but there are practical answers for their study. We don't need to discover hidden nuances about Whitefield's life. His example is straight and clear. The light is bright, and the candle gives warmth and provides motivation for Christian living.

A clear scriptural principle directs us in following his worthy example representing Christ. By no means do we worship the person or place him above our mutual association in salvation. God calls all believers to a similar commitment to the Lord. Whitefield's example, though, presents a wonderful model. The Apostle Paul said, "Those things, which ye have both learned, and received, and heard, and seen in me, do" (Phi. 4:9). We look to the human example of Whitefield's life as a pattern of Christ-likeness for ourselves.

WHITEFIELD IS AN EXAMPLE
OF WHOLE-HEARTED DEVOTION TO GOD

One of the obvious aspects of Whitefield's life was his devotion to Christ's calling on his life. We see this sincerity to God in his desperate struggle to find salvation. His daily devotional life began early; his dependence on God for his needs and direction was constant; his devotion to follow God's leadership is a recurrent theme throughout his life and ministry.[939] Belcher gave a greater understanding of his prayer life as he prepared for the preaching event:

> He was eminently a man of prayer; and had he been less prayerful, he would also have been less powerful. He came into the pulpit from the closet, where he had been communing with God, and could no more trifle with merry humor at such a time than could Moses when he came down from the mount to the people; or than the high-priest when he came out from the blazing symbols of the divine presence between the cherubim in the holy of holies; or Isaiah when he saw the Lord of hosts, high and lifted up, with his train filling the temple.[940]

Whitefield's early practice as a new believer was to read the Scripture and pray on his knees over each verse. He would use Matthew Henry's commentary to clarify any confusion he encountered in a passage.[941] Whitefield's hunger for the word was constant, and he never gave up his devotion to study and preparation. His furious pace drove him to repeat many sermons. On his last tour of the colonies, however, he could be found on his voyage preparing messages to preach.[942]

Philip posed questions concerning Whitefield's spiritual life:

> Did the study of oratory estrange him from his closet, or lessen his dependence on the Holy Spirit? Did his natural speaking skills divert him from living habitually in the light of eternity and the divine presence? Whitefield was a man who lived nearer to God and approached nearer to the perfection of oratory. He was too devotional to be cooled by rules, and too natural to be spoiled by art, and too much in earnest to win souls to neglect system (a set pattern of doing something).[943] Whitefield's devotion was self-sacrificial. He raised a fortune for his beloved Bethesda orphanage, but because he never pocketed any amount of significance for his personal use, he wanted to be free and clear of any accusation. His need for money to get started with home furnishings after his marriage demonstrated his unselfishness as he had to borrow furniture and personal necessities to furnish their meager home. He was often the conduit for charitable causes, including oppressed Christians; he did not hesitate to

---

939   Belcher, 506.
940   Ibid., 506.
941   Andrews, 423.
942   Fish, 181.
943   Philip, 560.

help people and quite often he would ask the huge crowds coming to hear him preach to contribute to these causes.[944]

Whitefield's commitment was a conduit for self-sacrifice in so many episodes of his life. Fish spoke of his integrity:

> Though vast sums of money passed through his hands, he refused the opportunity to become rich. Though many scandalous stories and jokes were told of Whitefield, there is not the slightest hint of any misconduct by him. He clearly enjoyed being famous but also feared it. Throughout his life, he purposely removed himself from positions in the secular world. He was at the core a man of integrity. He was transformed by the same new birth he preached to others.[945]

Whitefield practiced self-denial for the sake of others throughout his ministry. Belden revealed his selflessness: "His own personal sacrifices were proof of his utter religious sincerity—mortgaging his estate up to the hilt, despoiling his picture-gallery of masterpiece after masterpiece, living in obscure simplicity in order to pay for the passion of social reclamation, and reform that belief in Christ had brought him."[946]

His shining example of devotion is seen in Whitefield's perseverance. He had to cut back and go without preaching for several seasons in the last decade of his life, but never let the setbacks deter him. He was always on the go and died preaching, instead of pining away in a place where he no longer was of benefit to others.[947]

Benjamin Franklin paid tribute to Whitefield in the following letter to the Georgia Assembly: "I knew him intimately upwards of thirty years, his integrity, disinterestedness (objectivity and impartiality), and indefatigable zeal in prosecuting every good work, I have never seen equaled and shall never see it exceeded."[948]

Whitefield provided a model of constant vigilance to do God's will and never settled for anything less, a model that today's believer can and should follow. His consistent devotion is an example that can benefit all believers.

---

944   Mansfield, 181-183.

945   Fish, 204.

946   Belden, 242.

947   This statement is based on his perseverance to come back after long bouts of illness and his seeking to continue the ministry God called him to.

948   Dallimore, *George Whitefield: God's Anointed Servant in the Great Revival of the Eighteenth Century*, 181.

WHITEFIELD'S MINISTRY DISPLAYED
A CULTURAL APPEAL TO ALL

Whitefield's origins and the people he touched throughout his ministry are remarkable. He ran the gamut of all groups of people in every echelon of society. His humble beginning as a potboy in the Bell Inn allowed him to be comfortable with all groups of people in every place he traveled. He played many roles as a student at Oxford, as a promising young preacher, and he wound up as a respected and influential preacher who affected two continents. He was a trailblazing missionary in Georgia, a fellow preacher in the New England colonies, a doctrinal mainstay related to the Doctrines of Grace. In association with the upper classes, through his sponsorship by Lady Huntingdon, he became a chaplain to royalty, while remaining a great preacher whom people from all strata flocked to hear. He was a benevolent sponsor of Bethesda and a statesman and friend of governing officials (especially in the colonies), through the roles he played.[949]

Hoffer shared Whitefield's cultural appeal:

> A distinctive feature of Whitefield's life and ministry was to cut through all levels of society and be at home with any group of people. He loved the slaves in America and they loved him. He spoke for their cause and went among them to preach the gospel. In all, Whitefield would make seven trips to the colonies, interspersed with tours to Scotland and stops in Bermuda and Gibraltar. By the 1750's, the revival had spread to the backwoods of Virginia as Baptist and Methodist minsters reached out to settlers and slaves.[950]

Whoever they were, through coming to God as an undeserving sinner in need of Christ, they would experience an unlimited spiritual transformation by entering into the new birth and pursuing holiness. Whitefield contributed to an era of revolutionary change through an understanding of the equality salvation brings to everyone who comes to Christ.[951]

Whitefield followed in the footsteps of the Puritans and Quakers as an early advocate of treating slaves humanely. He was one of the first well-known religious leaders of modern times to address their spiritual

---

949   These are positions Whitefield held, described all through this work.

950   Hoffer, 97.

951   The truth of this observation is verified by the cross-cultural appeal and response to Whitefield's preaching and message.

needs in a serious and consistent way.[952]

Whitefield's ministry to the social outcasts at Kingswood Collier's mines indicated his willingness to go anywhere and to anyone. Actors ridiculed him, but many more respected him. The same was true of much of the royalty with whom he associated.[953]

The children especially loved Whitefield. He spoke to their hearts clearly, and he was their patron to those in need, as seen in the establishment of the Bethesda orphanage.[954] The children heard him gladly, and many heart-warming stories reveal his influence on their lives. Once when he visited a young boy's deathbed, the child testified to the assurance of his salvation when he said, "I want to go to Mr. Whitefield's God."[955]

It could be said of Whitefield that he fulfilled Paul's quest "to be all things to all men that by all means, I might save some" (I Cor. 9: 23b). Whitefield was comfortable in any situation with any group of people. He was seen sleeping by a campfire in a thick wilderness with a group going to Bethesda, hearing packs of wild wolves in the distance. He was seen trying to converse with a Native American chief about his soul and at Lady Huntingdon's interacting freely and properly with the highest-ranking people in England. His adaptability in every situation led him to feel at ease as he identified with everyone he came in contact with. His quest to be used by God led him to go to Georgia, where he related very well to the populace. The same place where John Wesley failed miserably was fertile ground for the gospel message under Whitefield's leadership. His graciousness to people of all cultural backgrounds was more than a gift: it was a strong compulsion.[956]

The modern day cry to target a group of people for ministry while ignoring others certainly does not have a scriptural foundation. Targeting specific groups of people was not the way Jesus conducted his ministry, and Whitefield did not try to reach a certain type of people only and it is certainly not the way God expects us to conduct church ministry.

A denominational meeting two decades ago featured two speakers

---

952 Dallimore, vol. 1, 588.

953 These responses are based on the varied reactions to Whitefield's preaching to all areas of society.

954 Cashin, 22-23.

955 Wakeley, 334.

956 The diversity of witnessing experiences Whitefield found himself immersed.

who shared how they did evangelism in their church. One speaker shared how his church was targeting only "baby boomers with the gospel." The fledgling mission didn't make it. The final speaker was a pastor of a large Southern Baptist church in Southern California. He approached reaching people from the right perspective. Pausing to reflect on what the previous speaker said on targeting baby boomers, he said, "We just boom everybody with the gospel in our church."[957] This method of evangelism worked very well for the church he served as pastor

We must follow Whitefield's example, reaching out to everyone. For in his reaching all sorts of people, he reached more people for Christ. He left a greater mark on the world than he would ever have done if he had targeted only a certain group of people. Reaching out to all groups of people is a significant example for believers in their witnessing and ministry to others.

WHITEFIELD WAS A MODEL
OF CALVINISTIC EVANGELISM

These two terms of Calvinism and evangelism have been perceived to be contradictory by those claiming to know everything about this system of theology. One has only to go back to the resource Calvin has been on the world through his teaching and writing. His teaching has been significant in all denominations, whether he is contradicted or admired.

Whitefield disproved the impression some people have of Calvinism being anti-evangelistic. He never let his belief in the Doctrines of Grace restrict his outreach efforts.[958] On the contrary, this emphasis delineated in his teaching actually enhanced his efforts. Lambert stressed how Whitefield exalted God's work in salvation:

> Adhering to strict Calvinism, Whitefield was a passive instrument who proclaimed what God was doing, leaving little room for human agency. The second awakening represented a sharp break. Men and women became the main actors, shaping the revivals through publicity and persuasion... Whitefield also believed in human— means including newspaper publicity,

---

957 Rob Zinn's Pastor of Immanuel Baptist Church in Highland, CA statement made at an Evangelism Meeting of the Gold Coast Baptist Association, Gold Coast Church Ventura, CA in the early 1990's.

958 Lawson, 67-68.

outdoor sermons, public debate–constituted vehicles by which God mediated His grace.[959]

Whitefield's deep held belief was that God's sovereignty is especially utilized in the preaching of the gospel through the means of God's calling out the elect for salvation.[960]

Many have used predestination and limited atonement, along with Calvinism's insistence on everyone's inability to come to Christ for salvation by free-will, as an opponent of evangelism. They have concluded, "You can't hold to these truths and be evangelistic." Whitefield's response would be, "Why not?" He did not know the identity of the elect, but he did know he was under the Great Commission. He knew people were lost without Christ and needed to hear the gospel to place their faith and trust in Christ for salvation. Lambert again related, "And because no one could be certain of election, all needed to hear and read God's Word."[961] Whitefield's call was to preach the gospel, not to discern who the elect were.

Whitefield actually became a stronger Calvinist as he grew older. He said he got his teaching from the confession of faith enumerated in the Thirty-Nine Articles of the Church of England. He was also influenced by the Tennents and Jonathan Edwards. He loved Scotland with its heavily Calvinistic influence, and is buried in a Presbyterian Church where one of his disciples, Pastor Jonathan Parsons, thundered out the Doctrines of Grace.[962] Whitefield saw no conflict between Calvinism and evangelism. The world's lost condition and hopelessness were strong motivators for him. Realizing people were without Christ only caused him to fulfill his calling to evangelistic endeavors.

Some have faulted Whitefield for not using a modern day altar call, but he chose other methods for relaying information to those whose hearts had been awakened. Those who were awakened to salvation handed him notes in some of his meetings, while he saw other people individually after his meetings. [963] At other times, he prayed with the

---

959 Lambert, 227.

960 Gillies, ed., *George Whitefield's Journals*, 575.

961 Lambert, 227.

962 The major contributors to Whitefield's Calvinism were his adherence to the Thirty-Nine Articles of the Church of England and his life-long use of Matthew Henry's commentary to supplement his intense study of the Bible. These set the foundation for other sources of influence as he aged.

963 Dallimore, vol. 2, 117.

masses who were moved to profess Christ.[964] The public invitation had not been popularized in his day, and he knew that coming forward in an assembly did not save people. It was enough innovation to have persuasive preaching. Alan Street verified that Whitefield gave no invitation, but gave an opportunity to talk later with him stating: "He urged people to make an appointment with him in private after he preached the gospel and exhorted them to repent and receive Christ. Often there were so many 'anxious inquirers' he could not eat or sleep."[965]

It was essential to Whitefield that people understand the Doctrines of Grace. His preaching in many sermons was thematically centered on the specific truths of Calvinism. No one can doubt Whitefield's passion for the lost and his commitment to evangelism, but many are puzzled that he married evangelism with Calvinism. This mixture was not surprising to him. He would say he was only emphasizing those New Testament doctrines highlighted by the Apostle Paul, particularly in Romans and other books of the New Testament.

Whitefield led the Calvinistic Methodist movement and was its spokesman for the association this group formed. He maintained a close relationship with groups within the movement until the time of his death.

Is there a need for Calvinistic evangelism today? Certainly we should see the need to help people understand their inability to save themselves and their need for a total dependence on God's gracious gift of Christ's sacrifice for their sins, along with their need for assurance of salvation. If these essentials are needed in the modern message of the gospel, there is a need for the type of evangelism with Calvinistic underpinnings that George Whitefield practiced. Dallimore clearly stated in a demonstrative way the gospel Whitefield preached:

> Whitefield speaks to us about the power of the Gospel. It was not the so-called "Social Gospel" but the Gospel of redeeming grace—the only Gospel—that wrought the great change two hundred years ago. In the knowledge of the Gospel Whitefield went with confidence to the semi-heathen Kingswood colliers or the equally godless aristocracy and to all other classes of mankind and witnessed the transformation of lives among all. The Gospel is the need of this present hour. Not the partial Gospel which characterizes so much of today's evangelicalism, but the whole Gospel that declares the

---

964   Alan R. Street, *The Effective Invitation* (Fleming H. Revell: Old Tappan, NJ, 1984), 90.
965   Ibid., 90.

majesty and holiness of God, the utter helplessness of man, the necessity of repentance, and a salvation that is manifested, not in a mere profession, but in the miracle of a new life. May Whitefield's example bring Christians back to the Gospel in its fullness and therewith in its power.[966]

Paige Patterson, president of Southwestern Baptist Theological Seminary, stated there are four basic reasons why we believe some of the main tenants of Calvinism, in regards to predestination:

Predestination is God's action: (1) To show from start to finish salvation is a work of God and we cannot contribute to it by good works, (2) To help us know God's salvation is eternal because He is the source of it, (3) To convince us we are not an accident but that God has a plan for our lives and when one accepts Christ they enter into that plan, and (4) God will accomplish his completed salvation of the world in His way according to his sovereign will. It will all turn out perfect at the return of Christ and end of the world because He is completely orchestrating it.[967]

Just as in Whitefield's preaching and practice, these themes need to be central to what we believe. The other extreme in this doctrinal issue is to have an attitude that the gospel can be accepted and rejected again and again. Free-will is abused through this belief, giving people control of their salvation, when in reality it is God who initiates salvation from start to finish.

WHITEFIELD DISPLAYED ENCOURAGEMENT
AND FELLOWSHIP CENTERED IN THE SCRIPTURE

Whitefield was an encourager and sought others of similar persuasion around the word. He would not be forced into conformity with any person or group. His fellowship extended to brethren who preached the gospel to the lost. He was at home with and relished the friendship of these and many others:

- Whitefield's friendship with the Wesleys went back to college days at Oxford

- He loved the Tennent family, their commitment to an itinerant ministry and their ability to train workers in that vocation.

- His admiration for Howell Harris stemmed from the fact that he was a field preacher.

---

966 Dallimore, vol. 2, 536.
967 A Message by Dr. Paige Patterson Southwestern Baptist Theological Seminary in a Spring Chapel service 2007 on Predestination and Free Will in Evangelism.

- He admired Jonathan Edwards for his influence in the community of Northampton and his commitment to doctrinal excellence.

- James Hervey and others supported him in England.

- The Erskine brothers were early friends in Scotland because of theological agreement with him in the Doctrines of Grace.

- William McCulloch and James Robe were his ardent allies in Scotland. They were responsible for the preparation of Whitefield's meetings in Scotland, particularly the Cambuslang area meetings of 1742.[968]

The driving force that brought Whitefield to these relationships was fellowship in the gospel and the fact that they were fellow laborers in the harvest. He felt more than kinship with these brethren; he found sweet communion with them because he knew God was using them as his servants.

Lady Huntingdon's association with Whitefield arose because of his doctrine and outreach to the masses. She discovered the Doctrines of Grace, built chapels and sponsored ministers who would preach the gospel through their emphasis on these cherished beliefs.[969]

God used doctrinal fellowship to unite people through Whitefield's ministry. This union in the gospel is why Whitefield, though ordained in the Church of England, would fellowship with any gospel preacher and could preach in their churches.

Tyerman describes the way Whitefield reached across all types of diverse religious parties for the gospel's sake:

> Whitefield was a man of no sect; the sphere of his labours had no boundary; holding office, as it were, in every church, his communion was with the pious of every name. In the erection of this cenotaph all may unite—the Episcopalian, who would say with Toplady, that "he was a true and faithful son of the Church of England,"—the Dissenter, who considers his whole course but practical independency,—the Calvinist, who admires his conscientious adherence to the truth,—and, likewise, the Wesleyan, who remembers him as, in life and death, the dearest friend of Wesley.[970]

Fellowship with believers cannot be forced or imposed by higher

---

968 These were all leaders in the awakening movements in both continents. He wrote to these leaders and fellowshipped with them in the meetings he conducted or the lifelong association he had with them.

969 Johnston, vol 2, 70.

970 Tyerman, vol. 2, 606.

denominational offices, but fellowship is enhanced when we find support through the preaching of the gospel to the world. We are strengthened by the unity we have in that work. The contrast is stark in this type of doctrinal fellowship. Without this fellowship of preaching the gospel in some denominations, one could honestly question the validity of continuing a fellowship that ignores or denies the preaching of the gospel as a basis for union. When we fellowship in the Word, we speak through the Scriptures and plan activities to help edify others in the Word of God. This type of fellowship is the greatest form of unity and is needed today.

WHITEFIELD EXCELLED IN PUTTING
NO BOUNDARIES ON THE GOSPEL

The limitations that others put on Whitefield's ministry were not ones he put on himself. He went many places and to all sorts of people with the gospel. His travels to America and back are monumental. He extended his ministry to the places where few would have thought of going, such as to the Colliers at Kingswood and the penal colony of Georgia to establish an orphanage. Whitefield extended his influence through his appointment as Chaplain to Lady Huntingdon. He died, not in his native country, but in America where he had a kinship with many. He was there to preach the gospel to the mission field God had given him, and God gave him many mission fields. Lambert illustrated the secret of Whitefield's crossing of these barriers with the message of the gospel in this effective way:

> Whitefield understood the importance of contextualizing his message. He preached gospel principles in language drawn from everyday life. To understand Whitefield's sermons, then, it is necessary to examine not just texts but contexts in which his audiences read and heard them. Whitefield knew the importance of framing his message in language familiar to his hearers. He endeavored to clothe his ideas in such plain language that the servant may understand, believing that if the poor and unlearned can comprehend, the learned and rich must.[971]

Fish also described how Whitefield influenced so many:

---

971 Lambert, 155.

Perhaps the most important fact to remember about Whitefield is the expanse of his ministry. Between 1736 and 1770 he preached more than 18,000 sermons to audiences both large and small. It is probable that as many as 80% of those living in America during that time actually heard Whitefield speak at least once. In all, his audiences numbered in the millions. Possibly, millions more were exposed to his words through newspapers, magazines, and printed versions of his sermons, journals and letters. Whitefield was definitely ahead of his time in terms of exposure and publicity. Not until the 20th century, with motion pictures, radio, television and the Internet has one person been able to reach so many people with none of the modern conveniences we have today.[972]

Hoffer believed the Grand Itinerant would have been famous today. He says:

Whitefield would have been a marvel on television, his dramatic presentation, his vocalization; his gestures magnified by the media and would be brought into the homes with perfect clarity… Whitefield's itinerancy is also mirrored in modern revival tours, starting with Billy Sunday's…continuing with Billy Graham's.[973]

The theme of the book of Acts is "nothing can stop the gospel geographically or culturally."[974] The book starts in Jerusalem and ends up in Rome, as if to trek through the entire book from a Jewish city to a Gentile one. How representative Acts is of this progression in Whitefield's ministry! He left his native country for the mission field of America, dying there.

The limitation we place on our lives is self-imposed. God provides the means and will supply the conviction when listeners hear the message if we will only go to others with the gospel. Whitefield went to others with the gospel this way and God opened many doors. A possible reason we don't see fruit in ministry is our failure to seize opportunities God gives us for ministry. We must constantly seek God to give us opportunities to share the gospel. He followed God's will to preach the gospel in new venues, and is long remembered because of his willingness to go through these doors of opportunity.

---

972   Fish, 196.

973   Hoffer, 124.

974   Frank Stagg, *The Book of Acts: The Early Struggle for the Unhindered Gospel.* (Broadman: Nashville, 1955), 12-13.

WHITEFIELD PREEMINENTLY LEFT AN
INFLUENCE ON SOCIETY AND CHRISTENDOM

Whitefield was respected in all levels of society. His benevolent work with orphans, his willingness to continue with the work God called him to—in spite of his health problems and his constant preaching on a round-the-clock schedule—endeared him to many. Whitefield was a preeminent influential leader in the history of Christianity throughout two continents.

Churches need to help widows and orphans that are too often forgotten. Churches need to reach all levels of society and not be a church for only "certain types" of people but every strata of people in every culture.

We remember Whitefield because he was involved in all sorts of ministries to all sorts of people. He demonstrated, by his example, that Christians can have a significance through their testimony and influence.

We expand ministries through listening to God and utilizing the opportunities God gives us.[975] The legacy that Whitefield left behind, forgotten by much of the world, is still vast. His work survives today in the lives of the people he touched in Britain and America through their descendants.

Dallimore shared the history of the Tabernacle after Whitefield:

> The Tabernacle continued its work for more than a century after Whitefield's death. In 1869 the building was demolished and a smaller one was built in its place which survived till 1930. The Tottenham Court Road Chapel continued to attract large crowds, including several members of the nobility. Near the end of World War II, a German rocket destroyed the structure. A smaller building was built in the original site, which remains today.[976]

Whitefield's permanent influence is amazing, given what he did not leave behind. Fish related this influence with none of the modern supports used today, "When he died, George Whitefield left behind no distinctive theology, no college, and no denominational structure. His published sermons and journals are relatively few in number. How does one access the impact of a man whose work for God is often obscured by

---

975   The many open doors Whitefield went through with excitement for what the Lord would do through Him.

976   Fish, 195.

John Wesley, Charles Wesley, and Jonathan Edwards?"[977]

John Wesley is helpful in understanding Whitefield's place in the history of Christianity. He preached a memorial sermon November 18, 1770, in a service dedicated to Whitefield's memory. Wesley recounted his friend's life, accomplishments, and beliefs. He closed by saying, "Have we read or heard of any person since the apostles, who testified to the gospel of God, through so widely extended a space, through so large a part of the habitable world? Have we read or heard of any person who called so many thousands, so many myriad of sinners to repentance?"[978]

John Newton preached a sermon in tribute to George Whitefield on November 11, 1770. In his introduction of this work, he shared the unique style Whitefield had that the Lord gave him that no one could copy.[979] He acknowledged the model that Whitefield was for preachers: "But notwithstanding he was in other respects a signal and happy pattern and model for preachers. He introduced a way of close and lively application to the conscience for which I believe many of the most admired and eminent preachers now living will not be ashamed, or unwilling to acknowledge themselves his debtors."[980]

Whitefield serves as a model for dynamic preaching and effective ministry to this day. His influence will never be diminished. We remember him as one of the greatest preachers in any generation. He pioneered mass evangelism. He showed how a gospel ministry cares for the social needs of people with the Bethesda orphanage. Whitefield did not let 18th century travel or lodging hinder him. His preaching style and the response to his sermons will probably be what is remembered most about him, and its effect will never be forgotten. Whitefield did God's will at any cost and accomplished the calling God placed on His life. He serves as a testimony to how God uses someone who is willing to yield their life completely to Him. We need to go and do likewise!

---

977   Ibid., 196.
978   Ibid., 196.
979   Tyerman, vol. 2, 624-625.
980   Dallimore, vol. 2, 534.

GLOSSARY OF TERMS

ALDERSGATE: The street where a Moravian chapel in Fetter Lane was located. Peter Bohler, the leader, ministered there. It was sacred to John Wesley for it was where he testified to conversion after hearing the reading of Luther's preface to the Romans and identifying himself as being that man, like Luther, in need of salvation. He described his heart as strangely warmed. After this experience ,Whitefield sought Wesley out to use him in ministry to the miners at Kingswood Colliers near Bristol.

THE ARMINIAN METHODIST MOVEMENT: In contrast to the Calvinist Methodist movement, it was the theology widespread due to John Wesley's influence. The belief exalted the free-will of man as opposed to the sovereignty of God in salvation. The belief was that a person could lose the salvation they once possessed through disobedience or denial of Christ. The doctrine of predestination was heavily opposed by the Arminian views and was one of the chief beliefs Wesley initially disagreed with Whitefield over.

ARMINIANISM: The belief of Jacob Arminius highlighting the free-will of man as opposed to God's sovereignty. The view heavily relies on man's free will to accept or reject God. The view is used to justify a person losing a relationship with God that they once had because of that person's free will to reject salvation in Christ by belief or by works. John Wesley subscribed to this theology through the influence of the Moravians.

THE ASSOCIATE PRESBYTERY: The association that was primarily spearheaded by Ralph and Ebenezer Erskine who sought to assert the true doctrines of the Reformation as first preached in Scotland under John Knox. They also separated from the state churches because of perceived Episcopal practices within the established church in Scotland particularly in the appointment of pastor's and self-governance of the congregation. They enlisted churches to disassociate with the state church and align themselves with this movement. When Whitefield chose to preach in and cooperate with several state churches, he was criticized for it. The Erskines did not cooperate with any of Whitefield's meetings after he made the decision to preach in churches unaffiliated with the Associate Presbytery on his first visit to Scotland.

THE AWAKENING MOVEMENT: A term more prevalent in America to describe the impact of the gospel on several areas, most notably New England, but not restricted to that area. It resulted in an interest in spiritual things, mass conversions and preaching under preachers like George Whitefield and Jonathan Edwards. It roughly spanned two decades from 1735-1756. The awakening movement was more prevalent under Whitefield in the early days of his ministry. His last two decades resulted in a reduction of field preaching because of health concerns.

CALVINISM: The theology articulated by John Calvin as a system of belief related to God's sovereignty and grace in salvation. Taken from his *Institutes of Christian Religion*, it was the initial theology of the Reformation. The system has five points represented in the acrostic TULIP: Total Depravity, Unconditional Election, Limited Atonement, Irresistible Grace and Perseverance of the Saints. The five points were answers to Arminian theology through the Council of Dort in 1618 and the influence of Jacob Arminius in Holland and the Dutch Reformed Church. The main points have been used to detect one's view toward salvation. These doctrines were popular in Whitefield's day and were adopted by him and rejected by John Wesley, who subscribed to Arminian theology.

CALVINISTIC EVANGELISM: The type of evangelism practiced by Whitefield and Edwards looked to God to awaken the heart, drawing people to a need for His salvation. The awakening resulted in repentance and forgiveness. The Calvinistic expression of God being the sole originator of salvation and a person's response to His gracious choice was prominent in this style of evangelism. Calvinistic evangelism is in contrast to Arminian evangelism practiced in the 2nd Great Awakening and Charles Finney's ministry in the first half of the 18th century. The free will of man deciding to trust in Christ was more of an emphasis in this type of evangelism.

CALVINISTIC METHODIST: The movement primarily organized by Howell Harris and George Whitefield to promote fellowship with other Calvinistic gospel preachers in England. Whitefield was the first moderator of the group. The fellowship was formed before societies John Wesley organized. Calvinists today do not identify themselves as Methodist because of Wesley's turning to Arminianism. They prefer to be identified more with the reformed movement.

CENOTAPH: A monument erected in honor of a person or group of people whose remains are elsewhere or in the general location. Whitefield's Cenotaph is located in the church in where is buried at The Old South Church in Newburyport, Massachusetts.

COW HEEL: A dish made from heel of an ox or cow that is stewed to a jelly. It is also known as "neat's foot." Whitefield disclosed it was one of his favorite dishes; he thought this would be a surprise to many that he dined on such cuisine.

DEBTORS' COLONY: The specific designation was given for the colony of Georgia. Settlers came to Georgia with safe passage to settle the land in return for forgiveness of the debt. Although life was hard in the pioneer colony where settlers were exposed to disease, threat of invasion and danger, it was an alternative to time spent in prison for payment of the debt. Australia was settled in similar fashion by those released from prison or in payment for a crime. Several children were made orphans and found themselves left all alone after parents succumbed to these elements. Whitefield also brought orphans with him from England to the Bethesda orphanage.

A DEVOUT CALL TO A SERIOUS AND HOLY LIFE: The work by William Law was used by the Holy Club in Oxford to promote deeds of holiness and piety in ministry to people. The book is devoid of teaching the new birth and led members leaving school after graduation unconverted. William Law eventually opposed Whitefield's ministry, probably for his emphasis on the new birth.

THE DOCTRINES OF GRACE: The term used to describe the doctrines of the Reformation as they pertain to salvation derived from Calvinism. The doctrines maintained that man is saved by God's grace, which is offered to us in Christ by God's sovereign will.

THE ENGLISH ACT OF TOLERANCE: The granting of religious freedom in England through the Glorious Revolution under King William and Queen Mary in 1688. The act came on the heels of Charles II's rule of England, as a Protestant, followed by James II 's reversal through his attempt to impose Catholicism once again on England. The act was a welcome relief under Protestant rule that resulted in England being a Protestant country forever.

THE ENLIGHTENMENT MOVEMENT: A philosophical movement of the 18th century, characterized by belief in the power of human reason and by innovations of thought in political, religious and educational worlds. Most of the clergy in the Church of England were influenced in Whitefield's day by this teaching that led to a departure from the authority of Scripture and the preaching of the gospel resulting in the new birth.

EPISCOPALIAN: The form of government by the Church of England meaning "rule by bishops." It is the common name for the Church of England in America, although some Anglican churches claim they are the "Church of England" in America and do not cooperate with the Episcopalian church.

THE ERSKINES: These two brothers (Ralph and Ebenezer) separated from the established church in Scotland. They had a more conservative and Calvinistic viewpoint. They corresponded with Whitefield initially, but when he preached in state churches and cooperated with these churches, they turned against him.

FREE-WILL BAPTISTS: This Baptist group is Arminian in their view of personal salvation. They believe the free-will of man determines his free choice to accept or deny Christ in their salvation experience. They were founded by Benjamin Randall, who was Whitefield's last convert to Christ. Randall, who was already under conviction after attending some of Whitefield's meeting, trusted Christ to save him after learning of Whitefield's death. It is interesting Whitefield as a Calvinist led one to Christ who founded one of the only Arminian groups of Baptists.

THE GREAT AWAKENING: The general term used to describe the periods of revival of religion resulting in mass conversions and intense religious interest in England and America. The movement took place primarily during Whitefield's ministry and briefly during the Wesleys' long ministry in England. The generally agreed date for the awakening was 1735, with the inception of the awakening at Northampton, Massachusetts and it ended with the beginning of The Seven Years' War in 1756.

THE GREAT COMMISSION: The last command Jesus gave his followers and a belief that is still applicable to today for all believers, as it was given in Matt. 28:19-20. The commission is to make disciples, baptize them and ground them in the faith.

THE HALFWAY COVENANT: An agreement in the early Puritan churches of American, resulting in those turning twelve automatically being added to the church rolls, regardless of their converted or unconverted state. This man-made covenant resulted in unconverted church members. Many were converted in the Northampton revival beginning in 1735 under the leadership of the pastor of the Congregational church, Jonathan Edwards. Edwards grandfather, Solomon Stoddard had initiated this covenant in the church where Edwards succeeded him as pastor in Northampton.

HIGH CHURCH: A style of worship in the Church of England that relies heavily on liturgy, the Book of Common Prayer, and aspects of the service that are similar to Catholicism. The worship is filled with a formal style of ritual and routine in the order of service.

ITINERANT MINISTRY: A ministry led by ministers who were not pastors of specific churches, but preached throughout a certain area, many times in open meetings. The ministry was popularized by Whitefield and William Tennent's school for itinerant ministers, known as The Log College in Pennsylvania, which eventually evolved into New Jersey College and later Princeton University. Gilbert Tennent's son preached in many meetings with Whitefield. Whitefield was also called "The Grand Itinerant" by many of the day and by historians who evaluated his ministry.

THE LAYING ON OF HANDS: The practice was laden with biblical precedent denoting the setting aside of men usually for vocational tasks in Christian ministry. The Anglican Church used the practice to designate ordination into ministry. Whitefield was ordained for ministry in such a manner through Bishop Benson at the St. Mary de Crypt church.

MANUAL FOR WINCHESTER SCHOLARS: A Manual of Prayers for the use of the Scholars of Winchester College, by Thomas Ken, D.D. London: Printed for John Martyn, 1675. The manual was used by Whitefield and his fellow students at the St. Mary de Crypt School they attended.

MERRY ANDREWS: A clown, comic or play actor in colonial times traceable back to medieval times. In Whitefield's day, one taunting him at Moorfields was an exhibitionist stripping—off all his clothes to distract the crowd from Whitefield's preaching.

NEW LIGHTS: Ministers supporting the awakening movement and advocating the preaching of the gospel everywhere and the personal salvation of the new birth. Initially, Tennent, Edwards and Whitefield, representing the New Lights, became the voices of awakening as they preached the gospel to masses of people.

OLD LIGHTS: The initial group of ministers opposed to the awakening movement and Whitefield. They were supportive of the crown and advocate a valid ministry only in church buildings.

THE PIETIST MOVEMENT: A reactionary movement started in Germany to emphasize more of the inner spiritual life of believers. It was set against the formalism and confessional theology of the state churches in Europe coming out of the Reformation. It was led in part by Philipp Jacob Spener and began in the Lutheran church. August Franke promoted the movement through the founding of his Halle schools. The Moravians were deeply pietistic and influenced the Wesleys, beginning with John's conversion and dependence on spiritual impulses some would view as extra-biblical such as the casting of lots. The name defines spiritual piety as an inward virtue designed to emulate the life of Christ.

PRACTICAL HOLINESS: The condition opposed to sinless perfection. It is the process of growth in Christ-likeness through which believers live godly lives free from sin's entrapment through temptation.

THE PRESS: The term refers to the act of taking men into the navy by force, with or without notice. It was used by the Royal Navy during the 18th and early 19th centuries during wartime as a means of crewing warships. Merchant sailors as well as sailors from other nations were impressed. Several of the ships Whitefield sailed on during his thirteen voyages across the Atlantic employed this practice.

THE PURITAN MOVEMENT: The group of ministers and theologians who in the latter part of the 16th century, started to reform the Church of England through a more biblical emphasis in their theology and church practice. The movement also popularized Calvinism in England and Reformation theology. They believed in staying in the church and purifying it from within, which is the reason for their name's designation.

REPROBATION: The reversing of truth that calls good evil and evil good according to Isaiah 5:20. The designation used by some Calvinists for people they believe to be reprobate is to be incapable of saving faith in Christ and evidence of not being the elect. The difficulty came in determining who was actually reprobate. Reprobation usually relates to moral behavior stemming from rejection of God, his moral law and the gospel of salvation in Christ.

THE SEPARATIST MOVEMENT: The more extreme movement in the general time of the Puritan movement. The Separatists advocated separation from the Church of England because of excessive government regulation of religion and the belief that the King was not the head of the Church of England. The Baptists, Pilgrims and Quakers were leaders in this movement. The Pilgrims' reason for coming to America was religious liberty not granted to them by the King and established church.

SERAPH: Another word for "angel," highlighting their joyful function of announcing good news and applied in a musical sense. Whitefield was identified by this description in his preaching. The pastor is called "an angel of the church" in Jesus' message to the seven churches of Asia in Revelation 2 and 3. Whitefield referred to his forceful preaching as "lifting up his voice like a trumpet."[981]

SINLESS PERFECTION: The belief that evolved from Arminianism. It maintains through holiness and being set apart separate from sin one can achieve this status. It maintained a person reach a point of never sinning again. Wesley was blamed for this aberration being the logical outcome of his teaching on holiness. He denied these charges and his denial resulted in Whitefield's cooperation with Wesley in the last decade of Whitefield's life.

THE SOLEMN LEAGUE AND COVENANT: A statement, dating from the 1640s, that was part of the Scottish opposition to Charles I imposing episcopacy on Scotland. Charles II made opposition illegal, but some Scottish Presbyterians clung to it and were known as the Covenanters.

THE TABERNACLE: The main chapel Whitefield used in London in the 1740's to hold meetings indoors. It was remodeled in the 1750's to be a more permanent structure, and it survived into the 19th century.

---

981 Gillies, 169, 258.

THE THIRTY-NINE ARTICLES OF THE CHURCH OF ENGLAND: In essence this is a doctrinal statement of the Church of England as found in the Book of Common Prayer. An important point for Whitefield in his Calvinist views was that article 9,10 and 17 are very Calvinistic in nature. They are discussed in chapter 8 as to their specific doctrinal affirmations. They refer to Predestination, Election and Eternal Security.

THE WESLEYAN MOVEMENT: Followers of Christ under John Wesley's leadership first formed societies and chapels under his leadership. They formed the Methodist Church after his death. They held to an Arminian view of salvation, free will and the possibility of losing salvation.

UNIVERSAL REDEMPTION: This view of Arminianism and other sincere believers was popularized by Wesley. Those holding to this view believe Christ's atonement has the capability of bringing salvation to everyone who believes in Christ. This view was opposed to Particular election which says that Christ death was only for the elect and sufficient for only those who believe in Him. Adherents believe Christ did not die for those who will not believe.

WESLEYAN SOCIETIES: These were groups that existed within the Church of England led by Wesley and his followers. They promoted the ideas of the awakening and spiritual devotion to Scripture in contrast to the formalism of the Church of England. They were the source of the strength and organization of the Wesleyan movement that resulted in the Methodist church. Small accountability groups were a characteristic of these societies.

WHIT-MONDAY: Also known as Pentecost Monday and Monday of the Holy Spirit. It is the holiday celebrating the day after Pentecost, a movable feast in the Christian calendar. Whitefield refers to preaching at Moorfields in open air to a hostile crowd on this specific day.

WILLIAM WILBERFORCE: The great English statesman in Parliament who made it his life-long quest to abolish slavery in England. Wilberforce was heavily influenced by his pastor John Newton, an admirer of Whitefield. Wilberforce attended meetings at the Tabernacle as a child in some of the final years of Whitefield's ministry there.

PHOTO GALLERY

Figure 1- Whitefield Memorial Church, Park Road,
Gloucester. Display of Whitefield's preaching to crowds.

Figure 2- The Pulpit where Whitefield preached
his first sermon inside St. Mary de Crypt church
in Gloucester, the church of Whitefield's youth.

Figure 3- Whitefield's old chair preserved at the Rodborough Tabernacle, in Gloucestershire.

Figure 4-Unique Portrait of Whitefield at the Tottenham Court Chapel in London.

Figure 5- The commemorative pulpit at Hanham Mount marking the place where Whitefield inaugurated field preaching to the Miners of Kingswood Colliers outside of Bristol.

Figure 6- Kennington Common: An early outdoor preaching spot for Whitefield.

Figure 7- Moorfield's Tabernacle where Whitefield faced
fierce opposition in preaching.

Figure 8- Whitefield Chapel at Bethesda
which is now the Bethesda Academy.

Figure 9- Portrait of Selina,
Countess of Huntingdon
(Lady Huntingdon)
at Bethesda. She was the
great benefactor of the
early Methodist movement.

Figure 10- The location of
the old court house in Philadelphia
where Whitefield preached
his first sermon in America.

Figure 11- Commemorative statute of
Whitefield preaching at the
University of Pennsylvania
in Philadelphia.

Figure 12- Boston Common where Whitefield preached to a
great majority of Boston on several occasions.

Figure 13- Interior of the Old South Church in Newburyport, Mass.
where Whitefield is buried in the basement, under the pulpit.

Figure 14- Former parsonage of Old South Church where Whitefield died.

Figure 15- The crypt where Whitefield is buried
in the basement of the Old South Church.

Dan Nelson performs impersonations of George Whitefield. This
is at Southwestern Baptist Theological Seminary chapel service in
Fort Worth, Texas, Nov. 8, 2006.

BIBLIOGRAPHY

BIBLE VERSIONS

The Bible, King James Version. Nashville, TN: Holman Bible, 1999.

BOOKS

Andrews, J. R. *George Whitefield A Light Rising in Obscurity.* London: Morgan and Chase, 2nd ed., 1930.

Beaurepaire, Anthony. *George Whitefield and the Great Evangelical Awakening: An Illustrated History.* London: Protestant Truth Society, 1972.

Belcher, Joseph. *George Whitefield, A Biography with Special Reference to His Labours in America.* New York: American Tract Society, 1938.

Belden, Albert D. *George Whitefield-The Awakener: A Modern Study of the Evangelical Revival.* London: Sampson, Low and Marston, 1930.

Billingsley, Amos Stevens. *The Life of the Great Preacher Rev. George Whitefield.* "Prince of the Pulpit Orators, with the Secret of Success and Specimens of His Sermons." Philadelphia, PA: P.W. Ziegler, 1878.

Cashin, Edward J. *Beloved Bethesda: A History of George Whitefield's Home for Boys, 1740-2000.* Atlanta: Mercer University Press, 2001.

Comfort, Ray. *Whitefield Gold.* Bridge-Logos: Alachua, FL: 2006.

Dallimore, Arnold A. *George Whitefield: God's Anointed Servant in the Great Revival of the Eighteenth Century.* Wheaton, IL: Crossway Books, 1990.

_____*George Whitefield: The Life and Times Of, Volume I.* London: Banner of Truth Trust, 1970.

_____ *George Whitefield The Life and Times Of, Volume II.* London: Banner of Truth Trust, 1980.

Dargan, Edwin Charles. *A History of Preaching.* Grand Rapids, MI: Baker Book House, 1954.

Demaray, Donald E. *Pulpit Giants: What Made Them Great.* Chicago: Moody Press, 1973.

Fant, Clyde E. and William Pinson, editors. *20 Centuries of Great Preaching, Volume II.* "Wesley to Finney." Waco, TX: Word, 1971.

Fawcett, Arthur. *The Cambuslang Revival: The Scottish Evangelical Revival of the Eighteenth Century.* Carlisle, PA: Banner of Truth, 1996.

Fish, Bruce and Becky. *George Whitefield, Pioneering Evangelist.* Uhrichsville, OH: Barbour Books, 2000.

Ferm, Robert. *Cooperative Evangelism.* Grand Rapids, MI: Zondervan, 1958.

Gillies, John. *Memoirs of Rev. George Whitefield.* Hartford, England: Hunt & Son, 1853.

Gillies, John, ed. *George Whitefield's Journal.* London: Banner of Truth Trust, 1960.

Gledstone, James Patterson. *Supreme Among Preachers.* Belfast: Ambassador Publications, reprint, 1998.

Gray, Joseph M. *Prophets of the Soul.* New York: The Abingdon Press, 1936.

Gunther, Peter F., ed. *Great Sermons by Great Preachers.* Chicago: Moody Press, 1960.

Haykin, Michael G. ed. *The Revived Puritan: the Spirituality of George Whitefield.* Dundas, Ontario: Joshua Press, 2000.

Hardman, Keith J. *Seasons of Refreshment.* Grand Rapids, MI: Baker Books, 1994.

_____. *The Spiritual Awakeners.* Chicago: Moody Press, 1983.

Hardy, E. N. *George Whitefield: The Matchless Soul Winner.* New York: American Tract Society, 1938.

Henry, Stuart C. *George Whitefield: Wayfaring Witness.* New York: Abingdon Press, 1957.

Hill, David C. *Messengers of the King.* Minneapolis: Augsburg Publishing House, 1968.

Hoffer, Peter James. *When Benjamin Franklin Met the Reverend Whitefield: Enlightenment, Revival and the Power of the Printed Word.* Baltimore, MD: John Hopkins University Press, 2011.

Hood, Paxton. *The Eighteenth Century Revival.* Belfast: Ambassador, reprint 1997.

Hughes, Maldwyn H. *Wesley and Whitefield.* London: Epworth, 1922.

Johntson, E. A. *George Whitefield: A Definitive Biography. Volume 1,* Tentmaker: Trent, England, 2008.

_____. *George Whitefield: A Definitive Biography. Volume 2,* Tentmaker: Trent, England, 2008.

Kidd, Thomas S. *George Whitefield: America's Spiritual Founding Father.* New Haven, CT: Yale University Press, 2014.

_____. *The Great Awakening: The Roots of Evangelical Christianity in Colonial America.* New Haven, CT: Yale University Press, 2007.

Kirton, John William. *Wesley and Whitefield: The Two Great Evangelists of the Last Century: Their Lives, Their Work, and Their Times.* Birmingham, United Kingdom: Morgan and Scott, 1884.

Lambert, Frank. *Pedlar in Divinity: George Whitefield and the Transatlantic Revivals, 1737-1770*. Princeton, NJ: Princeton University Press, 1994.

Law, William. *A Serious Call to a Devout and Holy Life*. London: Wyvern Books, 1961.

Lawson, Steve *The Evangelistic Zeal of George Whitefield*. Samford, FL: Reformation Trust, 2013.

Mahaffey, Jerome Dean. *Preaching Politics: The Religious Rhetoric of George Whitefield and the Founding of a New Nation*. Waco, TX: Baylor Press, 2007.

_____. *The Accidental Revolutionary: George Whitefield and the Creation of America*. Waco TX: Baylor Press, 2011.

Mansfield, Stephen. *Forgotten Founding Father: The Heroic Legacy of George Whitefield*. Nashville, TN: Highland Books/Cumberland House Pub., 2001.

Marsden, George M. *Jonathan Edwards, A Life*. New Haven, CT: Yale University Press, 2003.

May, G. Lacey. *Studies in Church History: Some Eighteenth Century Churchmen*. London: Society for Promoting Christian Knowledge, 1920.

McConnell, Francis John. *Evangelicals, Revolutionists and Idealists*. New York: Abingdon-Cokesbury Press, 1942.

Mead, Frank S. *The Ten Decisive Battles of Christianity*. New York: Bobbs-Merrill, 1935.

Miller, Perry. *The New England Mind: From Colony to Province*. Cambridge, MA: Harvard University Press, 1953.

Miller, Basil. *Ten Famous Evangelists*. Grand Rapids, MI: Zondervan Publishing House, 1949.

Ninde, Edward Summerfield. *George Whitefield: Prophet-Preacher*. New York: Abingdon Press, 1924.

Philip, Robert. *The Life and Times of George Whitefield*. London: George Virtue, Ivy Lane: 1842.

Pollock, John. *Billy Graham: The Authorized Biography*. New York: McGraw-Hill, 1966.

_____. *George Whitefield and the Great Awakening*. Garden City, NJ: Doubleday, 1972.

Ryle, J. C. *Christian Leaders of the 18th Century*. Carlisle, PA: Banner of Truth, reprint 1978.

_____. *Select Sermons of George Whitefield, with an Account of His Life*. Carlisle, Pennsylvania: Banner of Truth, 1958.

Scougal, Henry. *The Life of God in the Soul of Man*. Harrisburg, VA: Sprinkle Publications, 1986.

Simon, John, S. *The Revival of Religion in England in the Eighteenth Century*. London: Robert Culley Publishers, 1907.

Smith, Timothy L., ed. *Whitefield and Wesley on the New Birth*. Grand Rapids, MI: Francis Asbury Press, 1986.

Spurgeon, Charles Haddon. *Religious Zeal Illustrated and Enforced by the Life of the Rev. George Whitefield*. London: The Gospel Atlas, 1855.

Stagg, Frank. *The Book of Acts: The Early Struggle for the Unhindered Gospel*. Nashville, TN: Broadman, 1955.

Stout, Harry S. *The Divine Dramatist: George Whitefield and the Rise of Modern Evangelicalism*. Grand Rapids, MI: W.B. Eerdmans, 1991.

Street, Alan R. *The Effective Invitation Old Tappan*. NJ: Fleming H. Revell Co., 1984.

Sweet, William Warren. *The Story of Religion in America*, New York: Harper and Brothers, 1939.

Temple, Sarah Coleman, *Georgia's Journeys*, Athens, GA: University of Georgia Press, 1963.

Tracy, Joseph. *The Great Awakening, A History of Revival in the Time of Edwards and Whitefield*. Carlise, PA: Banner of Truth, 1997.

Tyerman, Luke. *The Life of the Rev. George Whitefield*. Volume 1, London: Hodder & Stoughton, 1877, Azie, TX: Need of the Times Publishers, reprint 1995.

_____. *The Life of the Rev. George Whitefield*. Volume 2, Azie, TX Need of the Times Publishers, reprint 1995.

Wakeley, J. B. *Anecdotes of Rev. George Whitefield Sketch*. London: Hodder and Stoughton, 1877.

Wood, A. Skevington. *The Inextinguishable Blaze*. London: The Paternoster Press, 1960.

INTERNET SITES

Ann Arbor, MI; Oxford (UK): Text Creation Partnership, 2003-07, http://name.umdl.umich.edu/A47224.0001.001, (accessed September 23, 2015).

Edwards, John "Charles Wesley's Reflections on George Whitefield," August 20, 2008, Elegy on the life of George Whitefield, 1771, (accessed Sept. 29, 2015). http://www.christian-faith.com/forjesus/charles-wesleys-thoughts-of-george-whitefield.

Middleton, Roy "Introduction to the Works of Ralph Erskine"1991, Free Presbyterian Publications, 1991, (accessed Sept. 30, 2015). http://www.fpchurch.org.uk/2014/08/ralph-erskine-1685-1752.

Sparrow, Tony William Seward (1702-1740) Methodist Martyr, "A Brief History of Badsey and Aldington," badsey.net. June 16, 2007, (accessed September 29, 2015). http://www.badsey.net/past/seward.htm.

Steel, Richard "John Wesley's Synthesis of the Revival Practices of Jonathan Edwards, George Whitefield, Nicholas Von Zinzendorf," Wesley Theological Journal, November 4, 2002, (accessed September 23, 2015). http://www.freerepublic.com/focus/religion.

Watts, Isaac "Why Do We Morn Departed Friends," Words: Hymns and Spiritual Songs 1707, Music: Dundee, 1615, The Cyber Hymnal, Page Design: Richard W. Adams, 1996-2015, (accessed September 30, 2015). http://www.hymntime.com/tch/htm/w/h/y/whydowem.htm.

MESSAGES

Autrey, C. E, "The First Great Awakening": A paper at The Awakenings Conference, Golden Gate Baptist Theological Seminary, Mill Valley, CA 1980.

MacArthur, John, Question and Answer Session, Shepherd's Conference: 2007 Pastor's Conference, Grace Community Church Panorama City, CA.

Patterson, Paige. "Predestination and Free Will in Evangelism," Taken from a Spring Chapel service 2007, Southwestern Baptist Theological Seminary, Fort Worth, Texas.

Wesley, John. "A Sermon on the Death of the Rev. Mr. George Whitefield," Preached on Sunday, November 18, 1770. Library, Emory University, 1953.

Zinn, Rob. A Message on Evangelism, Pastor of Immanuel Baptist Church in Highland, California: Evangelism Meeting of the Gold Coast Baptist Association, Gold Coast Church Ventura, CA in the early 1990's.

Index

ABOUT THE AUTHOR

Dan Nelson has served as pastor of First Baptist Church of Camarillo, California, in the greater Los Angeles area for the last 33 years.

He has also served as pastor of First Baptist Church Burney, California, and Seminary Baptist Church of Hintonville, Mississippi. Dan has served in the Northwest Baptist Convention for two years as Associate to the Evangelism Director in Portland, Oregon. He has also worked as an evangelist through the California Southern Baptist Convention in Fresno on student-led revival teams. Dan has preached in over 40 evangelistic meetings and revivals in his ministry.

Dan is a native of Mississippi, born in Hattiesburg, and he grew up in Agricola. He holds the Doctor of Ministry degree from Southwestern Baptist Theological Seminary in Fort Worth, Texas, a Doctor of Philosophy degree from California Graduate School of Theology in Glendale, California, the Master of Divinity degree from New Orleans Baptist Theological Seminary in New Orleans Louisiana and attended Golden Gate Baptist Theological Seminary in Mill Valley, California. He is a graduate of William Carey University in Hattiesburg, Mississippi with a B.A. degree.

He has been married to his wife Janice for 42 years. They have two daughters, Krista and Kimberly, living in Texas and Oregon. Dan is an active contributor to blog sites and publications with various articles. He is a regular contributor to *SBC Today* with many articles on biographies, sermons and topical studies. He is an avid bicyclist and an instructor in indoor cycling (spin class) at several local gyms.

Dan has been active in the Southern Baptist Convention denominational structure, serving on the Board of Trustees at Southwestern Baptist Theological Seminary in Fort Worth, Texas, and as National Alumni Chairman for New Orleans Baptist Theological Seminary in New Orleans, Louisiana.

Dan's first book was *Baptist Revival: Reaffirming Baptist Principles in Today's Changing Church Scene* followed by *Game On All the Time: Growing up in the Home of a Legendary Football Coach: L. R. Nelson.* This work, *A Burning and Shining Light: The Testimony and Witness of George Whitefield* is the product of many years of research and development in presenting the most recent comprehensive historical record of Whitefield's ministry.

Dan Nelson and his assistant, "GW"

Previous page- Dan Nelson at George Whitefield's grave

Contact Information

Contact Dan Nelson at gospel4you@fbccamarillo.com or (805) 484-2879 for speaking, questions, and comments.

Contact LifeSong Publishers at Laurie@LifeSongPublishers.com for copyright or other questions.

Visit www.LifeSongPublishers.com for more spiritually encouraging and challenging books.